AF316985

SECURING THE CLOUD ECOSYSTEM

Muhammed Olanrewaju

Globally Distributed & Available

Contents

Preface

The rapid evolution of cloud computing has transformed the way businesses and individuals store, manage, and process data, reshaping the digital landscape in ways we could not have imagined a decade ago. From startups to multinational corporations, educational institutions to government agencies, organizations are leveraging cloud services to drive efficiency, agility, and innovation. The cloud has provided unparalleled scalability, cost reduction, remote accessibility, and business continuity, allowing enterprises to expand their operations globally without the constraints of traditional IT infrastructures. However, with these advancements comes an entirely new set of cybersecurity risks, regulatory challenges, and operational complexities that organizations must navigate to maintain data integrity, privacy, and resilience.

The rise in cloud adoption has introduced a new frontier of security challenges—data breaches, compliance risks, insider threats, and sophisticated cyberattacks have escalated to unprecedented levels. Malicious actors are continuously evolving their tactics, exploiting cloud misconfigurations, weak authentication mechanisms, and vulnerable APIs to gain unauthorized access to critical systems. Supply chain attacks, ransomware threats, and AI-driven cyber warfare further amplify the risks, proving that conventional security measures are no longer sufficient in a cloud-driven world. As businesses and governments continue their digital transformation, the need for robust, scalable, and adaptive cloud security frameworks has never been more urgent. Without a well-defined cloud security strategy, organizations risk financial losses, reputational damage, regulatory penalties, and operational disruptions that could jeopardize their long-term success.

Securing the Cloud Ecosystem was born out of the necessity to provide a structured, practical, and forward-thinking approach to cloud security. This book is designed to serve security professionals, IT leaders, business executives, compliance officers, and cloud enthusiasts who seek to understand the evolving cloud security landscape, best practices, compliance requirements, and emerging technologies that will shape the future of cloud protection. Whether you are a CISO tasked with securing multi-cloud environments, a DevSecOps engineer embedding security into cloud-native applications, or a business leader navigating compliance obligation, this book provides valuable insights and actionable strategies to help you build a resilient and secure cloud infrastructure.

Rather than offering just technical insights, this book provides a holistic perspective, integrating security strategies, compliance challenges, risk management frameworks, and the impact of AI and automation on cloud security. Each chapter is structured to guide readers from fundamental security principles to advanced threat defense mechanisms, ensuring that readers at all levels of expertise can derive value from its contents. The book delves into identity and access management (IAM), cloud security tools, compliance best practices, incident response strategies, and the future of decentralized security models, equipping readers with the knowledge needed to proactively protect their cloud environments.

The future of cloud security will be defined by intelligence, automation, and decentralization. As cloud adoption grows, zero-trust security models, AI-driven security analytics, and blockchain-based security solutions will redefine how organizations protect their digital assets. Businesses that fail to adapt to these changes will be left vulnerable, while those that embrace innovation, enforce proactive security measures, and invest in AI-driven defenses will gain a significant advantage in securing their cloud ecosystems.

I hope this book serves as a valuable resource, a guide for cloud security decision-making, and a roadmap for organizations looking to fortify their cloud infrastructures against emerging threats. Cloud security is not a one-time implementation but a continuous journey, requiring constant vigilance, adaptation, and innovation. The key to long-term success lies in staying ahead of threats, understanding the evolving cybersecurity landscape, and building a resilient cloud security strategy that aligns with both business goals and regulatory requirements.

As we move forward into this next phase of cloud security evolution, I encourage you to adopt a proactive security mindset, invest in emerging technologies, and embrace the principles of continuous security improvement. The cloud offers endless possibilities, but only those who secure it effectively will truly reap its full potential.

Foreword

Cloud computing has redefined the technology landscape, providing organizations with unparalleled scalability, agility, and cost-efficiency. The cloud has transformed how businesses operate, enabling seamless remote collaboration, on-demand resource allocation, and the rapid deployment of innovative services. With cloud technology, enterprises can reduce capital expenditures, enhance business continuity, and accelerate digital transformation, allowing them to stay ahead in today's fast-paced digital economy. However, with these opportunities come significant security challenges—as the cloud expands, so does the attack surface for cybercriminals seeking to exploit vulnerabilities in cloud infrastructure, applications, and data storage.

The rise of cyber threats in cloud environments has made security a top priority for businesses worldwide. Cybercriminals are increasingly targeting misconfigured cloud services, weak authentication mechanisms, and supply chain dependencies, using sophisticated techniques such as ransomware, credential theft, and cloud-native malware to compromise sensitive data and disrupt business operations. Regulatory pressures are also intensifying, with governments enforcing stricter data protection laws and compliance mandates to ensure cloud security meets the highest standards. In this rapidly evolving landscape, organizations can no longer afford to take a reactive approach to cloud security. They must adopt proactive defense mechanisms, intelligent threat detection, and robust compliance frameworks to safeguard their cloud ecosystems.

In *Securing the Cloud Ecosystem*, Muhammed Olanrewaju takes us on an insightful and well-researched journey into the critical components of cloud security. This book is not just about understanding cloud security threats, it provides actionable solutions, strategic frameworks, and expert insights to help businesses build resilient, scalable, and future-ready cloud environments. Olanrewaju presents a holistic approach to cloud security, covering the fundamental principles of cloud security architecture, identity and access management (IAM), cloud compliance challenges, and AI-driven security automation. He also explores the role of Zero Trust, blockchain security, and post-quantum cryptography, ensuring that readers are well-equipped to navigate both present and future cloud security challenges.

What makes this book unique is its balanced approach, combining technical depth, regulatory compliance considerations, and emerging security innovations to create a comprehensive guide for securing cloud ecosystems. Unlike many cybersecurity books that focus solely on theoretical concepts, this book bridges the gap between strategy and implementation, making it a practical and highly relevant resource for professionals across various industries. Whether you are a CISO, security engineer, cloud architect, compliance officer, or business leader, this book will provide you with the knowledge, tools, and frameworks necessary to navigate the complex world of cloud security.

With cyber threats evolving at an unprecedented pace, security professionals and decision-makers must stay ahead of the curve by continuously enhancing their cloud security posture, adopting intelligent security solutions, and reinforcing governance frameworks. This book provides a roadmap for organizations looking to strengthen their cloud defenses, implement AI-driven security automation, and future-proof their cloud environments against emerging risks.

I highly recommend *Securing the Cloud Ecosystem* to anyone looking to fortify their cloud infrastructure, understand evolving cyber threats, and embrace cutting-edge security solutions. This book is an essential read for professionals who want to stay ahead in the ever-changing cybersecurity landscape and proactively defend their cloud environments against the next generation of cyber threats.

Introduction

The digital revolution has dramatically transformed how organizations and individuals store, manage, and process data, ushering in an era of unprecedented connectivity, scalability, and efficiency. At the heart of this transformation is cloud computing, a technology that has redefined the IT landscape, enabling businesses to scale operations seamlessly, optimize costs, and foster global collaboration. The cloud has empowered organizations to reduce infrastructure overhead, improve business continuity, and accelerate digital innovation. However, with these benefits come complex security challenges, ranging from data breaches and regulatory compliance risks to sophisticated AI-driven cyberattacks.

Cloud adoption continues to surge across industries, with enterprises, governments, and small businesses increasingly relying on Software as a Service (SaaS), Infrastructure as a Service (IaaS), and hybrid cloud models to streamline operations, enhance customer experiences, and drive competitive advantage. Yet, as cloud environments expand, so do their attack surfaces—creating new opportunities for cybercriminals to exploit misconfigurations, compromised credentials, and vulnerable APIs. Traditional security measures, designed for on-premise systems, are no longer sufficient to protect the modern cloud ecosystem. Cyber adversaries are becoming more advanced, leveraging automation, AI-powered malware, and supply chain attacks to target high-value cloud assets.

In today's highly interconnected world, cloud security is no longer optional, it is a fundamental necessity. Organizations that fail to implement robust security strategies risk data leaks, financial losses, reputational damage, and regulatory penalties that could disrupt business continuity. As cloud services become the backbone of critical infrastructure, ensuring data integrity, secure access, and compliance with industry regulations is now a top priority for businesses, policymakers, and security professionals.

Securing the Cloud Ecosystem is a comprehensive guide to understanding, implementing, and future-proofing cloud security strategies. This book delves into the core principles of cloud security, provides insightful case studies, and examines emerging trends that will shape the future of cloud protection. From Zero Trust Architecture (ZTA) and AI-driven security automation to blockchain-powered security models and post-quantum cryptography, this book explores the tools, frameworks, and best practices needed to build a resilient cloud security posture. It provides a structured approach to securing cloud infrastructures, covering topics such as the shared responsibility model in cloud security, best practices for identity and access management (IAM), detecting and mitigating cloud security threats using AI-driven analytics, ensuring compliance with global data protection regulations, incident response and disaster recovery strategies, and future security trends, including decentralized security architectures, homomorphic encryption, self-healing cloud infrastructures, and quantum-resistant encryption models.

This book is designed for a diverse audience, including CISOs, cybersecurity analysts, cloud architects, compliance officers, DevSecOps engineers, IT managers, and business executives. Whether you are a seasoned security professional or new to cloud security, you will find practical insights, actionable solutions, and industry-proven methodologies to enhance cloud security resilience.

As cloud technology continues to evolve, only organizations that prioritize security, adopt proactive threat detection measures, and integrate AI-driven defense mechanisms will thrive in this digital era. The journey to cloud resilience starts with understanding the risks, implementing robust security frameworks, and staying ahead of emerging cyber threats. This book will equip you with the knowledge, tools, and strategies to build, maintain, and secure cloud environments in an increasingly unpredictable cybersecurity landscape. It is a call to action for security leaders and IT professionals to take control of their cloud security strategies, embrace innovation, and safeguard the digital infrastructure of the future. Let's get started on this critical journey toward securing the cloud ecosystem.

Chapter 1
Understanding the Cloud Ecosystem

Cloud computing has transformed the way organizations store, process, and manage data. It eliminates the need for costly on-premise infrastructure by providing scalable and flexible solutions that allow users to access computing resources on demand. The cloud ecosystem is a complex network of technologies, services, and infrastructures designed to facilitate seamless computing experiences. As businesses and individuals continue to shift towards digital operations, understanding the fundamentals of cloud computing is essential for security, efficiency, and sustainability.

The journey of cloud computing began with early mainframe computers, where centralized computing was the norm. Over time, the industry moved towards client-server architectures, where organizations operated their own dedicated servers to manage applications and data. The introduction of virtualization allowed multiple operating systems to run on a single machine, significantly improving resource utilization and paving the way for modern cloud computing. The cloud era was further revolutionized by the emergence of tech giants like Amazon, Microsoft, and Google, which provided cloud-based services that enabled organizations to operate without the need for extensive physical infrastructure. Today, cloud computing is at the heart of digital transformation, supporting industries such as healthcare, finance, education, and e-commerce.

A fully functional cloud ecosystem consists of multiple components working together to deliver a seamless experience. Compute resources, such as virtual machines, containers, and serverless functions, provide the necessary processing power. Cloud storage solutions offer different types of data management, including block storage, object storage, and file storage. Networking infrastructure ensures connectivity and security through virtual private networks (VPNs), firewalls, and content delivery networks (CDNs). Security and compliance tools help organizations protect their cloud environments by offering encryption, identity management, and regulatory monitoring. At the center of this ecosystem are cloud service providers such as Amazon Web Services (AWS), Microsoft Azure, and Google Cloud Platform (GCP), which deliver a range of computing solutions tailored to different business needs.

Cloud computing services are categorized into three primary models: Infrastructure as a Service (IaaS), Platform as a Service (PaaS), and Software as a Service (SaaS). IaaS provides virtualized computing resources such as storage, networking, and virtual machines, allowing businesses to manage their workloads without investing in physical infrastructure. PaaS offers a platform for software development, enabling developers to build, test, and deploy applications without worrying about underlying hardware. SaaS delivers fully managed applications to end users over the internet, removing the need for local installations and maintenance. Each of these models serves different purposes, and organizations select them based on their operational requirements and levels of control.

The deployment of cloud services varies based on security, cost, and performance considerations. Public cloud environments, offered by third-party providers, are widely used due to their cost-effectiveness and scalability. However, organizations that require greater control and security often opt for private cloud infrastructures, which provide dedicated computing resources. Hybrid cloud solutions combine elements of both public and private clouds, allowing businesses to balance flexibility with security. Additionally, community clouds cater to specific industries or groups that share similar security and compliance needs, such as government agencies or healthcare institutions. The choice of deployment model depends on an organization's priorities and the nature of its data and applications.

The adoption of cloud computing brings numerous benefits, making it a preferred choice for businesses worldwide. One of its key advantages is cost efficiency, as companies can eliminate expenses associated with maintaining on-premise servers and only pay for the resources they use. Scalability is another major benefit, as cloud environments allow businesses to expand or reduce their computing resources based on demand. Flexibility and accessibility are enhanced since employees can access cloud-based applications and data from anywhere, supporting remote work and collaboration.

Cloud services also ensure automatic software and security updates, reducing the burden on IT teams. Furthermore, business continuity is strengthened through built-in disaster recovery solutions, enabling companies to restore operations quickly in the event of data loss or system failure.

Despite its advantages, cloud computing presents certain risks that organizations must address. Security vulnerabilities remain a significant concern, as cloud environments are prime targets for cyber threats, including data breaches, unauthorized access, and malware attacks. Compliance issues arise as businesses must adhere to regulatory standards, such as GDPR, HIPAA, and the Nigerian Data Protection Regulation (NDPR), to ensure data privacy and security. Downtime and reliability concerns can affect operations, especially if cloud service providers experience outages or technical failures. Vendor lock-in is another challenge, where businesses become dependent on a single cloud provider, limiting their flexibility to switch to alternative solutions. Additionally, data privacy remains a contentious issue, as organizations must trust third-party providers to handle their sensitive information securely.

Understanding the cloud ecosystem is the foundation for making informed decisions about cloud adoption. By recognizing the different service models, deployment strategies, key components, and potential risks, businesses can optimize their cloud strategies to enhance security, efficiency, and overall performance. Cloud adoption is no longer a luxury but a necessity in today's digital landscape. As businesses increasingly migrate to cloud environments, they must do so with a strong understanding of the underlying infrastructure and potential risks. Organizations that fail to grasp the intricacies of the cloud ecosystem often face challenges such as inefficient resource allocation, poor security implementation, and compliance failures. This is why understanding how the cloud operates, its benefits, and its risks is not just for IT professionals, it is crucial knowledge for business leaders, security experts, and even end-users who interact with cloud-based services daily.

One of the fundamental aspects of cloud computing is its ability to enhance operational efficiency. By shifting workloads to the cloud, organizations can reduce the burden of maintaining physical infrastructure, leading to cost savings and improved productivity. The pay-as-you-go model of cloud services ensures that businesses only pay for the resources they use, eliminating unnecessary expenditures. This economic model is particularly beneficial for startups and small businesses that lack the financial resources to invest in expensive on-premise servers. Large enterprises also benefit from cloud elasticity, which allows them to scale computing power up or down based on demand. For example, an e-commerce company can increase its server capacity during peak shopping seasons and scale down when demand normalizes, optimizing costs while maintaining performance.

Another major advantage of cloud computing is its impact on business agility. Traditional IT infrastructures often require extensive planning, procurement, and setup before applications can be deployed. In contrast, cloud services provide instant access to computing resources, enabling businesses to launch new applications and services in a matter of minutes. This agility is particularly valuable in today's fast-paced market, where the ability to innovate quickly can determine a company's success. Cloud computing allows organizations to experiment with new technologies without committing to expensive hardware, fostering innovation across various industries.

The flexibility of cloud computing extends to workforce management, particularly with the rise of remote and hybrid work environments. Cloud-based collaboration tools such as Google Workspace, Microsoft 365, and Slack enable employees to work from any location with an internet connection. This accessibility ensures that businesses can operate efficiently regardless of geographical constraints. During the COVID-19 pandemic, many organizations relied on cloud technology to facilitate remote work, underscoring its importance in ensuring business continuity. Even as companies return to in-office operations, the adoption of cloud-based collaboration tools remains prevalent, proving that cloud computing has reshaped the modern workplace.

However, as organizations enjoy the benefits of cloud adoption, they must remain aware of the challenges associated with it. One of the primary concerns is security. The shift from traditional on-premise systems to cloud environments introduces new vulnerabilities that cybercriminals exploit. While cloud providers invest heavily in security measures, businesses are still responsible for protecting their data and applications. Misconfigurations, weak access controls, and inadequate security policies often lead to breaches, making cloud security a shared responsibility between the provider and the user. Organizations must implement robust security frameworks, such as identity and access management (IAM), encryption, and multi-factor authentication, to protect their cloud assets.

Regulatory compliance is another critical consideration in cloud adoption. Different industries are subject to various data protection laws that dictate how customer information should be handled. For example, financial institutions must comply with regulations such as the General Data Protection Regulation (GDPR) in Europe, while healthcare organizations adhere to the Health Insurance Portability and Accountability Act (HIPAA) in the United States. In Nigeria, the Nigerian Data Protection Regulation (NDPR) governs how businesses collect, store, and process personal data. Failure to comply with these regulations can result in hefty fines, reputational damage, and legal consequences. As a result, organizations must ensure that their cloud environments meet industry-specific compliance requirements and implement best practices for data governance.

Downtime and service availability are also concerns when relying on cloud providers. While major cloud providers boast high availability and uptime guarantees, outages can still occur. A service disruption at a cloud provider's data center can affect thousands of businesses, leading to financial losses and operational delays. In recent years, several high-profile cloud outages have highlighted the risks of relying solely on a single provider. To mitigate this risk, businesses should implement redundancy strategies, such as multi-cloud or hybrid cloud deployments, to ensure continuity in case of service disruptions. Backup and disaster recovery plans are essential components of a resilient cloud strategy, helping organizations restore operations quickly after unexpected failures.

Vendor lock-in is another challenge that organizations must consider when adopting cloud services. Many cloud providers offer proprietary tools and platforms that make it difficult for businesses to migrate to alternative providers. While these tools often provide significant advantages in terms of integration and functionality, they can also create dependency on a single vendor. If a business later decides to switch providers, the process can be complex and costly. To minimize vendor lock-in, organizations should adopt open standards, prioritize portability, and design cloud architectures that allow for easy migration when necessary.

Despite these challenges, cloud computing continues to evolve, offering new innovations that enhance security, efficiency, and performance. The rise of artificial intelligence (AI) and machine learning (ML) in cloud environments has enabled businesses to automate processes, analyze large datasets, and detect cybersecurity threats in real time. AI-powered security solutions can identify unusual patterns and potential threats before they escalate, helping organizations strengthen their cloud defenses. Similarly, advancements in edge computing allow businesses to process data closer to its source, reducing latency and improving performance for applications that require real-time processing.

Blockchain technology is also making an impact in cloud security by providing decentralized and tamper-proof data storage solutions. Businesses are exploring blockchain for securing transactions, enhancing supply chain transparency, and ensuring data integrity in cloud environments. While still in its early stages, blockchain integration with cloud computing presents new opportunities for improving security and trust in digital transactions.

Quantum computing is another emerging technology that could reshape cloud security in the future. While quantum computers have the potential to break traditional encryption methods, researchers are actively developing quantum-resistant cryptographic algorithms to safeguard cloud data. As cloud computing continues to evolve, businesses must stay informed about emerging trends and technologies to adapt their security strategies accordingly.

1.1 The Role of Cloud Governance in Security and Compliance

As cloud computing adoption increases, organizations must establish robust governance frameworks to manage security risks, compliance obligations, and operational efficiency. Cloud governance refers to the policies, processes, and controls that ensure cloud resources are managed securely and effectively. Without proper governance, businesses may face security breaches, compliance violations, and inefficiencies that could lead to financial and reputational damage.

One of the critical aspects of cloud governance is defining roles and responsibilities within an organization. Cloud environments operate on a shared responsibility model, where the cloud provider is responsible for securing the underlying infrastructure, while the customer is responsible for securing their applications, data, and access controls. Businesses must clearly outline security responsibilities within their teams to prevent gaps that cybercriminals can exploit. Implementing a Cloud Center of Excellence (CCoE); a dedicated team responsible for cloud security, compliance, and cost optimization can help organizations maintain a structured governance framework.

Compliance management is another crucial part of cloud governance. As organizations process and store sensitive customer data in the cloud, they must comply with local and international data protection laws. **Automated compliance monitoring tools** help businesses track regulatory adherence in real time, alerting them to misconfigurations and potential violations. Many cloud providers offer built-in compliance tools that allow organizations to generate audit reports, monitor data access logs, and ensure compliance with industry standards such as GDPR, HIPAA, and NDPR.

Effective cloud governance also includes **cost management** strategies to prevent excessive cloud spending. Many businesses struggle with "cloud sprawl," where unused or underutilized cloud resources drive up costs unnecessarily. Organizations can implement cost optimization tools that analyze cloud usage patterns, recommend resource scaling, and automate cost-saving measures such as rightsizing virtual machines and shutting down idle instances.

Organizations that neglect cloud governance often face security vulnerabilities, inefficient operations, and regulatory penalties. By establishing well-defined policies, leveraging automation, and maintaining visibility into cloud operations, businesses can ensure that their cloud environments remain secure, compliant, and cost-efficient.

1.2 The Human Factor in Cloud Security

While cloud security often focuses on technology, the human element remains one of the most significant factors influencing security outcomes. Human error is a leading cause of cloud security incidents, including misconfigured cloud storage, weak passwords, and phishing attacks. Cybercriminals often exploit human vulnerabilities rather than technical flaws, making security awareness training a critical component of cloud security strategies.

Misconfigurations are among the most common cloud security risks. Organizations frequently fail to properly configure cloud storage, databases, and identity access controls, leaving sensitive information exposed. A notable example is the recurring Amazon S3 bucket misconfiguration issue, where businesses accidentally leave their storage open to the public, exposing customer data. To mitigate such risks, companies should use automated configuration management tools that scan cloud environments for misconfigurations and enforce security best practices.

Another human-related risk is the use of weak or reused passwords for cloud accounts. Many security breaches occur because employees use easily guessable passwords or reuse the same credentials across multiple accounts. Implementing multi-factor authentication (MFA) and password management policies can reduce the likelihood of credential-based attacks.

Social engineering attacks, such as phishing, remain a significant threat to cloud security. Attackers craft deceptive emails, messages, or websites to trick employees into revealing login credentials or downloading malware. Regular security awareness training can help employees recognize phishing attempts and avoid falling victim to scams. Organizations should also deploy email security gateways and anti-phishing tools to filter out malicious emails before they reach users.

Insider threats, whether intentional or unintentional, also pose a risk to cloud environments. Disgruntled employees, negligent staff, or compromised accounts can lead to data leaks or security breaches. Implementing role-based access control (RBAC), user activity monitoring, and privileged access management (PAM) can help limit the risk of insider threats.

The human factor in cloud security cannot be ignored. While technological solutions play a crucial role, fostering a security-conscious culture within an organization is just as important. Regular training, strong security policies, and automated tools can help reduce human-related security risks and strengthen cloud security posture.

The cloud ecosystem is a dynamic and complex environment that offers unparalleled opportunities for businesses to scale, innovate, and optimize their operations. However, adopting cloud computing requires a deep understanding of its architecture, security challenges, and governance requirements. Organizations must balance the benefits of cloud adoption with the risks of security breaches, compliance violations, and operational inefficiencies.

A successful cloud strategy involves **continuous learning, proactive security measures, and a strong governance framework**. As cyber threats continue to evolve, businesses must remain vigilant, leveraging automation, AI-driven security solutions, and human awareness training to secure their cloud environments. With the right approach, organizations can harness the power of cloud computing while minimizing risks and ensuring compliance with industry regulations.

14

Chapter 2
Threat Landscape in Cloud Computing

Cloud computing has revolutionized the way businesses operate, offering unparalleled scalability, flexibility, and cost efficiency. However, with these benefits come significant security risks. As more organizations migrate sensitive data and mission-critical workloads to the cloud, cybercriminals have adapted their tactics to exploit cloud-specific vulnerabilities. The threat landscape in cloud computing is vast, ranging from misconfigurations and data breaches to sophisticated cyberattacks like ransomware and insider threats. Understanding these risks is crucial for organizations seeking to protect their cloud environments from malicious actors.

One of the most pervasive threats in cloud computing is data breaches. Cloud storage often contains highly sensitive information, including customer records, financial details, and intellectual property. A single breach can have devastating consequences, leading to financial losses, legal ramifications, and reputational damage. Many data breaches in the cloud stem from misconfigurations, where organizations inadvertently expose databases, storage buckets, or virtual machines to the public. For instance, misconfigured Amazon S3 buckets have led to numerous high-profile breaches, exposing millions of sensitive records. Attackers use automated tools to scan for exposed cloud storage and extract valuable data within minutes. Organizations must implement encryption, access controls, and automated configuration management to prevent such incidents.

Another major risk in cloud computing is account hijacking, where attackers gain unauthorized access to cloud accounts by exploiting weak credentials, phishing attacks, or credential stuffing techniques. Once inside, they can steal data, launch further attacks, or deploy ransomware. Multi-factor authentication (MFA) is a critical defense against account hijacking, as it requires additional verification beyond just a username and password. Cloud providers also offer security features such as identity and access management (IAM) policies to limit user privileges and reduce the potential impact of a compromised account.

Denial-of-Service (DoS) and Distributed Denial-of-Service (DDoS) attacks are also significant concerns for cloud environments. In a DoS attack, attackers overwhelm a system with excessive traffic, rendering it unavailable to legitimate users. DDoS attacks amplify this by using a network of compromised devices (botnets) to flood cloud servers with malicious traffic. These attacks can disrupt business operations, causing downtime and financial losses. Cloud service providers offer DDoS mitigation services, such as AWS Shield and Azure DDoS Protection, to help organizations detect and respond to these attacks in real-time.

One of the most destructive threats in cloud computing is ransomware, a type of malware that encrypts files and demands payment for their release. Cloud environments are not immune to ransomware attacks, as cybercriminals target cloud storage, virtual machines, and backup systems. In some cases, attackers use double extortion tactics, where they not only encrypt the data but also threaten to leak it unless a ransom is paid. To defend against ransomware, organizations should implement regular backups, endpoint detection, and behavior-based security monitoring to detect suspicious activities before encryption occurs.

Insider threats remain a critical challenge in cloud security. Unlike external attackers, insiders already have legitimate access to cloud resources, making their actions harder to detect. An insider could be a disgruntled employee, a contractor with excessive permissions, or even an unwitting user who falls victim to social engineering attacks. Implementing role-based access control (RBAC) and privileged access management (PAM) can help mitigate the risk of insider threats by restricting access to sensitive data and monitoring high-risk accounts.

Cloud environments also face the risk of supply chain attacks, where attackers target cloud service providers or third-party vendors to compromise their customers. A notable example is the SolarWinds attack, where attackers inserted malicious code into a trusted software update, affecting multiple organizations. These attacks highlight the importance of vendor risk management and conducting security audits on third-party providers before integrating their services into cloud infrastructures.

Another growing concern is API security vulnerabilities. Many cloud applications rely on APIs (Application Programming Interfaces) to interact with different services and systems. If an API is poorly secured, attackers can exploit it to gain unauthorized access to cloud resources, modify data, or execute malicious commands. Common API security issues include broken authentication, inadequate rate limiting, and insecure data exposure. Organizations should enforce API security best practices, such as OAuth authentication, API gateway protections, and regular security testing to mitigate these risks.

Cloud misconfigurations are among the most prevalent and preventable security risks. Many organizations fail to properly configure security settings for their cloud resources, leaving them vulnerable to attacks. Common misconfigurations include exposed storage buckets, overly permissive IAM roles, and unpatched virtual machines. Attackers actively scan for misconfigured cloud services using tools like Shodan and Censys, making it crucial for organizations to conduct regular security audits, apply the principle of least privilege, and use cloud security posture management (CSPM) tools to identify and fix misconfigurations.

In addition to these threats, phishing attacks remain a top concern in cloud security. Cybercriminals craft convincing emails that trick employees into revealing their login credentials or downloading malware. Business Email Compromise (BEC) scams have become increasingly sophisticated, where attackers impersonate executives or vendors to request fraudulent payments or sensitive information. Organizations should implement email security gateways, user training programs, and AI-driven phishing detection tools to combat these threats.

To address the evolving threat landscape, businesses must adopt a proactive cloud security strategy that includes continuous monitoring, real-time threat intelligence, and automated security responses. Cloud-native security solutions such as Security Information and Event Management (SIEM) systems, Extended Detection and Response (XDR), and Cloud Workload Protection Platforms (CWPP) can help organizations detect and respond to threats before they escalate. Additionally, Zero Trust security models, which assume that no user or device should be trusted by default, are gaining popularity as an effective approach to securing cloud environments.

The complexity of cloud security means that organizations cannot rely solely on cloud providers to protect their data. While major providers like AWS, Azure, and Google Cloud offer extensive security features, responsibility for securing cloud workloads is shared between the provider and the customer. Businesses must take an active role in securing their cloud assets, enforcing security best practices, and staying updated on emerging threats.

The threat landscape in cloud computing is constantly evolving, with attackers developing new techniques to exploit cloud vulnerabilities. Organizations must stay ahead by implementing strong security frameworks, investing in cybersecurity training for employees, and leveraging AI-driven security tools. By understanding and addressing these risks, businesses can confidently embrace cloud computing while minimizing potential threats.

Cyber threats in cloud computing are not static; they evolve as attackers develop more sophisticated techniques to exploit vulnerabilities. Organizations must take a holistic approach to cloud security, combining proactive threat detection, automated defense mechanisms, and human-centric security awareness programs. The increasing reliance on cloud-based services means that even a single security lapse can have far-reaching consequences, affecting not just a single organization but an entire network of interconnected businesses, vendors, and customers.

One of the emerging attack vectors in cloud security is container security vulnerabilities. As organizations adopt containerization technologies such as Docker and Kubernetes, attackers are finding ways to exploit misconfigured containerized environments. Containers, while highly efficient for deploying applications at scale, introduce new attack surfaces, such as container escape attacks, where an attacker can break out of an isolated container to gain access to the host system. In some cases, vulnerable container images may contain embedded malware or backdoors, which can compromise cloud infrastructure once deployed. To mitigate these risks, organizations must scan container images for vulnerabilities, enforce runtime security policies, and adopt privilege principles for containerized workloads.

Another key area of concern is cloud identity threats. The increased adoption of cloud-based identity and access management (IAM) solutions means that identity is now the primary security perimeter. Cybercriminals increasingly target IAM misconfigurations, stolen credentials, and weak authentication mechanisms to gain unauthorized access to cloud environments. Privilege escalation attacks, where attackers gain elevated permissions through poorly configured IAM policies, pose a significant threat. Implementing role-based access control (RBAC), enforcing multi-factor authentication (MFA), and continuously monitoring IAM logs can help mitigate these threats. Organizations should also conduct regular IAM audits to identify and remove unused accounts, overly permissive roles, and outdated credentials.

With the rapid adoption of serverless computing (e.g., AWS Lambda, Azure Functions), attackers are shifting their focus to exploiting serverless functions. Since serverless applications execute code in a fully managed cloud environment, developers may overlook security measures, assuming the provider is responsible for everything. However, insecure function permissions, unvalidated inputs, and outdated dependencies can create vulnerabilities that attackers can exploit. Function event injection attacks, where attackers manipulate the input triggers of serverless functions to execute unauthorized actions, have become a growing concern. Implementing strict input validation, principle of least privilege access, and monitoring serverless execution logs are key defenses against such attacks.

Another threat organizations should not overlook is data exfiltration via cloud APIs. Many cloud applications rely on APIs to communicate with third-party services, and poorly secured APIs can be exploited to steal data, manipulate configurations, or disrupt services. Attackers often perform API scraping, unauthorized API calls, or inject malicious payloads to compromise cloud services. Businesses should limit API access using OAuth authentication, enforce rate limiting, and implement API gateways to filter and monitor API traffic.

The rise of AI-driven cyber threats also presents new challenges in cloud security. Cybercriminals are now leveraging machine learning (ML) and artificial intelligence (AI) to automate attacks, making them faster and harder to detect. AI-powered attacks can bypass traditional security measures, generate convincing phishing emails, or analyze cloud infrastructure for weaknesses in real time. In response, organizations must adopt AI-driven cybersecurity tools that can detect anomalous behavior, flag suspicious activity, and automate threat mitigation.

One of the most underrated risks in cloud security is shadow IT—the use of unauthorized cloud applications and services by employees without the knowledge of the IT department. Shadow IT creates security blind spots, as unapproved cloud applications may not have proper security controls, compliance measures, or data protection mechanisms in place. This increases the risk of data leaks, compliance violations, and unauthorized access. Organizations must implement cloud access security brokers

(CASB) to monitor and control the use of unauthorized cloud services while providing visibility into cloud-based activities.

Another persistent issue in cloud computing is inadequate logging and monitoring. Many security incidents go undetected for weeks or months because organizations fail to monitor their cloud environments effectively. Security teams must adopt real-time monitoring solutions, centralized log management, and automated alerting systems to detect and respond to threats before they escalate. Cloud providers offer security information and event management (SIEM) solutions, such as AWS CloudTrail, Azure Security Center, and Google Security Command Center, which help organizations track user activity, identify anomalies, and generate security reports.

Organizations should also recognize the importance of proactive cloud penetration testing. While many businesses rely on their cloud provider's built-in security features, conducting regular penetration tests and red teaming exercises can uncover hidden vulnerabilities before they are exploited. Ethical hackers can simulate real-world attack scenarios, helping security teams strengthen defenses and improve incident response readiness.

A common mistake that increases cloud security risks is the lack of proper cloud backup and disaster recovery planning. Many organizations assume that because their data is in the cloud, it is automatically safe. However, cloud providers operate on a shared responsibility model, meaning that while they secure the infrastructure, data protection and backups remain the customer's responsibility. Businesses should implement frequent, automated backups with encryption, ensuring that backup data is stored separately from production environments to prevent ransomware infections.

As the cloud threat landscape continues to evolve, organizations must adopt a multi-layered security approach that combines proactive threat detection, automation, and strong governance frameworks. Cybersecurity is no longer an afterthought but a core business function that must be continuously improved. By understanding and addressing this cloud security risks, businesses can confidently embrace cloud computing while ensuring resilience against cyber threats.

2.1 The Role of Threat Intelligence in Cloud Security

As cloud threats continue to evolve, organizations must take a **proactive approach to** cybersecurity rather than a reactive one. Threat intelligence plays a crucial role in enabling businesses to anticipate, detect, and mitigate cloud security threats before they cause damage. Threat intelligence refers to the collection, analysis, and application of data on emerging threats, attack techniques, and threat actors. It helps security teams stay ahead of cybercriminals by providing real-time insights into malicious activities targeting cloud environments.

Cloud threat intelligence is gathered from multiple sources, including global security communities, dark web monitoring, cloud security logs, and machine learning-driven threat analysis. Organizations can leverage threat intelligence platforms (TIPs) that aggregate and analyze data from various sources to identify patterns of attack, assess risks, and automate response mechanisms. Cloud service providers like AWS, Azure, and Google Cloud integrate AI-powered threat intelligence into their security services to help detect unusual behaviors, brute-force attempts, and unauthorized access attempts in real time.

By incorporating threat intelligence feeds, organizations can proactively block IP addresses associated with known malicious actors, prevent zero-day exploits, and deploy security patches before vulnerabilities are exploited. Additionally, integrating Security Orchestration, Automation, and Response (SOAR) tools allows businesses to automate threat detection and response workflows, reducing the time required to contain security incidents.

A critical advantage of threat intelligence is its role in predictive security analytics. Instead of waiting for a security breach to occur, businesses can use predictive analytics to analyze trends, anticipate new attack vectors, and strengthen cloud security postures accordingly. Threat intelligence also enhances incident response, allowing security teams to respond faster and mitigate damage efficiently when an attack does occur.

Despite its benefits, threat intelligence is only effective if organizations have a clear strategy for implementing and using it. Security teams must be trained to interpret threat intelligence reports and integrate findings into their security frameworks. Furthermore, businesses should adopt a continuous learning approach, staying updated with global cybersecurity trends, new malware strains, and emerging threat actors targeting cloud environments.

2.2 The Impact of Artificial Intelligence and Machine Learning on Cloud Security Threats

While AI and machine learning (ML) have enhanced cloud security, cybercriminals are also leveraging these technologies to launch more sophisticated attacks. AI-powered attacks are particularly concerning because they adapt to security defenses, automate malicious tasks, and analyze security patterns to identify weak points in cloud environments.

One of the ways attackers use AI is in automating phishing campaigns. Traditional phishing attempts rely on mass email distribution, but AI-driven phishing customizes messages based on a target's online behavior, email interactions, and cloud application usage. This makes AI-based phishing more convincing and harder to detect. AI can also generate deep-fake videos and voice recordings to impersonate executives, tricking employees into revealing credentials or approving fraudulent transactions.

Another area where attackers use AI is bypassing security defenses. AI-driven malware can learn from security patterns, modifying itself to evade detection by cloud security tools. Some advanced malware uses polymorphic techniques, continuously altering its code structure to bypass antivirus and endpoint detection systems. Attackers also use AI-powered brute force algorithms to crack passwords faster than traditional methods, making cloud authentication systems more vulnerable.

On the defensive side, organizations are leveraging AI-driven security tools to detect anomalies, monitor user behavior, and automate incident response. AI-powered User and Entity Behavior Analytics (UEBA) tools track deviations in user activity, helping detect insider threats or unauthorized access attempts. Machine learning models can analyze large volumes of cloud security logs to identify patterns associated with cyberattacks, enabling real-time threat prevention.

AI is also used in automated security patching, reducing human intervention in vulnerability management. By continuously scanning cloud workloads, AI-driven security solutions can identify software weaknesses, recommend patches, and even apply fixes autonomously before attackers exploit them.

Despite these advancements, AI is not a silver bullet in cloud security. It requires human oversight, as AI models can produce false positives or miss novel attack strategies. Security teams must combine AI-driven security solutions with manual threat analysis to build a robust defense against AI-powered cyber threats.

The cloud threat landscape is evolving at an unprecedented pace, requiring organizations to adopt proactive security strategies. Cybercriminals are leveraging automation, AI, and advanced attack techniques to exploit vulnerabilities in cloud infrastructures. Businesses that fail to implement a strong security posture risk data breaches, financial losses, regulatory penalties, and reputational damage.

To mitigate these risks, organizations must invest in AI-powered threat intelligence, enforce strong identity security measures, and continuously monitor cloud activity for anomalies. The importance of real-time threat detection, automated incident response, and continuous employee security training cannot be overstated. Cloud security is a shared responsibility, meaning that both cloud providers and customers must work together to implement and enforce best practices.

As cyber threats become more sophisticated, organizations must stay ahead by embracing Zero Trust security models, leveraging AI-driven security tools, and integrating threat intelligence into their cloud security strategies. Only by understanding the cloud threat landscape and taking proactive security measures can businesses safely navigate the complexities of cloud computing.

Chapter 3
Cloud Security Architecture and Best Practices

As organizations continue to embrace cloud computing, designing a secure cloud architecture is no longer optional; it is a necessity. The cloud security architecture serves as the foundation for protecting data, applications, and workloads in the cloud while ensuring compliance with regulatory standards. Without a robust security framework, businesses are vulnerable to cyber threats such as data breaches, unauthorized access, insider threats, and denial-of-service attacks. A well-designed cloud security architecture must incorporate identity and access management, encryption, network security, monitoring, and compliance enforcement to create a resilient and threat-resistant cloud environment.

A secure cloud architecture follows the principle of defense-in-depth, which involves implementing multiple layers of security controls to mitigate risk at every level of cloud infrastructure. This strategy ensures that if one layer is compromised, additional layers of protection remain intact, preventing unauthorized access and minimizing the impact of potential breaches. The shared responsibility model in cloud computing dictates that while cloud providers secure the underlying infrastructure, customers are responsible for securing their applications, configurations, and data. This means organizations must be proactive in setting up security policies, enforcing access controls, and monitoring cloud environments for threats.

One of the critical components of cloud security is identity and access management. Unauthorized access is one of the leading causes of cloud security incidents, making it essential to establish strict authentication and authorization mechanisms. Organizations should implement multi-factor authentication to add an additional layer of protection beyond usernames and passwords. Role-based access control ensures that users only have access to the resources necessary for their job functions, minimizing the risk of insider threats or credential abuse. Regular audits of access permissions help identify unnecessary privileges and reduce the risk of unauthorized access to sensitive data.

Data protection and encryption are at the core of cloud security architecture. Organizations must ensure that their data remains confidential, whether it is at rest, in transit, or being processed in the cloud. Encryption technologies such as AES-256 for stored data and TLS 1.3 for data transmission help safeguard sensitive information from unauthorized access. Effective key management systems ensure that encryption keys are securely stored and accessed only by authorized systems. Data loss prevention mechanisms further strengthen security by detecting and preventing unauthorized transfers of sensitive information.

Cloud network security is another fundamental aspect of a well-designed cloud security architecture. Organizations must segment their cloud environments to reduce the risk of lateral movement by attackers. Virtual private clouds and network security groups allow businesses to isolate critical workloads from public-facing services, ensuring that only authorized traffic can reach sensitive systems. Firewalls, intrusion detection systems, and virtual private networks provide an added layer of protection by filtering incoming and outgoing traffic to prevent malicious access. Continuous monitoring of network activity allows organizations to detect anomalies and respond to potential threats in real time.

Application security plays a vital role in protecting cloud workloads from cyberattacks. Many breaches occur due to vulnerabilities in cloud-hosted applications, making it crucial for organizations to follow secure coding practices and conduct regular security assessments. Cloud applications must be designed with security in mind, ensuring they are protected from common attack techniques such as SQL injection, cross-site scripting, and API vulnerabilities. Developers should integrate security testing into the software development lifecycle, leveraging automated tools to identify and remediate vulnerabilities before applications are deployed. Web application firewalls provide additional protection by blocking malicious requests that attempt to exploit security flaws.

Monitoring and threat detection are essential for maintaining a secure cloud environment. Organizations must continuously track user activity, system logs, and network traffic to identify potential security incidents. Security information and event management systems aggregate security logs from various sources, providing a centralized platform for detecting suspicious behavior. AI-powered threat detection tools analyze patterns of activity to identify potential threats before they escalate into major security incidents. Automated incident response mechanisms can contain attacks in real time, reducing the time it takes to mitigate security breaches.

Regulatory compliance is a key consideration for businesses operating in the cloud. Organizations must align their cloud security practices with industry regulations such as GDPR, HIPAA, NIST, and the Nigerian Data Protection Regulation. Compliance management tools help businesses track regulatory requirements, conduct audits, and generate compliance reports. Failure to comply with data protection laws can result in financial penalties and reputational damage, making it imperative for businesses to implement security controls that meet legal obligations.

The Zero Trust security model has emerged as the best practice for securing cloud environments. Unlike traditional security approaches that rely on perimeter defenses, Zero Trust assumes that no user or device should be automatically trusted, regardless of whether they are inside or outside the network. Every access request is verified based on identity, device health, and contextual factors before granting access to cloud resources. Zero Trust policies enforce continuous authentication and least privilege access, reducing the risk of unauthorized access. By adopting a Zero Trust framework, organizations can minimize attack surfaces and strengthen security across their cloud infrastructure.

A proactive approach to cloud security requires organizations to establish best practices that reduce the likelihood of security incidents. Regularly updating cloud workloads, applications, and virtual machines with the latest security patches helps prevent attackers from exploiting known vulnerabilities. Implementing cloud security posture management tools enables organizations to automate security checks, identify misconfigurations, and enforce security policies across their cloud environments. Secure backup strategies ensure that critical data is protected from ransomware attacks and accidental loss. Multi-cloud security strategies help organizations prevent vendor lock-in while diversifying risk across different cloud providers.

As cloud technologies continue to evolve, cloud security architectures will need to adapt to new challenges. The increasing integration of artificial intelligence and machine learning in cybersecurity will enable organizations to automate threat detection and incident response with greater accuracy. Quantum computing, while still in its early stages, poses potential risks to encryption algorithms, making it important for businesses to explore quantum-resistant cryptographic methods. Confidential computing is gaining traction as a means to protect data even during processing, reducing exposure to unauthorized access. The future of cloud security will be shaped by emerging technologies that enhance automation, improve detection capabilities, and offer stronger encryption methods to protect cloud assets.

Cloud security is an ongoing process that requires continuous assessment, adaptation, and improvement. Organizations must remain vigilant against evolving cyber threats and adopt a security-first mindset when designing their cloud infrastructure. The ability to detect and respond to threats in real time, enforce strong identity controls, and integrate automated security solutions will determine the effectiveness of a cloud security strategy. By implementing best practices and leveraging advanced security technologies, businesses can create a resilient cloud environment that supports innovation while maintaining the highest levels of security.

Cloud security is an ongoing process that requires continuous assessment, adaptation, and improvement. Organizations must remain vigilant against evolving cyber threats and adopt a security-first mindset when designing their cloud infrastructure. The ability to detect and respond to threats in real-time, enforce strong identity controls, and integrate automated security solutions will determine the effectiveness of a cloud security strategy. However, security is not just about implementing the latest tools and technologies; it requires a cultural shift within organizations. Employees at all levels must be aware of security best practices, as human error remains one of the weakest links in cybersecurity. Organizations must invest in regular security training, incident response drills, and awareness programs to ensure that staff can recognize phishing attempts, understand the importance of strong passwords, and follow secure data handling procedures. A well-trained workforce significantly reduces the risk of security incidents caused by negligence or lack of awareness.

Another crucial aspect of cloud security architecture is visibility and control over cloud workloads. Many businesses operate in multi-cloud or hybrid cloud environments, where different cloud platforms, data centers, and on-premise systems work together to support operations. This complexity makes it difficult to maintain a unified security posture. Organizations must deploy cloud security posture management solutions to gain comprehensive visibility across their cloud environments. These tools provide automated security assessments, identify misconfigurations, and help enforce compliance policies. By maintaining a centralized view of cloud assets, organizations can quickly detect and remediate vulnerabilities before they are exploited by attackers.

Automation is becoming an integral part of modern cloud security strategies. As cyber threats evolve, traditional manual security practices are no longer sufficient to keep up with the speed and scale of cloud environments. Security automation enables businesses to respond to threats in real-time, reducing the time attackers have to exploit vulnerabilities. Automated security response mechanisms, such as AI-driven threat detection and self-healing systems, allow organizations to proactively defend against cyberattacks. For instance, machine learning algorithms can analyze network traffic patterns and detect anomalies indicative of an ongoing attack. Automated security policies can isolate affected resources, revoke access permissions, and initiate incident response procedures without requiring human intervention. This level of automation not only improves security efficiency but also minimizes the potential impact of security breaches.

Cloud-native security solutions are also transforming how organizations approach cloud security. Unlike traditional security models designed for on-premise environments, cloud-native security focuses on integrating security directly into cloud applications and infrastructure. Cloud-native security tools provide deeper integration with cloud providers' security services, allowing for better threat detection and response. For example, serverless security solutions help protect workloads running in function-as-a-service environments, while container security tools ensure that Docker and Kubernetes deployments remain secure. Organizations that adopt cloud-native security approaches benefit from faster incident response times and enhanced protection tailored to their cloud environments.

Resilience is another key factor in designing a strong cloud security architecture. While prevention is important, organizations must also prepare for security incidents by implementing robust disaster recovery and business continuity plans. Cloud providers offer various backup and recovery options, but businesses must take an active role in ensuring their data is recoverable in the event of an attack or failure. A multi-layered backup strategy, including immutable backups, air-gapped storage, and automated recovery testing, ensures that critical data remains protected from ransomware and other destructive attacks. Additionally, organizations should establish clear incident response protocols, defining roles and responsibilities for security teams, executives, and external partners in the event of a security breach. A well-prepared response plan reduces downtime, minimizes financial losses, and protects customer trust.

Threat intelligence is another critical component of cloud security. As cyber threats become more sophisticated, organizations must stay informed about emerging attack techniques and threat actors. Threat intelligence feeds provide real-time insights into known vulnerabilities, malware trends, and ongoing cyber campaigns. Security teams can use this information to proactively strengthen defenses, apply security patches, and fine-tune security policies. Many cloud security platforms now integrate AI-driven threat intelligence, allowing businesses to automate threat detection and mitigation. By leveraging real-time intelligence, organizations can stay ahead of cybercriminals and reduce the risk of falling victim to advanced persistent threats.

The future of cloud security architecture will continue to be shaped by technological advancements, regulatory changes, and evolving cyber threats. Organizations must remain agile and adaptable, continuously refining their security strategies to address new risks. As artificial intelligence and machine learning continue to play a larger role in cybersecurity, businesses must explore how these technologies can be leveraged to enhance cloud security operations. Additionally, the rise of edge computing and IoT devices introduces new security challenges that organizations must consider when designing cloud security architectures.

Quantum computing is expected to disrupt the field of cybersecurity, as traditional encryption methods may become vulnerable to quantum attacks. Organizations should begin preparing for quantum-resistant cryptographic solutions to ensure long-term data protection. Furthermore, confidential computing is gaining traction as a means to protect sensitive data even during processing, reducing exposure to unauthorized access. These advancements highlight the need for organizations to remain proactive and forward-thinking in their cloud security strategies.

Ultimately, cloud security is not a one-time effort but an ongoing commitment. Businesses that prioritize security as a core component of their cloud strategy will be better positioned to mitigate risks, protect customer data, and maintain trust in an increasingly digital world. By adopting a comprehensive security architecture that includes identity protection, encryption, continuous monitoring, automation, and threat intelligence, organizations can build a resilient cloud environment capable of withstanding modern cyber threats.

3.1 The Importance of Security by Design in Cloud Environments

One of the most overlooked aspects of cloud security architecture is the principle of Security by Design, where security measures are integrated into cloud environments from the ground up rather than added as an afterthought. Many organizations prioritize functionality, scalability, and deployment speed while treating security as a secondary concern. This reactive approach often results in costly security breaches, compliance violations, and operational disruptions. By embedding security into the design phase of cloud infrastructure, organizations can create a more robust and resilient cloud security posture.

Security by Design ensures that security controls are implemented at every layer of cloud infrastructure, from networking and identity management to data encryption and application security. For example, implementing secure software development lifecycle (SDLC) practices ensures that applications deployed in the cloud are built with security considerations from the start. Secure coding standards, vulnerability testing, and automated security scans should be integrated into DevOps pipelines to identify and remediate vulnerabilities before deployment. This approach, often referred to as DevSecOps, promotes a security-first mindset across development and IT teams, ensuring that security is not seen as a roadblock but as an essential part of the development process.

In addition to securing applications, infrastructure-as-code (IaC) security plays a crucial role in Security by Design. Organizations that use automation tools to provision cloud resources must ensure that security configurations are embedded into infrastructure deployment scripts. Misconfigured cloud environments are one of the leading causes of security breaches, often due to human error. By defining security policies as code, organizations can enforce consistent security standards across cloud deployments, reducing the risk of misconfigurations and compliance violations.

Another key component of Security by Design is default security settings. Many cloud services come with security settings that need to be manually configured by users, leaving room for potential misconfigurations. Organizations should adopt the principle of secure defaults, ensuring that cloud resources are provisioned with the highest level of security by default. This includes enforcing encryption, enabling logging and monitoring, and restricting public access to cloud storage and databases. Cloud providers offer security configuration templates and compliance frameworks that help businesses implement secure-by-default policies, but organizations must take an active role in validating and enforcing these settings.

Security by Design also extends to zero trust architecture, which eliminates implicit trust within cloud environments. Traditional security models rely on perimeter-based defenses, assuming that threats exist outside the network while internal users and systems are inherently trusted. However, this approach is ineffective in cloud computing, where workloads are distributed across multiple cloud providers, locations, and endpoints. Zero trust security ensures that every request for access is authenticated, authorized, and continuously verified, regardless of whether it originates from inside or outside the network. Implementing zero trust policies, such as continuous identity verification and micro-segmentation, strengthens cloud security by reducing attack surfaces and limiting the impact of potential breaches.

3.2 The Role of Cloud Access Security Brokers (CASBs) in Strengthening Security

As organizations continue to adopt multi-cloud and hybrid cloud environments, managing security policies, access controls, and compliance requirements across different cloud platforms becomes increasingly complex. **Cloud Access Security Brokers (CASBs)** have emerged as a critical solution to bridge the security gap between cloud service providers and enterprise security requirements. CASBs provide visibility, compliance enforcement, data security, and threat protection for cloud applications, ensuring that organizations can securely manage their cloud environments without compromising productivity or agility.

One of the primary functions of CASBs is visibility into cloud usage and data movement. Many organizations struggle with shadow IT, where employees use unsanctioned cloud applications without the knowledge of the IT department. Shadow IT increases security risks, as these unauthorized applications may lack proper security controls and compliance measures. CASBs help organizations identify, monitor, and control the use of cloud applications, providing a comprehensive view of cloud activity to prevent data leaks and unauthorized access.

In addition to visibility, CASBs enhance data security by enforcing encryption, access control, and data loss prevention (DLP) policies. Organizations often store sensitive customer data, intellectual property, and confidential business information in cloud environments. Without proper security measures, this data is vulnerable to breaches and insider threats. CASBs allow businesses to apply encryption policies at the file level, ensuring that sensitive data remains protected even if it is transferred outside the organization. DLP capabilities enable organizations to monitor and restrict the movement of sensitive data, preventing unauthorized users from sharing or downloading confidential files.

CASBs also play a crucial role in compliance enforcement. Organizations operating in regulated industries must adhere to various security and privacy laws, such as GDPR, HIPAA, and the Nigerian Data Protection Regulation (NDPR). Ensuring compliance with multiple cloud providers can be challenging, as each platform has different security controls and configurations. CASBs provide automated compliance reporting and enforcement, helping businesses align their cloud security practices with industry regulations. By integrating CASBs into their cloud environments, organizations can streamline compliance efforts, reduce regulatory risks, and demonstrate adherence to legal requirements.

Another key feature of CASBs is advanced threat protection. Cyber threats such as malware, ransomware, and account hijacking remain persistent challenges in cloud security. CASBs leverage AI-driven threat intelligence and behavior analytics to detect and respond to suspicious activities in real-time. By analyzing user behavior, CASBs can identify anomalies such as unusual login locations, excessive data downloads, or attempted access to restricted files. These proactive security measures help organizations prevent data breaches and mitigate insider threats before they escalate.

Incorporating CASBs into a cloud security architecture strengthens an organization's overall security posture by providing visibility, data protection, compliance enforcement, and threat detection across cloud environments. As businesses continue to expand their cloud footprints, CASBs will remain an essential tool for managing cloud security challenges and ensuring that cloud applications are used securely and in accordance with corporate policies.

Building a secure cloud architecture requires a multi-layered security approach that integrates Security by Design, Zero Trust principles, and automated security enforcement mechanisms. Organizations must move beyond traditional security models and embrace modern cloud security frameworks that focus on continuous verification, proactive threat detection, and automated remediation. Security must be embedded into every layer of cloud infrastructure, from identity management and network security to data encryption and compliance enforcement.

As cyber threats continue to evolve, organizations must remain agile and proactive, continuously updating their security strategies to adapt to new risks. Emerging technologies such as AI-driven security analytics, confidential computing, and quantum-resistant encryption will shape the future of cloud security, enabling businesses to stay ahead of sophisticated attacks. Security teams must leverage automation, threat intelligence, and advanced cloud security tools to detect and respond to security incidents in real time.

Ultimately, cloud security is a shared responsibility between cloud providers and customers. While cloud service providers offer robust security features, businesses must take an active role in securing their cloud workloads, enforcing strict access controls, and implementing comprehensive security policies. By adopting best practices, leveraging cutting-edge security solutions, and fostering a security-first culture, organizations can create a resilient cloud environment that supports business growth while safeguarding critical assets.

Chapter 4
Regulatory Compliance and Cloud Security Standards

The rapid adoption of cloud computing has transformed the way businesses operate, offering flexibility, scalability, and cost efficiency. However, this shift has also introduced complex legal and regulatory challenges, particularly concerning data protection, privacy, and security. Organizations leveraging cloud technologies must navigate an evolving landscape of compliance requirements to ensure that their data handling practices align with regional and industry-specific regulations. Failure to comply with these standards can result in legal penalties, financial losses, and reputational damage. Understanding cloud security regulations and implementing the necessary security frameworks is crucial for organizations to maintain compliance while safeguarding sensitive data.

Regulatory compliance in cloud computing is driven by the need to protect customer data from unauthorized access, breaches, and misuse. Governments and regulatory bodies worldwide have established data protection laws that define how businesses must collect, store, and process information in the cloud. Regulations such as the General Data Protection Regulation (GDPR) in Europe, the Health Insurance Portability and Accountability Act (HIPAA) in the United States, and the Nigerian Data Protection Regulation (NDPR) in Nigeria impose strict requirements on organizations handling personal data. These regulations mandate organizations to implement security measures such as encryption, access controls, and breach notification policies to ensure the confidentiality, integrity, and availability of data stored in the cloud.

One of the primary challenges businesses face in achieving cloud compliance is the shared responsibility model of cloud computing. While cloud service providers secure the underlying infrastructure, customers are responsible for protecting their applications, configurations, and data. This means that organizations must take an active role in securing their cloud environments by enforcing access restrictions, monitoring user activities, and ensuring compliance with regulatory policies. Cloud providers offer compliance certifications and security frameworks to help businesses meet regulatory requirements, but ultimate responsibility lies with the customer.

Data sovereignty is another critical factor in cloud compliance. Many countries enforce data localization laws, requiring businesses to store and process data within national borders to prevent foreign entities from accessing sensitive information. These regulations can impact cloud adoption strategies, as businesses must select cloud providers with data centers in compliance with local laws. Organizations operating in multiple regions must navigate cross-border data transfer laws, ensuring that data flows between different jurisdictions comply with international regulations. Implementing data residency controls and encryption mechanisms helps businesses maintain compliance while leveraging the global capabilities of cloud services.

To address compliance challenges, organizations must align their cloud security practices with established security frameworks and standards. The National Institute of Standards and Technology (NIST) Cybersecurity Framework provides a structured approach to identifying, protecting, detecting, responding to, and recovering from security threats in cloud environments. The ISO/IEC 27001 standard outlines best practices for information security management, helping organizations establish a robust security posture. The Center for Internet Security (CIS) Benchmarks offer cloud-specific security controls for platforms such as AWS, Microsoft Azure, and Google Cloud, guiding organizations in configuring their cloud resources securely.

Achieving compliance in cloud environments requires continuous monitoring and enforcement of security policies. Organizations must implement security information and event management (SIEM) solutions to track security incidents, detect anomalies, and generate compliance reports. Automated compliance tools streamline the auditing process by assessing cloud configurations against regulatory requirements and providing real-time alerts for policy violations. Cloud access security brokers (CASBs) help enforce compliance policies by monitoring data movement, preventing unauthorized access, and ensuring that cloud applications adhere to security standards.

Another essential aspect of cloud compliance is incident response and breach notification policies. Regulations such as GDPR mandate that organizations report security breaches within a specific timeframe to regulatory authorities and affected customers. Developing a cloud-specific incident response plan ensures that businesses can quickly detect, contain, and mitigate security incidents. Establishing a clear chain of communication between security teams, cloud providers, and legal authorities enables organizations to respond to compliance violations efficiently.

Cloud security compliance is not a one-time effort but an ongoing process that requires organizations to stay informed about regulatory updates, emerging threats, and evolving best practices. Many regulations are continuously updated to address new cybersecurity challenges, meaning businesses must adopt a proactive compliance strategy rather than a reactive one. This involves regularly reviewing security policies, updating access controls, and conducting risk assessments to identify vulnerabilities in cloud environments. By implementing a culture of compliance, organizations can ensure that security and data protection measures are integrated into everyday operations rather than being treated as an afterthought.

One of the most significant factors influencing regulatory compliance in cloud computing is the dynamic nature of cloud environments. Unlike traditional on-premise infrastructures, cloud systems are highly scalable and often experience frequent changes in configurations, workloads, and user access. This makes it challenging for businesses to maintain a static compliance framework. Automated compliance tools and continuous monitoring solutions play a crucial role in addressing this challenge by providing real-time insights into security configurations, detecting compliance violations, and generating audit reports. These tools help organizations remain compliant by ensuring that cloud environments align with industry regulations at all times, even as infrastructure changes occur.

Third-party risk management is another critical component of cloud security compliance. Many businesses rely on cloud service providers, software vendors, and external consultants to manage cloud workloads, increasing the complexity of regulatory compliance. Organizations must conduct thorough due diligence when selecting cloud vendors, ensuring that they meet security and compliance standards required by law. Service Level Agreements (SLAs) should outline compliance responsibilities, data ownership policies, and incident response protocols to prevent misunderstandings in the event of a security breach. Establishing clear contractual obligations with cloud providers helps businesses maintain compliance while mitigating risks associated with third-party dependencies.

Encryption and data protection strategies are fundamental to maintaining compliance in cloud environments. Many data protection regulations, including GDPR and NDPR, mandate that organizations encrypt sensitive information both at rest and in transit to prevent unauthorized access. However, encryption alone is not sufficient to ensure compliance. Organizations must implement robust key management practices to control access to encryption keys, preventing unauthorized decryption of sensitive data. Hardware security modules (HSMs) and cloud-native key management systems (KMS) provide secure storage and management of encryption keys, ensuring that encryption processes align with compliance requirements.

Access control policies also play a significant role in cloud compliance. Many regulatory standards require organizations to enforce the principle of least privilege, ensuring that users and applications only have access to the data and resources necessary for their roles. Multi-factor authentication (MFA), identity and access management (IAM), and role-based access control (RBAC) are essential security measures that help enforce access restrictions in cloud environments. By continuously monitoring user activities and logging access events, businesses can detect unauthorized access attempts and prevent security breaches before they occur.

In addition to enforcing access controls, organizations must implement data classification policies to manage sensitive information in compliance with regulatory requirements. Data classification involves categorizing data based on its sensitivity, risk level, and regulatory obligations. For example, personally identifiable information (PII) should be subject to stricter security controls than general business data. Cloud security tools can automate data classification processes, applying security policies based on predefined data protection requirements. Proper data classification ensures that compliance measures are tailored to the sensitivity of information stored in the cloud, reducing the risk of data exposure and regulatory violations.

Incident response and breach notification policies are essential components of regulatory compliance. Many data protection laws require businesses to report security breaches within a specified timeframe to regulatory authorities and affected individuals. Organizations must develop a comprehensive incident response plan that includes breach detection mechanisms, containment strategies, and legal notification procedures. Cloud providers offer security services such as threat intelligence, automated alerts, and forensic analysis tools that help businesses respond to security incidents quickly and effectively. By preparing for potential data breaches in advance, organizations can minimize regulatory penalties and maintain trust with customers.

Achieving cloud security compliance also requires continuous employee education and training. Many security breaches occur due to human error, such as misconfigurations, weak passwords, and falling victim to phishing attacks. Security awareness training programs help employees recognize cybersecurity threats, follow the best practices for data protection, and comply with regulatory requirements. Regular training sessions ensure that staff remain updated on the latest compliance policies and understand their roles in maintaining cloud security.

The integration of artificial intelligence (AI) and machine learning (ML) in compliance management is transforming how organizations maintain regulatory adherence. AI-powered compliance tools analyze vast amounts of security data, identify potential compliance violations, and provide recommendations for remediation. Machine learning models can detect patterns of suspicious activity, helping businesses identify risks before they escalate into regulatory violations. By leveraging AI-driven compliance solutions, organizations can automate security monitoring, improve threat detection, and enhance their overall compliance strategy.

The future of cloud security compliance will be shaped by emerging technologies and evolving regulatory landscapes. Governments and regulatory bodies continue to introduce new data protection laws to address cybersecurity challenges, requiring businesses to stay agile in their compliance efforts. Cloud security frameworks will become increasingly reliant on automation, AI, and blockchain technology to enhance transparency, enforce compliance policies, and secure cloud environments against cyber threats. Organizations that prioritize compliance as an ongoing process rather than a one-time requirement will be better positioned to navigate regulatory challenges and maintain a strong security posture in the digital era.

4.1 The Role of Compliance Automation in Cloud Security

As cloud infrastructures grow in complexity, manually ensuring regulatory compliance becomes increasingly difficult and resource intensive. Organizations must constantly monitor security configurations, audit access controls, and verify data protection mechanisms to align with evolving regulatory requirements. Compliance automation has emerged as a powerful solution to simplify this process, allowing businesses to continuously enforce security policies, detect compliance violations in real time, and generate audit reports with minimal manual intervention. By leveraging compliance automation tools, organizations can enhance efficiency, reduce human error, and maintain regulatory adherence even as cloud environments scale.

Compliance automation solutions integrate with cloud platforms to monitor security settings, detect misconfigurations, and ensure that policies such as encryption, access control, and data retention are consistently applied. These tools provide real-time compliance assessments, alerting security teams to deviations from regulatory requirements before they become critical vulnerabilities. For example, automated compliance platforms can scan cloud environments for unauthorized public storage permissions, unencrypted data repositories, or inactive user accounts with privileged access. By identifying and remediating these issues automatically, businesses can proactively mitigate compliance risks and strengthen their security posture.

Another key advantage of compliance automation is the ability to generate audit-ready reports that simplify regulatory inspections. Many compliance frameworks, such as GDPR, HIPAA, and ISO 27001, require businesses to maintain detailed records of security controls, incident response actions, and data protection measures.

Compliance automation tools streamline this process by collecting security logs, documenting policy enforcement, and generating reports that demonstrate adherence to regulatory standards. This reduces the burden on compliance teams, allowing them to focus on strategic security initiatives rather than manual documentation and audits.

Machine learning and artificial intelligence further enhance compliance automation by identifying patterns and anomalies that may indicate compliance risks. AI-driven compliance tools analyze vast amounts of cloud security data to detect suspicious behavior, predict potential compliance failures, and recommend corrective actions. These technologies enable businesses to stay ahead of emerging threats and evolving regulations, ensuring that cloud security remains proactive rather than reactive. As regulatory requirements continue to evolve, compliance automation will play a crucial role in helping organizations adapt to new mandates while maintaining a secure cloud environment.

4.2 Third-Party Risk Management and Regulatory Compliance

Organizations rarely operate in isolation when using cloud services. Most businesses rely on third-party vendors, cloud service providers, and external contractors to manage and support cloud-based applications. While these partnerships enhance operational efficiency, they also introduce significant compliance risks. Many regulatory frameworks hold organizations accountable for data protection, even when data is processed or stored by third-party providers. This makes third-party risk management a critical component of cloud security compliance.

Businesses must conduct thorough due diligence when selecting cloud service providers to ensure that they meet regulatory security requirements. This involves assessing a provider's security certifications, reviewing data handling policies, and verifying compliance with industry regulations. Cloud providers that adhere to recognized security standards such as ISO 27001, SOC 2, and GDPR demonstrate a commitment to data protection and compliance. However, organizations must go beyond certifications and conduct regular audits to validate a provider's security practices.

Service Level Agreements (SLAs) play a key role in defining compliance responsibilities between organizations and their cloud providers. SLAs should clearly outline data ownership, security obligations, breach notification procedures, and regulatory compliance requirements. Establishing contractual agreements that specify compliance responsibilities ensures that both parties understand their roles in maintaining data security. Additionally, organizations should negotiate data residency requirements to ensure that cloud providers store and process data in locations that comply with regional regulations.

Continuous monitoring of third-party vendors is essential for managing compliance risks. Many businesses implement third-party risk management platforms that track vendor security performance, assess compliance adherence, and provide risk scores based on security incidents or policy violations. Automated security assessments allow organizations to evaluate vendors in real-time, reducing the risk of compliance failures caused by third-party mismanagement. Regular audits, security assessments, and risk evaluations help businesses maintain visibility into third-party security practices and ensure compliance across the entire cloud supply chain.

Another consideration in third-party risk management is the risk of supply chain attacks, where cybercriminals target cloud service providers to compromise multiple customers. The **SolarWinds breach**, for example, demonstrated how attackers can infiltrate widely used software vendors to gain access to corporate and government networks. To mitigate such risks, businesses should adopt a **zero-trust approach to third-party access**, implementing the least privilege access controls, monitoring external access activities, and segmenting cloud resources to prevent lateral movement in the event of a breach.

By taking a proactive approach to third-party risk management, organizations can strengthen their cloud security compliance framework while minimizing regulatory exposure. Ensuring that cloud vendors and external partners adhere to strict security standards, enforce compliance policies, and align with legal obligations protects businesses from regulatory fines, data breaches, and reputational damage.

Regulatory compliance is an essential aspect of cloud security that requires continuous monitoring, proactive enforcement, and collaboration between businesses, cloud service providers, and third-party vendors. As data protection laws become more stringent and cyber threats evolve, organizations must implement compliance automation, third-party risk management frameworks, and AI-driven security solutions to maintain adherence to regulatory standards. Businesses that fail to comply with data protection regulations risk severe penalties, legal repercussions, and loss of customer trust.

To achieve long-term compliance in cloud environments, organizations must integrate compliance into their overall security strategy. This involves adopting security best practices such as encryption, access control, automated compliance assessments, and incident response planning. By leveraging compliance automation, businesses can streamline auditing processes, reduce operational overhead, and ensure that cloud environments remain secure against cyber threats. Additionally, maintaining strong partnerships with cloud service providers and enforcing third-party security requirements help businesses minimize external risks and ensure regulatory alignment.

58

Chapter 5
Securing Cloud Storage and Data Protection Strategies

Cloud storage has become an integral component of modern IT infrastructure, allowing businesses to store vast amounts of data without the limitations of physical hardware. However, as organizations migrate sensitive information to the cloud, securing cloud storage has become a critical concern. Data breaches, unauthorized access, misconfigurations, and compliance violations pose significant risks to cloud-stored data. To mitigate these risks, organizations must implement robust data protection strategies, including encryption, access control, data loss prevention, and secure backup solutions. A well-structured cloud storage security framework ensures that data remains confidential, available, and protected against evolving cyber threats.

One of the fundamental principles of securing cloud storage is data encryption. Encryption protects data by converting it into an unreadable format, ensuring that only authorized users with the correct decryption keys can access the original content. Organizations should encrypt data at rest, in transit, and during processing to prevent unauthorized access. Cloud service providers offer built-in encryption mechanisms, allowing businesses to secure their data without significant overhead. Encryption algorithms such as AES-256 for storage and TLS 1.3 for network transmission provide industry-standard protection against data interception and leaks. However, encryption is only effective if managed correctly, making key management an essential aspect of cloud security. Secure key management systems (KMS) and hardware security modules (HSMs) provide controlled access to encryption keys, reducing the risk of compromise.

Access control mechanisms play a crucial role in preventing unauthorized users from accessing cloud storage. Organizations must implement Identity and Access Management (IAM) policies to enforce the principle of least privilege, ensuring that users and applications only have access to the data necessary for their roles. Multi-factor authentication (MFA) adds an extra layer of security, requiring users to verify their identity before accessing cloud storage. Role-based access control (RBAC) and attribute-based access control (ABAC) further enhance security by defining permissions based on job responsibilities and specific security attributes. Regular audits of access logs and permissions help organizations identify excessive privileges, inactive accounts, and unauthorized access attempts.

One of the most common risks in cloud storage security is misconfigurations. Many cloud storage breaches occur due to publicly exposed storage buckets, databases, and object storage that were mistakenly configured to allow external access. Cybercriminals actively scan for misconfigured cloud storage using tools like Shodan and Censys, making it imperative for organizations to continuously monitor and assess storage configurations. Cloud security posture management (CSPM) solutions automate the detection of misconfigurations, providing real-time alerts and recommendations for remediation. Organizations must ensure that storage repositories are private by default, enforce strict access control lists (ACLs), and disable unnecessary public sharing features to reduce exposure.

Data loss prevention (DLP) strategies are essential for safeguarding sensitive data in the cloud. DLP solutions help organizations detect and prevent unauthorized data transfers, ensuring that confidential information is not shared outside approved channels. Cloud-native DLP tools analyze file content, metadata, and user behavior to identify potential data leakage incidents. Policies can be set to restrict data downloads, enforce automatic encryption, and block the sharing of sensitive files through email or external collaboration tools. DLP solutions also help businesses comply with data protection regulations by ensuring that personal identifiable information (PII) and financial data are securely handled.

Backup and disaster recovery planning are critical components of cloud data protection. Ransomware attacks, accidental deletions, and cloud service outages can lead to data loss if proper backup strategies are not in place. Organizations should adopt a 3-2-1 backup strategy, where three copies of data are maintained on two different storage media, with one stored offsite or in an immutable backup repository. Cloud providers offer automated backup solutions, enabling businesses to schedule incremental backups, versioning, and replication across multiple geographic locations. In addition to backups, organizations must conduct disaster recovery (DR) testing to ensure that critical systems can be restored quickly in the event of an incident.

Cloud storage security also requires organizations to monitor and log all storage activities to detect anomalies and suspicious access patterns. Security information and event management (SIEM) solutions provide centralized logging and real-time analysis of storage events, helping security teams identify unauthorized access attempts, data exfiltration, and malicious insider threats. AI-driven anomaly detection tools can flag unusual behaviors, such as large-scale data downloads, unauthorized file modifications, or access from unfamiliar locations, triggering automated response mechanisms to mitigate potential threats.

Compliance with data protection regulations is another key factor in cloud storage security. Laws such as GDPR, HIPAA, CCPA, and NDPR impose strict requirements on how businesses handle customer data. Organizations must ensure that data retention policies align with legal mandates, implementing data anonymization, tokenization, and retention limits to minimize regulatory risks. Compliance management tools integrated with cloud storage provide automated auditing, ensuring that stored data adheres to security and privacy standards.

As organizations continue to adopt cloud-first strategies, secure file sharing and collaboration must also be considered. Cloud collaboration platforms enable employees to work remotely and share files seamlessly, but improper sharing settings can expose sensitive data to unauthorized parties. Organizations should implement enterprise-grade file sharing solutions with built-in encryption, access expiration controls, and activity tracking to secure collaborative workflows. Implementing zero-trust policies ensures that every file access request is authenticated and authorized, reducing the risk of unauthorized data exposure.

Emerging technologies such as confidential computing, homomorphic encryption, and blockchain-based data integrity solutions are expected to enhance cloud storage security. Confidential computing allows data to remain encrypted even during processing, minimizing exposure to external threats. Homomorphic encryption enables computations on encrypted data without decryption, offering privacy-preserving cloud data analytics. Blockchain solutions provide tamper-proof audit trails for cloud storage transactions, ensuring data integrity and non-repudiation. These advancements will shape the future of cloud security, providing businesses with innovative tools to protect their most valuable digital assets.

Securing cloud storage requires a multi-layered security approach that includes encryption, access control, data loss prevention, backups, monitoring, and compliance enforcement. By integrating these security measures, organizations can protect their cloud-stored data from cyber threats, accidental exposure, and regulatory violations. As cybercriminals continue to target cloud environments, businesses must remain proactive in their security strategies, leveraging automation, AI-driven threat detection, and advanced encryption techniques to safeguard critical information.

Securing cloud storage requires a multi-layered security approach that integrates encryption, access control, data loss prevention, backups, monitoring, and compliance enforcement. However, implementing these measures effectively demands a strategic mindset, continuous evaluation, and an understanding of the evolving threat landscape. Cloud security is not a static process but an ongoing effort that requires organizations to stay ahead of emerging risks, technological advancements, and regulatory changes. As cybercriminals develop new attack techniques, businesses must constantly refine their cloud storage security strategies to mitigate risks and protect critical data assets.

One of the most persistent threats to cloud storage is ransomware, a type of malware that encrypts files and demands payment for decryption. Ransomware attacks have become more sophisticated, with attackers now using double extortion tactics, where they not only encrypt data but also threaten to leak it publicly if the ransom is not paid. Cloud environments are not immune to ransomware, as attackers can exploit weak access controls, misconfigured cloud storage, or compromised credentials to gain entry. To defend against ransomware, organizations should implement immutable backups, which prevent data from being modified or deleted once stored. Additionally, endpoint detection and response (EDR) solutions, AI-driven threat intelligence, and behavior-based anomaly detection can help identify ransomware activity before files are encrypted.

Another major risk in cloud storage security is insider threats, which include both malicious insiders and negligent employees who unintentionally expose sensitive data. Unlike external attacks, insider threats are harder to detect because the individuals involved already have authorized access to cloud resources. Insider threats can take various forms, such as employees misusing access privileges, disgruntled workers leaking confidential data, or negligent users mishandling sensitive files. Organizations must enforce strict role-based access control (RBAC), implement user behavior analytics (UBA) to monitor suspicious activities, and establish zero-trust security models that continuously verify user identities and access requests. Security awareness training is also critical, as educating employees about phishing attacks, social engineering, and proper data handling procedures can reduce the risk of accidental data exposure.

The rapid growth of multi-cloud and hybrid cloud environments introduces additional complexity to securing cloud storage. Many organizations use multiple cloud providers, combining services from AWS, Microsoft Azure, Google Cloud, and private cloud infrastructures. While this approach provides flexibility and reduces reliance on a single provider, it also creates security challenges, such as inconsistent security configurations, difficulty in tracking data movement across different platforms, and increased attack surfaces. To address these challenges, businesses must adopt cloud security posture management (CSPM) solutions, which provide unified visibility across multi-cloud environments, enforce consistent security policies, and automate compliance monitoring. Organizations should also implement data discovery and classification tools that help identify where sensitive data resides, ensuring that it is properly secured across all cloud platforms.

Regulatory compliance remains a critical aspect of cloud storage security, especially as governments and industry bodies introduce stricter data protection laws. Many regulations require organizations to maintain data integrity, ensure access transparency, and provide customers with the ability to delete or retrieve their personal information upon request. Failure to meet these requirements can result in severe financial penalties and reputational damage. Businesses operating in regulated industries such as healthcare, finance, and government must implement data governance frameworks, conduct regular security audits, and use automated compliance management tools to ensure that cloud storage meets legal obligations. Keeping up with evolving regulations requires a proactive approach, where businesses continuously update security policies, review data protection measures, and collaborate with cloud service providers to address compliance challenges.

Artificial intelligence and machine learning are playing an increasingly important role in enhancing cloud storage security. AI-powered security tools can analyze vast amounts of cloud activity logs, identify patterns of suspicious behavior, and trigger automated security responses before threats escalate. For example, AI-driven anomaly detection can identify when an unauthorized user attempts to access sensitive cloud storage, while machine learning-based security analytics can distinguish between normal user behavior and potential insider threats. By integrating AI-driven security automation, organizations can reduce response times, minimize human error, and improve overall cloud security resilience.

Confidential computing and homomorphic encryption are emerging as next-generation solutions for securing cloud-stored data. Confidential computing enables organizations to encrypt data even while it is being processed, ensuring that sensitive information remains protected at all times. This technology is particularly valuable for industries that handle highly sensitive data, such as healthcare, finance, and government sectors. Similarly, homomorphic encryption allows computations to be performed on encrypted data without decrypting it, enabling secure data analytics and machine learning without exposing raw data to potential threats. As these technologies continue to mature, they will provide new layers of protection for organizations looking to strengthen their cloud storage security.

Ultimately, securing cloud storage is not just about implementing individual security measures but about building a culture of security within an organization. Security teams, IT professionals, developers, and end-users all play a role in protecting cloud-stored data. By fostering a security-first mindset, businesses can ensure that security becomes an integral part of daily operations rather than an afterthought. This includes educating employees on data protection best practices, enforcing strict security policies, and leveraging cutting-edge security technologies to protect sensitive information from ever-evolving cyber threats.

5.1 The Role of Threat Intelligence in Cloud Storage Security

As cyber threats evolve, organizations must take a proactive approach to securing cloud storage by integrating threat intelligence into their security strategies. Threat intelligence involves gathering and analyzing data on emerging attack techniques, threat actors, and vulnerabilities to predict and prevent cyberattacks. In cloud storage security, threat intelligence provides insights into potential risks such as ransomware campaigns, data exfiltration techniques, and misconfiguration exploits, allowing security teams to strengthen defenses before an attack occurs.

One of the primary advantages of threat intelligence in cloud storage security is its ability to identify suspicious behavior and anomalous activities before they escalate into full-scale breaches. AI-driven threat intelligence platforms analyze cloud activity logs, detecting unusual access patterns, unauthorized file downloads, and lateral movement attempts by attackers. For example, if a user suddenly attempts to download large volumes of data from cloud storage at an unusual hour or from an unrecognized location, the system can flag this as a potential data theft attempt and trigger automated security measures such as revoking access or requiring additional authentication.

Threat intelligence also plays a crucial role in preventing supply chain attacks, were cybercriminals compromise cloud service providers, third-party applications, or cloud-integrated tools to gain access to sensitive data. Organizations must monitor global threat intelligence feeds, stay informed about new vulnerabilities affecting their cloud service providers, and apply security patches and updates promptly to mitigate risks. Integrating real-time threat intelligence with cloud security posture management (CSPM) solutions enhances visibility and ensures that cloud storage environments are protected against the latest attack techniques.

Another key application of threat intelligence in cloud storage security is automated incident response. By leveraging machine learning and AI-driven security automation, businesses can create predictive security models that detect potential breaches before they occur. For instance, if threat intelligence data indicates an increase in credential stuffing attacks, organizations can preemptively enforce multi-factor authentication (MFA), reset compromised passwords, and block malicious IP addresses from accessing cloud storage. This proactive defense mechanism reduces the attack surface and strengthens cloud data security.

5.2 Emerging Technologies in Cloud Storage Protection

As cloud adoption increases, security researchers and technology companies are developing **next**-generation solutions to enhance cloud storage protection. Emerging technologies such as confidential computing, homomorphic encryption, and blockchain-based data integrity verification are set to revolutionize how organizations secure cloud-stored data. These technologies aim to minimize data exposure, enhance privacy, and prevent unauthorized access, even in cases were attackers compromise cloud storage infrastructure.

One of the most promising innovations in cloud storage security is confidential computing, which ensures that data remains encrypted even during processing. Traditionally, encryption protects data at rest and in transit, but during computation, data is typically decrypted, creating a temporary window of vulnerability. Confidential computing leverages trusted execution environments (TEEs) to allow cloud workloads to run on secure, isolated hardware enclaves where data remains encrypted throughout processing. This technology significantly enhances privacy and security for sensitive applications such as financial transactions, healthcare data analytics, and government communications.

Another cutting-edge advancement in cloud storage security is homomorphic encryption, which allows computations to be performed on encrypted data without decrypting it. This innovation is particularly valuable for industries that require secure data analytics and cloud-based machine learning while maintaining strict data confidentiality requirements. For example, financial institutions can use homomorphic encryption to analyze customer transaction data in the cloud without exposing raw financial records to third-party cloud providers. While homomorphic encryption is still in its early stages, ongoing research is expected to make it a mainstream security technology in the coming years.

Blockchain technology is also emerging as a powerful tool for ensuring data integrity in cloud storage. Blockchain-based storage solutions use decentralized, tamper-proof ledgers to record and verify every change made to cloud-stored files. This ensures that data cannot be altered or deleted without an auditable record, making it ideal for legal documents, medical records, and financial statements. Blockchain-powered immutable logging mechanisms enhance compliance efforts by providing a transparent, verifiable history of data modifications, helping organizations meet regulatory audit requirements.

Additionally, self-healing storage systems are being developed to enhance cloud data resilience. These systems use AI-driven automation to detect file corruption, ransomware encryption, or unauthorized modifications and restore the original version from secure backup repositories without human intervention. This technology is particularly useful for mitigating the impact of ransomware attacks, where businesses can quickly recover encrypted files without paying ransom demands.

Cloud storage security is a multifaceted challenge that requires a combination of traditional security best practices and emerging technologies. Organizations must continuously assess and refine their security strategies, integrating threat intelligence, automation, and advanced encryption techniques to stay ahead of cyber threats. The growing sophistication of cyberattacks means that businesses cannot afford to rely solely on reactive security measures—proactive defense mechanisms such as AI-powered threat detection, automated compliance monitoring, and predictive analytics must be incorporated to prevent security incidents before they occur.

As cloud security continues to evolve, businesses must also invest in user education and awareness. Employees, contractors, and third-party vendors must understand the importance of secure data handling, access control policies, and phishing prevention techniques to reduce the risk of insider threats and human error. Security is a shared responsibility, and fostering a culture of cybersecurity awareness within an organization is just as important as implementing technical security controls.

Chapter 6
Identity and Access Management (IAM) in Cloud Security

In the world of cloud computing, securing access to systems, applications, and data is one of the most critical aspects of cybersecurity. Identity and Access Management (IAM) is the framework that governs how users and systems authenticate, authorize, and manage their access to cloud resources. As cloud environments become more complex and distributed, IAM plays a crucial role in preventing unauthorized access, enforcing security policies, and minimizing insider threats. Weak or misconfigured identity controls can expose cloud infrastructure to breaches, privilege escalation attacks, and data theft. Implementing a strong IAM strategy ensures that only the right individuals and systems have the appropriate level of access, reducing security risks and enhancing compliance with industry regulations.

IAM solutions are designed to control who can access what, when, and how within a cloud environment. The primary components of IAM include user authentication, authorization, access control policies, role-based permissions, and identity governance. A well-structured IAM system ensures that users and applications are verified before accessing cloud resources, reducing the risk of compromised accounts being exploited. Organizations must enforce multi-factor authentication, which requires users to verify their identity using multiple credentials, such as passwords, biometrics, or one-time authentication codes. MFA significantly strengthens security by making it more difficult for attackers to gain access using stolen credentials.

Another critical aspect of IAM is the least privilege access, a principle that restricts user permissions to only what is necessary for their specific role. Excessive access rights increase the attack surface, as compromised accounts with broad privileges can be exploited to move laterally within a cloud environment. Organizations should implement role-based access control and attribute-based access control to define permissions based on job responsibilities and specific attributes such as location, device type, or risk level. Regularly reviewing IAM policies and revoking unnecessary permissions helps reduce the risk of insider threats and accidental data exposure.

Managing IAM in multi-cloud and hybrid environments introduces additional complexity, as different cloud providers use unique identity frameworks. Businesses must ensure that IAM policies are consistent across all cloud platforms, using identity federation and single sign-on solutions to provide seamless authentication without compromising security. Identity federation allows users to access multiple cloud services with a single set of credentials, reducing the risk of password fatigue and unauthorized account sharing.

Organizations should integrate IAM with cloud access security brokers to enforce access policies, monitor user behavior, and detect anomalies that could indicate credential compromise.

One of the biggest threats to cloud security is privileged access misuse. Privileged accounts, such as administrators, developers, and system engineers, have elevated permissions that allow them to modify configurations, access sensitive data, and manage cloud workloads. If compromised, privileged accounts can be used to execute devastating attacks, including data breaches, ransomware deployment, and system takeovers. Organizations must implement privileged access management solutions to monitor, control, and restrict the use of privileged accounts. PAM solutions enforce just-in-time access, which grants temporary privileges only when needed, reducing the risk of persistent privileged access abuse.

IAM also plays a key role in identity governance and compliance. Many regulatory frameworks, such as GDPR, HIPAA, ISO 27001, and NDPR, require organizations to enforce strict identity and access controls to protect sensitive data. Automated identity lifecycle management ensures that users' access permissions are adjusted when they change roles, leave the company, or no longer require access. Implementing continuous access auditing, logging, and reporting helps businesses demonstrate compliance, detect anomalies, and identify potential security violations.

With the rise of artificial intelligence and machine learning, IAM solutions are becoming more adaptive and intelligent. AI-driven IAM can analyze user behavior, detect anomalies, and automatically trigger security responses when suspicious activities occur. For example, if an IAM system detects a user logging in from an unfamiliar country, it can block access, enforce additional authentication steps, or alert security teams. Machine learning models can also assess risk levels dynamically, granting or restricting access based on real-time security assessments rather than static permissions.

The Zero Trust security model has gained popularity as a modern approach to IAM. Traditional security models rely on perimeter defenses, assuming that users inside the corporate network are trusted while external users are potential threats. However, in cloud environments, the perimeter is no longer well-defined, as users access cloud resources from multiple devices, locations, and networks. Zero Trust operates on the principle of "never trust, always verify," requiring continuous authentication, strict access control, and micro-segmentation to limit the movement of attackers within cloud environments. IAM is a core component of Zero Trust, ensuring that every user, device, and application is continuously verified before accessing cloud resources. Implementing conditional access policies allows organizations to dynamically adjust access privileges based on risk factors such as device security posture, location, and behavior patterns. Identity verification must be enforced at every access point, reducing the likelihood of unauthorized users gaining entry even if they have stolen credentials.

To strengthen IAM security in the cloud, organizations must adopt a proactive approach that includes enforcing multi-factor authentication, implementing the least privilege access, continuously auditing IAM policies, and integrating AI-driven security analytics. Many security breaches originate from compromised credentials, making identity management one of the highest priorities in cloud security. Organizations should also educate employees on security best practices, emphasizing password hygiene, phishing awareness, and proper handling of access credentials. A well-trained workforce can serve as the first line of defense against identity-related threats, reducing the risk of human error and social engineering attacks.

As cloud adoption continues to grow, identity and access management will remain a cornerstone of cloud security. Businesses that invest in robust IAM frameworks, leverage AI-driven analytics, and embrace Zero Trust principles will be better positioned to protect their cloud environments from unauthorized access and evolving cyber threats. The future of IAM will likely include biometric authentication, decentralized identity models, and even blockchain-based identity verification systems, offering enhanced security and privacy for cloud users. Organizations that prioritize IAM as a core component of their cloud security strategy will not only safeguard their cloud resources but also improve regulatory compliance, streamline user access, and build greater trust with customers and partners.

As cloud adoption continues to grow, identity and access management will remain a cornerstone of cloud security. Businesses that invest in robust IAM frameworks, leverage AI-driven analytics, and embrace Zero Trust principles will be better positioned to protect their cloud environments from unauthorized access and evolving cyber threats. However, as IAM evolves, so do the tactics used by cybercriminals. Attackers increasingly target identity-based vulnerabilities through credential stuffing, social engineering, and session hijacking. To counteract these threats, organizations must adopt advanced authentication techniques, including biometric authentication, passwordless login solutions, and adaptive authentication mechanisms that adjust security requirements based on real-time risk assessments.

One of the biggest challenges in IAM is balancing security with user convenience. Strict authentication policies can enhance security but may frustrate users and lead to compliance gaps if employees seek workarounds. Organizations must implement IAM strategies that provide strong security without compromising user experience. Adaptive authentication, which dynamically adjusts authentication requirements based on factors such as device reputation, geographic location, and behavioral analysis, helps maintain security while reducing friction for trusted users. AI-driven IAM solutions further enhance security by learning from user behavior, detecting anomalies, and automatically responding to potential threats without disrupting legitimate workflows.

As organizations scale their cloud operations, they must also consider IAM governance and automation. Manually managing user access across multiple cloud platforms is not only time-consuming but also increases the likelihood of human error, which can lead to security gaps. IAM automation streamlines identity provisioning and deprovisioning, ensuring that users are granted and revoked access in real time based on role changes, employment status, or project requirements. Automated IAM governance tools also help organizations enforce security policies consistently, generate audit logs for compliance, and reduce the risk of orphaned accounts that could be exploited by attackers.

Third-party integrations and cloud service providers further complicate IAM in modern cloud environments. Many businesses rely on third-party vendors, contractors, and software-as-a-service (SaaS) applications, each requiring different levels of access to cloud resources. Managing external identities securely is a growing concern, as excessive permissions granted to third-party applications or vendors can create security blind spots. Organizations should implement third-party risk management strategies, enforce the least privilege access, and monitor vendor activities through continuous access reviews. Security teams must also assess the security posture of third-party integrations before granting access, ensuring that external partners follow the best practices for identity management and data protection.

Another key area of focus in IAM is insider threats. While most security strategies focus on preventing external attacks, insider threats—whether malicious or accidental can be just as damaging. Employees, contractors, or administrators with excessive privileges pose a risk if their accounts are compromised or misused. IAM solutions should include user behavior analytics (UBA) to detect unusual activity patterns, such as excessive data downloads, multiple failed login attempts, or access requests outside of normal working hours. Implementing privileged access monitoring, session recording, and real-time alerts for high-risk actions can help mitigate insider threats before they escalate into security incidents.

As cloud environments become more decentralized, the future of IAM will likely see the rise of decentralized identity solutions and blockchain-based authentication mechanisms. Decentralized identity management shifts control of identity verification from central authorities to users, allowing individuals to manage their digital identities securely without relying on traditional identity providers. Blockchain technology enhances IAM security by providing immutable, tamper-proof identity records that prevent identity theft and credential forgery. These innovations, while still in their early stages, have the potential to reshape how organizations manage identities in the cloud, offering enhanced security, privacy, and user control.

Ultimately, IAM is a continuous process that requires organizations to stay ahead of emerging threats, adopt evolving security technologies, and implement policies that balance security with usability. As cloud security threats grow in sophistication, businesses must take a proactive approach to IAM, leveraging automation, AI-driven analytics, and Zero Trust principles to create a resilient and future-ready identity security strategy. Organizations that fail to prioritize IAM risk exposing their cloud environments to credential-based attacks, insider threats, and compliance violations, all of which can lead to financial and reputational damage.

6.1 The Impact of Artificial Intelligence on IAM

As cloud environments grow more complex, artificial intelligence (AI) is playing a transformative role in Identity and Access Management (IAM). Traditional IAM solutions rely on predefined rules and policies to govern access, but AI introduces the ability to adaptively assess risk, detect anomalies, and automate security decisions in real time. AI-driven IAM solutions analyze user behavior patterns, login histories, and access requests to identify deviations from normal activity and respond proactively to potential threats.

One of the primary advantages of AI in IAM is its ability to detect and mitigate credential-based attacks. Credential stuffing, brute force attacks, and phishing attempts remain among the most common methods attackers use to gain unauthorized access to cloud environments. AI-powered systems continuously analyze login attempts, comparing them against historical usage patterns to determine whether an access request is legitimate or suspicious. If an employee suddenly logs in from an unusual location, at an irregular time, or from an unrecognized device, AI can flag the activity, prompt additional authentication steps, or block the attempt altogether.

AI also improves adaptive authentication, where access control decisions are dynamically adjusted based on risk levels. Instead of using static access policies, AI-powered IAM solutions assess multiple factors such as device trustworthiness, network conditions, and past user behavior—to determine whether a user should be granted access, required to complete multi-factor authentication, or denied access altogether. This approach ensures that security measures are proportionate to the risk, improving security without introducing unnecessary friction for legitimate users.

Another crucial application of AI in IAM is insider threat detection. Many security breaches occur due to compromised credentials, misused privileges, or accidental data exposure by employees or contractors. AI-driven IAM continuously monitors user behavior, detecting deviations from normal activities that could indicate malicious intent or negligent actions. For example, if an employee suddenly accesses a large number of sensitive files, attempts to download bulk data, or modifies permissions outside of their usual job functions, AI can trigger alerts, restrict access, or require supervisor approval before proceeding. This level of automation enhances IAM by reducing reliance on manual reviews while ensuring that access policies remain responsive to real-world risks.

Beyond security, AI-driven IAM solutions streamline compliance efforts by automating audit and reporting processes. Many regulatory frameworks, such as GDPR and HIPAA, require businesses to track and document user access activities. AI helps simplify this process by generating real-time reports, highlighting unusual behaviors, and ensuring that audit logs remain tamper-proof and easily accessible. This reduces the burden on security teams while ensuring that organizations remain compliant with industry regulations.

6.2 Biometric Authentication and the Future of Identity Security

As password-based authentication continues to be a weak link in IAM security, many organizations are shifting towards biometric authentication to enhance security and reduce the risk of credential theft. Biometrics such as fingerprints, facial recognition, iris scanning, and voice recognition—offer a more secure and user-friendly alternative to traditional passwords. Unlike passwords, which can be stolen, guessed, or shared, biometric data is unique to each individual, making it significantly harder for attackers to exploit.

Cloud providers are increasingly integrating biometric authentication into their IAM solutions to enhance access control. Multi-factor authentication systems now frequently incorporate biometric verification as a second authentication factor, ensuring that even if an attacker obtains a user's password, they cannot gain access without the biometric component. This added layer of security reduces the success rate of phishing attacks, credential stuffing, and password reuse vulnerabilities.

One of the key benefits of biometric authentication is its ability to enable passwordless authentication, eliminating the need for traditional password-based logins altogether. Many organizations are adopting passwordless authentication solutions that rely on a combination of biometrics, device-based authentication, and cryptographic security keys. This approach not only enhances security but also improves user experience by eliminating password-related frustrations such as forgotten credentials, password resets, and frequent password changes.

However, biometric authentication also comes with security and privacy challenges. Unlike passwords, which can be changed if compromised, biometric data is permanent and cannot be easily replaced. If biometric credentials are stolen or leaked in a data breach, the affected individuals may face long-term security risks. Organizations must encrypt and securely store biometric data to prevent unauthorized access and ensure compliance with data protection regulations. Many IAM solutions now use on-device biometric storage rather than cloud-based storage, ensuring that biometric data remains under the user's control and is not transmitted across networks.

As IAM continues to evolve, the future of identity security will likely incorporate a combination of AI-driven risk assessment, behavioral biometrics, and decentralized identity management. Behavioral biometrics analyze how users interact with devices, such as typing

speed, mouse movements, and touch gestures, to create a unique identity profile that continuously verifies the user's authenticity. Decentralized identity solutions, powered by **blockchain technology**, allow users to manage their digital identities **without relying on central authorities**, reducing the risk of identity theft and unauthorized access.

The rapid evolution of cloud computing has made Identity and Access Management a critical pillar of cloud security, ensuring that only authorized individuals and systems can access cloud resources. However, as cyber threats become more sophisticated, organizations must go beyond traditional authentication mechanisms and adopt advanced identity security measures that leverage AI, behavioral analytics, and biometric authentication. The integration of AI-driven security automation enhances IAM by detecting anomalies in real time, enforcing adaptive authentication policies, and preventing identity-based attacks before they cause damage.

At the same time, the adoption of biometric authentication and passwordless security models is transforming how users interact with cloud systems. By reducing reliance on passwords, organizations can minimize credential theft risks and improve user experience while maintaining high levels of security. As IAM solutions continue to advance, organizations must also address the privacy and ethical concerns surrounding biometric data to ensure that identity security remains both effective and privacy conscious.

Decentralized identity management, blockchain-based authentication, and AI-driven identity verification will shape the future of IAM in cloud security. Businesses that embrace innovation, implement Zero Trust principles, and continuously refine their IAM strategies will be best equipped to protect their cloud environments against identity-based threats while ensuring seamless and secure access for legitimate users.

Chapter 7
Cloud Security Tools and Technologies

As cloud computing becomes an integral part of modern business operations; organizations must leverage advanced security tools and technologies to protect their cloud environments from evolving cyber threats. The complexity of cloud infrastructure, coupled with the increasing sophistication of cyberattacks, requires a multi-layered security approach that combines network security, endpoint protection, threat intelligence, and automated security responses. Cloud security tools are designed to address various aspects of cloud security, including access control, threat detection, compliance enforcement, and data protection. By integrating these technologies into their security strategy, businesses can enhance visibility, improve incident response, and mitigate security risks before they escalate into full-scale breaches.

One of the most fundamental cloud security tools is the cloud firewall, which acts as the first line of defense against unauthorized access and malicious traffic. Unlike traditional firewalls that operate at the perimeter of a corporate network, cloud firewalls are specifically designed to protect cloud workloads, virtual machines, and containerized applications. Cloud firewalls analyze incoming and outgoing traffic, applying security rules to block suspicious activity, detect intrusion attempts, and prevent data exfiltration. Many cloud providers offer next-generation firewalls (NGFWs) that incorporate deep packet inspection, AI-driven threat analysis, and zero-day attack detection, allowing businesses to proactively secure their cloud environments.

Intrusion detection and prevention systems (IDPS) are another critical component of cloud security. These tools continuously monitor cloud networks, analyzing traffic patterns and system behaviors to identify potential security breaches in real time. Intrusion detection systems (IDS) alert security teams when suspicious activity is detected, while intrusion prevention systems (IPS) automatically block malicious traffic before it reaches cloud resources. AI-driven IDPS solutions enhance security by learning from past attack patterns, predicting future threats, and adapting to emerging cyberattack techniques. By integrating IDPS with cloud-native security services, businesses can detect anomalies, prevent data breaches, and minimize downtime caused by security incidents.

Cloud security posture management (CSPM) solutions play a vital role in maintaining cloud security hygiene by automating the detection and remediation of misconfigurations. Many cloud breaches result from misconfigured access controls, publicly exposed storage buckets, and weak security settings that leave cloud environments vulnerable to exploitation. CSPM tools continuously scan cloud infrastructure, identifying security gaps, enforcing best practices, and ensuring compliance with industry standards such as

GDPR, HIPAA, and ISO 27001. These tools provide real-time visibility into cloud security risks, helping organizations prevent human errors, unauthorized data access, and compliance violations before they lead to costly breaches.

Security Information and Event Management (SIEM) solutions provide centralized logging, analysis, and reporting of security events across cloud environments. SIEM tools aggregate security data from multiple sources, including firewalls, IDPS, authentication logs, and endpoint security solutions, allowing security teams to detect threats, investigate incidents, and respond to cyberattacks more efficiently. AI-driven SIEM platforms leverage machine learning to correlate security events, identify attack patterns, and provide actionable insights for threat mitigation. By integrating SIEM with cloud access security brokers (CASBs), endpoint detection and response (EDR) tools, and behavioral analytics, businesses can create a holistic security ecosystem that enables rapid threat detection and incident response.

Endpoint Detection and Response (EDR) solutions are essential for securing cloud-connected devices, virtual machines, and remote endpoints. Traditional antivirus solutions are no longer sufficient to defend against modern threats such as fileless malware, ransomware, and advanced persistent threats (APTs). EDR tools provide continuous endpoint monitoring, real-time threat detection, and automated response mechanisms to neutralize threats before they spread within cloud environments. Many EDR platforms use behavioral analysis and AI-powered threat intelligence to identify anomalies, detect suspicious activities, and quarantine infected devices to prevent further damage. As remote work and cloud-based collaboration continue to rise, EDR solutions have become a critical security measure for protecting endpoints connected to cloud infrastructure.

Cloud Access Security Brokers (CASBs) act as intermediaries between users and cloud applications, enforcing security policies, monitoring data transfers, and detecting unauthorized access attempts. CASBs provide visibility into shadow IT, helping organizations identify unapproved cloud applications and risky user behaviors that may lead to data leaks or compliance violations. CASB solutions enforce data loss prevention (DLP) policies, ensuring that sensitive information is not exposed, shared with unauthorized parties, or transferred to insecure locations. By integrating CASBs with IAM, SIEM, and threat intelligence platforms, businesses can strengthen data protection, control cloud application usage, and prevent security breaches.

Artificial intelligence and machine learning are revolutionizing cloud security by enhancing threat detection, automating incident response, and predicting cyberattack trends. AI-driven security analytics can process massive amounts of security data, identifying patterns and anomalies that may indicate potential threats. Machine learning models continuously learn from new attack techniques, allowing security tools to evolve and adapt to emerging cyber threats. AI-powered automation also enables self-healing security systems, where cloud security tools automatically remediate misconfigurations, isolate compromised workloads, and neutralize threats without human intervention. These advancements significantly reduce response times, improve threat hunting capabilities, and enhance the overall resilience of cloud security architectures.

Zero Trust Network Access (ZTNA) is reshaping how organizations secure cloud applications by eliminating implicit trust and enforcing strict access controls. Unlike traditional security models that assume users within a network can be trusted, Zero Trust requires continuous authentication and authorization for every access request. ZTNA ensures that users, devices, and applications are verified before being granted access, reducing the risk of lateral movement in the event of a security breach. By integrating ZTNA with IAM, CASB, and micro-segmentation strategies, organizations can limit attack surfaces, prevent unauthorized access, and strengthen cloud security postures.

Cloud workload protection platforms (CWPPs) provide comprehensive security for cloud-native applications, containers, and serverless workloads. As organizations adopt Kubernetes, Docker, and serverless computing, traditional security tools are no longer sufficient to protect dynamic cloud environments. CWPP solutions offer runtime protection, vulnerability management, and automated compliance enforcement for cloud workloads. These tools ensure that applications remain secure from development to deployment, mitigating security risks associated with misconfigured containers, API vulnerabilities, and insecure software dependencies.

Cloud-native security tools are continuously evolving to address new threats, improve automation, and provide deeper visibility into cloud environments. The integration of AI-driven analytics, automated threat response, and Zero Trust principles is transforming how businesses secure their cloud infrastructure. Organizations that embrace advanced cloud security technologies, enforce security best practices, and invest in proactive threat intelligence will be better equipped to defend against cyberattacks, protect sensitive data, and maintain regulatory compliance in an increasingly complex cloud landscape.

Cloud-native security tools are continuously evolving to address new threats, improve automation, and provide deeper visibility into cloud environments. The integration of AI-driven analytics, automated threat response, and Zero Trust principles is transforming how businesses secure their cloud infrastructure. However, securing cloud environments is not just about deploying the latest tools; it requires a **comprehensive security strategy** that combines technology, policies, and human oversight. Organizations must continuously assess their security posture, update their defense mechanisms, and train personnel to recognize and respond to security incidents effectively.

One of the primary challenges in cloud security is **visibility across hybrid and multi-cloud environments**. Many businesses operate across multiple cloud platforms, integrating services from AWS, Microsoft Azure, Google Cloud, and private cloud providers. This fragmented infrastructure often results in security blind spots, where vulnerabilities go undetected. To address this challenge, organizations must adopt **unified security management platforms** that provide a **single pane of glass visibility** into all cloud assets. These platforms integrate security data from various cloud services, enabling security teams to **correlate events, detect threats, and enforce security policies consistently across different environments**.

Automated security orchestration and response (SOAR) solutions are becoming essential in modern cloud security operations. SOAR platforms integrate with SIEM, endpoint detection and response (EDR), and cloud security tools to automate incident response workflows, reducing the time required to detect, analyze, and contain threats. Instead of relying on manual security investigations, SOAR tools automatically correlate security events, assign threat severity levels, and initiate predefined response actions. For example, if an intrusion detection system identifies a brute-force attack on a cloud-based application, the SOAR platform can automatically block the attacker's IP address, revoke compromised credentials and generate an incident report. By leveraging automation, organizations can reduce the burden on security teams, minimize response times, and mitigate security risks more efficiently.

Another critical aspect of cloud security is real-time threat intelligence. Organizations must stay informed about emerging cyber threats, including new attack vectors, malware strains, and zero-day vulnerabilities that could compromise cloud environments. Threat intelligence feeds provide real-time updates on global cyber threats, enabling security teams to proactively adjust security controls and implement defensive measures before an attack occurs. Many cloud security platforms integrate with global threat intelligence networks, allowing businesses to automatically block known malicious domains, detect suspicious activities, and quarantine compromised systems based on up-to-date threat intelligence data.

Cloud security analytics is another powerful tool for enhancing security posture. AI-driven security analytics platforms use big data analysis, machine learning, and behavioral modeling to detect hidden threats, predict attack patterns, and identify security gaps that traditional security tools might overlook. By analyzing massive volumes of security logs, cloud security analytics can detect subtle signs of insider threats, account takeovers, and sophisticated cyberattacks before they escalate. These platforms also provide risk scoring for cloud assets, enabling security teams to prioritize vulnerabilities based on their potential impact.

As cloud security tools evolve, businesses must also consider the human element of cybersecurity. Even with the most advanced security technologies in place, human errors—such as misconfigurations, weak passwords, and phishing attacks—continue to be a leading cause of cloud security breaches. Organizations must invest in cybersecurity training programs, ensuring that employees, developers, and IT administrators understand cloud security best practices, recognize social engineering threats, and follow secure coding principles. Security awareness training should be an ongoing process, reinforced with simulated phishing tests, cloud security drills, and role-based security education.

The future of cloud security will be shaped by **emerging technologies such as** quantum computing, confidential computing, and decentralized identity management. Quantum computing has the potential to break traditional encryption methods, forcing organizations to adopt post-quantum cryptographic algorithms to protect cloud data. Confidential computing is another promising innovation, ensuring that sensitive data remains encrypted even during processing by using secure hardware enclaves. Meanwhile, decentralized identity management leverages blockchain technology to provide tamper-proof **digital identities**, reducing the risks associated with identity theft and credential misuse.

Cloud security is an ongoing process that requires businesses to remain vigilant, adapt to new threats, and continuously improve their security strategies. Organizations that invest in AI-driven security automation, real-time threat intelligence, and continuous security monitoring will be better equipped to defend against cyberattacks, maintain regulatory compliance, and protect critical cloud assets. However, technology alone is not enough—a strong security culture, proactive risk management, and clear security policies are essential components of a resilient cloud security framework.

7.1 The Role of Cloud Forensics in Security Incident Investigation

As organizations continue to rely on cloud computing, the ability to effectively investigate security incidents and breaches becomes a crucial aspect of cloud security. Cloud forensics is the process of collecting, analyzing, and preserving digital evidence from cloud environments to determine the cause of a security incident and prevent future attacks. Unlike traditional forensics, which focuses on on-premise infrastructures, cloud forensics introduces new challenges due to the distributed nature of cloud data, shared responsibility models, and legal jurisdiction concerns. Organizations must establish well-defined cloud forensic procedures to trace cyberattacks, identify unauthorized access, and maintain digital evidence integrity for regulatory compliance or legal proceedings.

One of the biggest challenges in cloud forensics is data volatility. In cloud environments, data is constantly being generated, modified, and deleted, making it difficult to capture and preserve forensic evidence. Attackers often take advantage of this dynamic nature to cover their tracks, making real-time event logging and security monitoring critical. To address this challenge, businesses must integrate cloud-native forensic tools that capture security logs, track user activity, and maintain immutable audit trails. Cloud service providers offer logging and monitoring services such as AWS CloudTrail, Microsoft Azure Monitor, and Google Cloud Operations Suite, which allow organizations to collect forensic evidence in real-time. These logs help security teams trace unauthorized activities, detect anomalies, and reconstruct the sequence of events leading up to a security breach.

Another critical component of cloud forensics is logging correlation and timeline reconstruction. Investigating a cloud security incident often requires security analysts to piece together information from multiple sources, including IAM logs, virtual machine activity, network traffic data, and API call records. AI-driven forensic tools simplify this process by correlating logs, identifying attack patterns, and reconstructing the attacker's actions across different cloud resources. By leveraging automated forensic analysis, organizations can quickly determine how a security breach occurred, what data was affected, and how to mitigate further risks.

Data integrity and legal considerations also play a key role in cloud forensics. Many data protection regulations require organizations to preserve digital evidence in a tamper-proof format for legal investigations. Cloud forensic tools use cryptographic hashing to ensure that evidence remains unchanged throughout the forensic process. Additionally, businesses operating in multiple regions must consider data sovereignty laws, ensuring that forensic investigations comply with jurisdictional requirements regarding data access, transfer, and storage. Legal agreements with cloud providers should clearly outline incident response procedures, forensic data access policies, and compliance obligations to ensure organizations can conduct forensic investigations without violating contractual or legal restrictions.

7.2 Automating Security Incident Response in Cloud Environments

As cyber threats grow in sophistication, businesses cannot afford to rely solely on manual incident response processes. Security automation has become a game-changer in cloud security, enabling organizations to detect, contain, and mitigate security incidents in real time without human intervention. Automated security incident response solutions reduce response times, minimize the impact of attacks, and free up security teams to focus on more strategic security initiatives.

One of the most powerful applications of security automation is automated threat containment and mitigation. AI-driven security platforms continuously analyze security logs and detect anomalies indicative of cyberattacks. When an attack is detected, automated response mechanisms isolate compromised cloud resources, block malicious traffic, and revoke unauthorized access permissions within seconds. For example, if a cloud firewall detects a distributed denial-of-service (DDoS) attack, it can automatically trigger rate-limiting rules, activate traffic filtering, and divert malicious requests to a mitigation service without human intervention. Similarly, if an IAM policy violation is detected, security automation tools can immediately disable the compromised account, enforce additional authentication checks, and notify security administrators to investigate further.

Another key aspect of automated security incident response is self-healing cloud infrastructure. Cloud environments can be configured to automatically restore affected resources to a secure state after a security incident. For example, if a virtual machine is compromised, automated security policies can terminate the affected instance, redeploy a clean version from a secure backup, and reconfigure security settings to prevent reinfection. This approach reduces downtime, ensures operational continuity, and minimizes the need for manual intervention in security recovery efforts.

Security orchestration, automation, and response (SOAR) platforms further enhance incident response capabilities by integrating multiple security tools into a unified automation framework. SOAR solutions enable businesses to automate threat intelligence sharing, streamline security investigations, and coordinate responses across cloud security tools. Instead of relying on separate security solutions for logging, threat detection, and response, SOAR platforms consolidate security events and apply predefined response playbooks to ensure that security incidents are handled efficiently.

As cyber threats become more persistent, organizations must also consider AI-powered predictive security in their incident response strategies. Predictive security analytics leverage machine learning to analyze historical security data and identify attack patterns before they escalate. By detecting early warning signs such as unusual network traffic spikes, unauthorized API access, or inconsistent login behaviors; AI-driven security systems can proactively trigger mitigation actions, reducing the risk of full-scale breaches. Predictive security models also help organizations prioritize security vulnerabilities, apply targeted patches, and strengthen defenses before attackers exploit weaknesses.

The combination of cloud forensics, automated incident response, and predictive security analytics represents the future of resilient cloud security operations. Businesses that embrace these advanced security capabilities will not only detect and respond to threats faster but also minimize security risks, ensure compliance, and maintain trust in their cloud environments.

As cybercriminals continue to evolve their attack techniques, organizations must remain proactive by investing in AI-driven security automation, forensic investigation tools, and cloud-native threat detection technologies. The ability to quickly investigate, contain, and recover from cloud security incidents will be a defining factor in determining which businesses can withstand the evolving cybersecurity landscape.

Chapter 8
Cloud Incident Response and Disaster Recovery

As cloud computing continues to dominate modern business operations; organizations must be prepared to handle security incidents and system failures efficiently. Cloud environments introduce unique challenges when it comes to incident response and disaster recovery due to their distributed nature, shared responsibility models, and the potential for data loss across multiple regions. A well-structured cloud incident response and disaster recovery (DR) plan ensures that businesses can quickly detect, respond to, and recover from cyber threats, outages, and data corruption while minimizing downtime and financial loss. The key to effective cloud resilience lies in proactive risk assessment, real-time security monitoring, and automated recovery mechanisms that allow businesses to restore operations without significant disruptions.

Incident response in cloud environments follows a structured approach that includes identification, containment, eradication, recovery, and lessons learned. The identification phase focuses on detecting security breaches, suspicious activities, and performance anomalies that indicate potential security incidents. Organizations must leverage cloud-native security monitoring tools, intrusion detection systems (IDS), and AI-driven threat intelligence to continuously monitor cloud workloads and detect early warning signs of cyber threats. Real-time alerting mechanisms help security teams respond promptly to security breaches, preventing attackers from escalating their activities. Cloud service providers offer log monitoring and security analytics services such as AWS CloudTrail, Google Security Command Center, and Microsoft Azure Security Center, which provide comprehensive visibility into cloud activity and potential threats.

Once a security incident is identified, the containment phase aims to limit the damage by isolating affected cloud resources, restricting user access, and blocking malicious traffic. Automated incident response solutions help organizations immediately deactivate compromised accounts, enforce multi-factor authentication, and quarantine infected virtual machines or containers to prevent the spread of malware or unauthorized access. Security orchestration and automation tools (SOAR) streamline this process by applying predefined response playbooks that ensure consistency in how incidents are handled.

The eradication phase involves removing malicious files, closing security vulnerabilities, and strengthening cloud security configurations to prevent a recurrence of the attack. Organizations must conduct forensic investigations to determine how attackers gained access and ensure that all traces of the attack are eliminated. Cloud forensic tools allow security analysts to trace attack vectors, analyze compromised accounts, and reconstruct attacker movements to understand the full scope of the breach. This information is critical in strengthening security measures and preventing future incidents.

Once the immediate threat is neutralized, the recovery phase focuses on restoring cloud services to normal operation. Disaster recovery strategies play a crucial role in ensuring business continuity, as they allow organizations to recover lost data, restore workloads, and resume operations with minimal downtime. Cloud service providers offer various disaster recovery solutions, including geographically distributed backups, automated failover mechanisms, and real-time replication of critical workloads. Businesses must implement a multi-layered backup strategy, ensuring that backups are stored securely, regularly tested, and remain resilient against ransomware attacks and accidental deletions.

Testing and validation are essential components of disaster recovery planning. Many organizations fail to verify whether their backup and restoration processes actually work until a real disaster occurs, leading to prolonged downtime and data loss. Conducting regular disaster recovery drills, simulating cyberattacks, and stress-testing cloud recovery systems helps organizations identify weaknesses in their DR plans and improve their ability to respond effectively to real-world incidents. Businesses should also document recovery time objectives (RTOs) and recovery point objectives (RPOs) to define acceptable levels of downtime and data loss, ensuring that their disaster recovery plans align with business continuity requirements.

Beyond technical recovery, the lessons learned phase is crucial for improving future incident response strategies. Organizations must conduct post-mortem analysis, document security incidents, and refine incident response procedures based on insights gained from past incidents. Continuous learning and adaptation help security teams stay ahead of emerging threats, improve response efficiency, and enhance collaboration between IT, security, and business stakeholders.

The rise of AI-powered incident response and predictive analytics is transforming how businesses handle cloud security incidents. AI-driven security automation enables organizations to predict potential incidents before they occur, initiate automated remediation actions, and improve threat detection accuracy. Predictive analytics leverage historical attack data and real-time threat intelligence to identify attack patterns, prioritize security risks, and implement preemptive defenses. By incorporating AI into incident response workflows, businesses can significantly reduce detection-to-response times, enhance threat visibility, and minimize security risks before they escalate into full-scale breaches.

Cloud disaster recovery is evolving with the adoption of serverless computing, edge computing, and multi-cloud redundancy strategies. Serverless architectures eliminate the need for traditional infrastructure recovery by allowing organizations to rebuild applications on demand using cloud functions and automated deployment pipelines. Edge computing introduces decentralized data processing, reducing reliance on centralized cloud data centers and improving disaster resilience in distributed environments.

Multi-cloud redundancy ensures that critical applications and data remain available across multiple cloud providers, mitigating the risks associated with cloud provider outages or regional disruptions.

Cloud incident response and disaster recovery require a proactive and well-coordinated approach that integrates real-time threat detection, automated response mechanisms, and strategic recovery planning. Organizations that invest in advanced cloud security automation, continuous monitoring, and resilient backup strategies will be better equipped to handle security incidents swiftly and effectively, ensuring that they maintain business continuity, protect customer data, and mitigate financial and reputational losses.

Cloud incident response and disaster recovery require a proactive and well-coordinated approach that integrates real-time threat detection, automated response mechanisms, and strategic recovery planning. However, beyond technical execution, organizations must also focus on the human and operational aspects of incident response and recovery. Security teams must be well-trained, agile, and equipped with the necessary resources to handle cloud security incidents efficiently. Many organizations make the mistake of assuming that their cloud provider will handle all aspects of disaster recovery, failing to recognize that under the shared responsibility model, businesses remain accountable for securing their own data, applications, and workloads.

To strengthen cloud incident response capabilities, organizations must establish clear roles and responsibilities for security teams, IT personnel, and business stakeholders. Incident response teams should have predefined escalation procedures, incident classification guidelines, and communication channels to ensure seamless coordination during a security event. Establishing a dedicated Security Operations Center (SOC) or partnering with a Managed Security Service Provider (MSSP) can provide businesses with 24/7 monitoring, rapid response capabilities, and forensic analysis expertise to handle complex cloud security incidents effectively.

One of the most critical challenges in cloud disaster recovery is data integrity and security during restoration. Many organizations assume that restoring data from a backup is sufficient to recover from a cyberattack, but without proper validation, corrupted, compromised, or outdated backups can introduce further risks. Businesses must implement backup integrity checks, versioning controls, and immutable backups to ensure that restored data is authentic and uncompromised. Immutable backups prevent unauthorized modifications, ensuring that data remains intact even in the event of a ransomware attack. Organizations should also apply zero-trust security principles to backup environments, restricting access to backup storage and continuously monitoring suspicious activities.

In addition to technical recovery efforts, organizations must consider the business and reputational impact of security incidents. Customers, partners, and regulatory bodies expect transparency and accountability when a security breach occurs. A well-prepared incident communication strategy ensures that affected stakeholders receive timely, accurate, and clear information about security incidents, minimizing confusion and reputational damage. Many data protection regulations, such as GDPR, CCPA, and NDPR, require organizations to notify customers and regulators within specific timeframes following a data breach. Failure to comply with these reporting requirements can result in significant financial penalties and legal consequences.

As cloud adoption continues to rise, compliance-driven incident response is becoming a growing concern for businesses operating in regulated industries such as finance, healthcare, and government sectors. Organizations must ensure that their incident response and disaster recovery plans align with industry-specific security frameworks, compliance mandates, and regional data protection laws. Conducting regular compliance audits, penetration testing, and cloud security assessments helps businesses identify gaps in their security posture and implement corrective actions to meet regulatory expectations.

The future of cloud disaster recovery will be driven by automation, AI-driven security analytics, and decentralized recovery architectures. Businesses are increasingly adopting AI-powered incident response solutions that detect threats in real time, automate containment actions, and provide actionable insights to security teams. AI-driven recovery solutions use predictive analytics to assess risks, identify optimal recovery paths, and automatically orchestrate cloud workload restoration with minimal downtime. Meanwhile, decentralized disaster recovery strategies, such as multi-cloud redundancy and blockchain-based data integrity verification, are emerging as highly resilient approaches to mitigating risks associated with cloud provider failures or regional outages.

Cloud security incidents are not a matter of if, but when. Organizations must continuously test, refine, and improve their incident response and disaster recovery strategies to stay ahead of evolving cyber threats. By combining real-time threat intelligence, automated security orchestration, and proactive disaster recovery planning, businesses can reduce the impact of cyber incidents, protect critical assets, and maintain operational resilience in an increasingly cloud-dependent world.

8.1 The Role of Cyber Insurance in Cloud Incident Response and Recovery

As cyber threats continue to grow in complexity, many organizations are turning to cyber insurance as an additional layer of protection against financial losses associated with cloud security incidents. Cyber insurance policies help businesses recover from data breaches, ransomware attacks, and system outages by covering costs related to incident response, forensic investigations, legal fees, regulatory fines, and customer notifications. While cyber insurance does not replace robust security measures, it serves as a financial safety net, enabling businesses to mitigate the financial impact of a cloud security breach and ensure business continuity.

One of the key considerations in cyber insurance for cloud environments is policy coverage and exclusions. Not all cyber insurance policies provide comprehensive coverage for cloud-based incidents, and organizations must carefully evaluate their policies to ensure that data loss, service disruptions, and compliance violations are included. Many insurers require businesses to demonstrate strong security practices, such as multi-factor authentication (MFA), encryption, regular security audits, and employee training, before providing coverage. Businesses that fail to meet these security requirements may face higher premiums or even denial of claims if an incident occurs.

Cyber insurance providers also assess an organization's disaster recovery and incident response capabilities before issuing coverage. Companies with well-documented cloud security policies, automated response mechanisms, and strong data protection measures are more likely to receive favorable policy terms and lower premiums. Additionally, insurers may require businesses to conduct penetration testing and cloud security assessments to validate their resilience against cyber threats.

Despite its benefits, cyber insurance should not be viewed as a substitute for strong cybersecurity controls. Many insurance policies do not cover losses resulting from human error, insider threats, or failure to implement security patches, emphasizing the need for businesses to maintain a proactive security posture. Organizations must balance cyber insurance with technical defenses, compliance strategies, and risk management frameworks to create a comprehensive cloud security strategy that minimizes the likelihood and impact of security incidents.

8.2 The Future of AI-Driven Disaster Recovery and Autonomous Security Response

Advancements in artificial intelligence (AI) and machine learning are revolutionizing cloud disaster recovery by enabling businesses to predict, prevent, and respond to security incidents with greater speed and accuracy. AI-driven disaster recovery systems use predictive analytics to identify vulnerabilities, forecast potential failures, and initiate automated recovery actions before a full-scale outage or security breach occurs. By analyzing historical cloud performance data and security logs, AI can detect patterns of abnormal behavior, allowing organizations to address weaknesses before they result in downtime or data loss.

One of the most promising developments in AI-driven security response is autonomous threat containment, where AI-powered security platforms detect and neutralize threats without human intervention. These systems continuously monitor cloud workloads, identify anomalies, and apply real-time security controls to prevent attacks. For example, if an AI-driven security solution detects unauthorized API access, unusual data transfers, or malware behavior, it can automatically revoke access, isolate the compromised workload, and initiate forensic analysis to investigate the root cause of the attack. This reduces the time between threat detection and response, minimizing damage and preventing attackers from escalating their actions.

AI also enhancing self-healing cloud architectures, where cloud systems automatically recover from failures and cyber incidents by detecting issues and reconfiguring resources without manual intervention. In a self-healing cloud environment, if a virtual machine is compromised, the system can automatically replace it with a clean instance, migrate workloads to unaffected servers, and restore data from secure backups. These capabilities improve business resilience by ensuring that cloud applications remain operational even in the face of cyberattacks, hardware failures, or cloud provider disruptions.

Additionally, AI-driven risk scoring and security analytics help organizations prioritize disaster recovery efforts by identifying the most critical assets and vulnerabilities. Rather than applying uniform security measures across all cloud resources, businesses can use AI to dynamically allocate security controls and disaster recovery resources based on real-time risk assessments. This adaptive security approach ensures that the most sensitive workloads receive the highest level of protection while optimizing resource utilization for overall cloud efficiency.

The integration of AI with blockchain-based data verification and decentralized cloud recovery networks is expected to further enhance cloud security and disaster resilience. Blockchain ensures tamper-proof data integrity, allowing businesses to verify the authenticity of recovered files and prevent ransomware-altered backups from being restored. Decentralized recovery networks distribute backup storage across multiple independent cloud providers, reducing reliance on a single provider and minimizing the risk of total system failure in the event of a cloud outage.

Ultimately, the combination of AI-driven automation, predictive security analytics, and self-healing cloud architectures is shaping the future of resilient cloud security operations. Organizations that embrace these technologies will not only respond to security incidents more efficiently but also anticipate and prevent disruptions before they occur. The ability to proactively defend cloud environments, automate recovery actions, and minimize downtime will be a key differentiator in maintaining operational stability and business continuity in an increasingly threat-prone digital landscape.

As cloud security threats continue to evolve, businesses must continuously refine their incident response and disaster recovery strategies to stay ahead of adversaries. By investing in AI-driven security automation, cloud-native forensic tools, and multi-cloud redundancy solutions, organizations can ensure that they are well-prepared to navigate the complexities of cloud security, recover from cyber incidents, and maintain trust with customers and stakeholders.

Chapter 9
Compliance Challenges in Cloud Security

As businesses migrate more of their operations to the cloud, compliance with regulatory frameworks and data protection laws becomes a crucial aspect of cloud security. Organizations must ensure that their cloud environments align with industry standards and legal requirements to protect sensitive data, prevent breaches, and avoid costly penalties. However, achieving compliance in cloud computing presents unique challenges due to the distributed nature of cloud infrastructure, cross-border data transfers, and shared security responsibilities between cloud service providers and customers. A failure to adhere to compliance regulations can result in legal consequences, reputational damage, and loss of customer trust.

One of the primary challenges in cloud security compliance is data sovereignty and jurisdictional laws. Many countries enforce data localization requirements, mandating that certain types of data, especially personal, financial, and healthcare information must be stored and processed within national borders. Regulations such as the General Data Protection Regulation (GDPR) in Europe, the

California Consumer Privacy Act (CCPA) in the U.S., and the Nigerian Data Protection Regulation (NDPR) impose strict guidelines on how businesses handle customer data. For organizations operating across multiple regions, navigating varying legal requirements can be complex, requiring careful selection of cloud providers, contractual agreements, and data governance policies to ensure compliance with each jurisdiction's laws.

The shared responsibility model of cloud computing further complicates compliance efforts. Cloud service providers, such as AWS, Microsoft Azure, and Google Cloud, secure the underlying cloud infrastructure, but customers are responsible for securing their applications, workloads, and data. Many compliance violations arise due to misconfigured cloud settings, excessive user permissions, and improper data storage practices, rather than vulnerabilities in the cloud provider's infrastructure. To address these risks, organizations must conduct regular security audits, enforce access controls, and implement cloud security posture management (CSPM) solutions to detect misconfigurations and policy violations in real-time.

Another critical compliance challenge is third-party risk management. Many businesses rely on Software as a Service (SaaS), Platform as a Service (PaaS), and third-party APIs to extend their cloud capabilities. While these integrations enhance functionality, they also introduce new security and compliance risks, as organizations must trust external vendors with sensitive data. A breach in a third-party service provider can expose confidential information and create compliance violations. Organizations must implement strict vendor risk assessment policies, require security certifications such as ISO 27001 and SOC 2, and enforce contractual agreements that outline security obligations, data protection measures, and incident response procedures for third-party providers.

Achieving compliance in cloud security also requires businesses to maintain detailed security logs and audit trails to demonstrate adherence to regulatory standards. Many compliance frameworks mandate that organizations track user activity, detect unauthorized access, and retain security logs for a specified period. Cloud providers offer logging and monitoring tools, such as AWS CloudTrail, Azure Monitor, and Google Cloud Audit Logs, to help businesses capture security events and generate compliance reports. However, managing and analyzing large volumes of security logs can be challenging, making it essential for organizations to integrate Security Information and Event Management (SIEM) solutions to automate compliance monitoring and detect anomalies in cloud environments.

Encryption and data protection are fundamental to compliance with cloud security. Many data privacy regulations require businesses to encrypt sensitive information both at rest and in transit to prevent unauthorized access. Cloud providers offer built-in encryption services, such as AWS Key Management Service (KMS) and Azure Key Vault, allowing businesses to encrypt databases, storage buckets, and network traffic. However, organizations must also manage encryption keys securely, as poor key management practices can lead to compliance failures. Implementing hardware security modules

(HSMs), zero-trust encryption models, and multi-layered key rotation policies helps businesses maintain strong encryption standards while complying with regulatory requirements.

Identity and Access Management (IAM) plays a significant role in ensuring compliance, as many regulatory frameworks require strict access control mechanisms to protect sensitive data. Role-based access control (RBAC) and attribute-based access control (ABAC) help organizations enforce the principle of least privilege, ensuring that users and applications only have access to the resources necessary for their roles. Multi-factor authentication (MFA) adds an additional layer of security, reducing the risk of unauthorized access due to credential theft or weak passwords. Continuous user activity monitoring, automated access reviews, and real-time access policy enforcement further strengthen compliance by preventing privilege abuse and detecting anomalous user behavior.

One of the most pressing concerns in cloud compliance is incident response and breach notification obligations. Many regulations, such as GDPR, require businesses to report security breaches within a strict timeframe, often within 72 hours of detection. Organizations must have a well-documented incident response plan that includes automated breach detection, forensic investigation capabilities, and legal notification processes to comply with reporting requirements. Failure to report a breach within the required timeframe can result in hefty fines, legal repercussions, and reputational damage.

AI and machine learning are increasingly being integrated into compliance management solutions, enabling businesses to automate regulatory compliance, detect security violations, and streamline audit processes. AI-powered compliance tools analyze cloud configurations, user activity, and security logs to identify compliance risks, generate audit reports, and recommend corrective actions. These intelligent systems reduce the manual effort required for compliance monitoring, allowing security teams to focus on strategic risk management and policy enforcement.

As cloud compliance continues to evolve, businesses must stay ahead of emerging regulatory trends, industry-specific security requirements, and evolving cyber threats. Governments and regulatory bodies are introducing stricter data protection laws, enhanced privacy controls, and greater accountability for cloud security failures. Organizations must remain agile and proactive, regularly updating security policies, conducting compliance assessments, and collaborating with cloud providers to meet evolving legal requirements.

Achieving cloud compliance requires a combination of strong security policies, automated compliance monitoring, third-party risk management, and continuous security awareness training. Businesses that prioritize compliance as a core component of their cloud security strategy will not only avoid legal and financial risks but also build customer trust, enhance operational resilience, and maintain a competitive advantage in the cloud-driven economy.

Cloud compliance is an ongoing process that requires organizations to remain vigilant, adaptable, and proactive in their security practices. While regulatory frameworks provide clear guidelines for protecting sensitive data in cloud environments, compliance is not just about meeting legal requirements, it is about building a culture of security, trust, and accountability. As cyber threats continue to evolve, organizations must recognize that compliance is not a one-time certification or checkbox exercise but a continuous effort to monitor risks, enforce security controls, and maintain regulatory alignment across dynamic cloud infrastructures.

One of the most overlooked aspects of compliance in cloud security is continuous security validation and auditing. Many organizations implement security measures at the initial deployment stage but fail to regularly reassess their cloud security posture. Misconfigurations, excessive user permissions, and outdated security policies can develop over time, creating hidden compliance gaps that go unnoticed until a security incident occurs. Businesses must adopt a continuous compliance monitoring approach, leveraging automated security assessments, cloud security posture management (CSPM) tools, and real-time policy enforcement mechanisms to ensure that their cloud environments remain secure and compliant at all times.

Another major compliance challenge is data residency and cross-border data transfers, particularly for multinational organizations that operate across multiple jurisdictions. Different countries have varying regulations regarding where data can be stored and how it can be processed, often requiring businesses to implement region-specific security controls. For instance, GDPR mandates that

0001

ne Galleria Blvd., Suite 1900, Metairie, LA 7
888-421-2397

CONTENTS

What is truth? This book may or may not answer that for you. Truth is like beauty; it is in the eyes of the beholder. It is not the purpose of this book to tell lies, so you will just read about different ways to tell the truth. In life, we often come across tidbits of useful, or sometimes useless, information. This book will have some of both.

Several years ago, I wrote the book *Words of Wisdom from Anonymous Wiseguys* under the pen name of John Marsh. It was a book about wisdom. It was also about stupidity. Using a question and answer format the book examined stupid questions; if there really is such a thing. Answers were given to the questions that were sometimes serious and at other times a wise guy would make a crack about the stupid question and literally give a stupid answer. Oh, what fun it is to make fun of other people and how they think about things.

This book is not intended to be politically correct. In fact, we may make fun of the political correct assumed answers. Names in this book are generic assumptions of perhaps, someone you know. Sometimes we will use the name of some soldier who may be doing something under the supervision of a sergeant or corporal. The smartest person is going to be Captain Scott. Although the good captain was a real officer in the American Civil War, he wasn't anything like what you will read in this book.

If you are offended by anything in this book, then you should put it down and burn it in your microwave oven. This book is not about you, but if you resemble anyone in this book, well then, congratulations.

Are you a wise guy? Then you may join the ranks of those who enjoy the answers. This book will follow the format of questions and answers most of the time. One of the chapters will be word puzzles to try to stump the wise guys. Good luck with that one.

The Yogi chapter in this book is about real people. It is all in good fun, even Yogi thought so. The Covid-19 chapter is so much fun to see how our government really helped us out of a pandemic. Who would have thought we would all follow these rules like cattle heading for the slaughter house.

This book contains the truth about common sense. The wise guys use satire, cynicism and sometimes double talk to help bring you to know the truth.

EASY QUESTIONS TO GET STARTED

Q. What is the hardest thing to learn in college?
A. How to open a beer bottle with a quarter.

Q. What are the sins of omission?
A. They are the sins we should have committed.

Q. If the sergeant asked for all morons to step forward what should I do?
A. Step forward so the sergeant won't be standing there alone.

Q. Will the encyclopedia tell you everything you will ever need to know?
A. Not if you're married.

Q. What is a bigamist?
A. A man who makes the same mistake twice at the same time.

Q. What should you do when you and your wife have a difference of opinion?
A. Don't tell her yours.

Q. I want to say something soft and sweet to my sweet heart. Do you have any suggestions?
A. Try custard pie and see how that goes.

Q. I've heard that a marriage license is the most expensive license there is. Is that true?

A. Yes, it costs $10 at the courthouse and the rest of your income for life.

Q. Can you name two convictions that carry a life sentence?

A. Murder and marriage.

Q. I noticed that my car insurance policy would not pay cash for an accident but just give me a replacement vehicle. Is this a good policy?

A. It's okay for your car but you might want to check the fine print on the life insurance policy you have on your wife.

Q. I've noticed that the tonic I bought from the salesman for my bad cough says that it works so well that I will never use any other. Do you think this is true?

A. Sure, but you might want to try something less fatal.

Q. Women always accuse a man when the toilet seat is left up. I don't think that is fair.

A. Neither does HQ staff. If a woman won't look at the toilet before using it, what else will she back her ass up to without looking?

Q. Is there any benefit to being grossly over-weight?

A. Yes, you will be less likely to be kidnapped.

Q. What is a reenactor?

A. Not to be confused with identity theft, he is pretending to be someone else.

Q. What is something you would like to give but not receive?

A. Advise.

Q. What is the proper amount of time to be engaged before getting married?

A. If it is more than six months the girl is still seeing if she can do better than you.

Q. What does a man gain by making numerous mistakes?

A. He gains experience. The rest of us gain funny stories.

Q. What do you call an optimist who practices what he preaches?

A. A pessimist.

Q. Do politicians seem like they are going somewhere?

A. Sure. First, they run for office and then they run for cover.

Q. Is a philanthropist a stamp collector?

A. Oh you simple-minded fool. No, he is someone who returns to the people publicly a small percentage of his wealth that he steels from them privately.

Q. What makes a person popular?

A. The ability to know a whole lot of uninteresting people.

Q. When will I hear people praise me for the things I have done?

A. You will have to wait for your funeral.

Q. What makes a person a radical?

A. They have a different opinion than you.

Q. What is a self-made man?

A. It's a horrible example of unskilled labor.

Q. Can you think of a reason why I shouldn't tip?

A. Why should you pay the wages of someone else's worker?

Q. Where can I find a person who thinks the world can't go on without him?
A. The cemetery is full of them.

Q. What is the best advise that I can give?
A. None. Keep your mouth shut if you know what's good for you.

Q. When company comes and stays at my house they tend to stay longer than I expected. How do I get them to leave without being rude?
A. Start treating them like family.

Q. How can an author increase his book sales?
A. Have the book banned at the local library, then sell copies out of the trunk of your car.

Q. What do you call a person who tries to teach stupid people?
A. A jackass whisperer.

Q. Why do dogs retrieve a ball when you throw it?
A. Dogs think you like to throw balls and it amuses them.

Q. Is poison ever safe to consume?
A. Yes, it is no longer poisonous after the expiration date. But more important- why do you want to know this?

Q. Which letter is silent in the word "scent," the S or the C?
A. The S is silent. It is always the first letter when 2 consonants are together at the beginning of a word. Example: pneumonia and psycho and philharmonic. The P is silent in every case.

Q. Do twins ever not like their twin?

A. Rarely, usually after finding out that one of them was not planned.

Q. Why is the letter W, in English, called a double U? Shouldn't it be a double V?

A. It's a double U because it is a vowel.

Q. Is oxygen considered to be a dangerous gas?

A. It should be, but it often takes 75 to 100 years to kill you.

Q. Is cleaning your house a waste of time?

A. Yes, because you are just moving the dirt around and that makes something else dirty.

Q. Can someone intentionally lose a game of rock, paper, scissors?

A. The answer is no, but I am sure you can.

Q. Can someone predict the future?

A. Your future self is watching you right now through memories.

Q. Doctors in 1953 predicted that Stephan Hawking had only two years to live. What ever happened to them?

A. They all died before he did. There is a lesson here. Do you see it?

Q. What is the answer to the question What, Where and When?

A. Replace the W with a T for each word. Now you have the answer.

Q. Do animals need glasses?

A. Many animals probably do need glasses. Why don't you go catch a possum and give him an eye test?

Q. How can I reduce the number of holes in a net?

A. Staff is not sure why you want to do this, but we can tell you this: rip a hole in a net and you will now have fewer holes in the net than you had before.

Q. Am I weird for living in my own world?
A. Not really. At least everyone knows you there.

Q. If flying is so safe, why do they call the airport the terminal?
A. Because that is where the bodies are taken after a crash.

Q. Are there really two sides to every divorce?
A. Yes, yours and the jerks.

Q. Do you know what record I broke today?
A. Your previous record for the number of days you've stayed alive.

Q. Why can't we have a smoking section in every restaurant?
A. For the same reason that every swimming pool does not have a peeing section.

Q. What is the hardest word to master in the English language?
A. The word is ass.

Q. Could you explain why ass is the hardest word to understand?
A. I suppose you think ass means butt. That could be true but it has so many more meanings. For instance, what is a lazy ass? If you say "my lazy ass husband" is he actually lazy without the word ass? The word ass has absolutely no meaning in this way. So, what is a long ass flight? A long flight, as there is not butt in the meaning of the word. You can actually add the word ass to any sentence for absolutely no change to the meaning of the sentence except that it sounds cool. Using the word ass can also change the meaning of a

word. For instance, a badass is actually good even though bad is bad but a dumb-ass is still dumb. If someone tells you to move your ass, now they are talking about your entire person not your butt. But if someone said they had a fast ass car, and you said, "fast my ass", you are saying no to the car being fast. Now if you divide ass such as half ass; that means something is done badly and a piece of ass is good to have.

Q. Is there anything else about the word ass?
A. You're either covering it, laughing it off, kicking it, busting it, kissing it, trying to get a piece of it, behaving like one or you live with one.

CHAPTER 2

FUNNY STUFF

Q. Do men and women see the same things?

A. No, men can't see wrinkles in clothes.

Q. Is it true that food makes a good substitute for sex?

A. Yes, but those who have tried it now can't even get into their own pants.

Q. What pills should never be taken together?

A. Off hand, laxatives and sleeping pills come to mind.

Q. My wife said I am like a fine wine. What did she mean?

A. Men start out like grapes and it's up to women to stomp the crap out of them until they turn into something acceptable to have with dinner.

Q. I am a little clumsy with a knife when I slice vegetables. What should I do?

A. Get someone else to hold them while you chop away.

Q. What should I do about a bad cough?

A. Take a large dose of laxatives, then you will be afraid to cough.

Q. My wife argues with me about leaving the toilet seat up. What can I do?

A. Avoid arguments by leaving the seat down and start peeing in the sink.

Q. Should I eat more natural foods?

A. You can take your chances but most people die of natural causes.

Q. Why will a man pay $2 for a $1 Item?

A. Because he needs the item, whereas a woman will pay $1 for a $2 item that she doesn't need.

Q. I'm having a party on Friday. What should I use for a centerpiece at the table?

A. Anything; as long as it was not prepared by a taxidermist.

Q. What should I do to keep potatoes from budding?

A. Buy Hungry Jack mashed potato mix, keep it in the pantry for up to a year. Keep it dry and you can go two years.

Q. Should I brush some beaten egg whites over piecrust before baking to yield a glossy finish?

A. Don't do it. Brushing egg whites is not on the directions of Mrs. Smith frozen pie.

Q. Is it true that you can cure a headache by rubbing a lime on your forehead?

A. You are getting bad advice. Mix the lime with tequila, chill and drink.

Q. What should I do with leftover wine?

A. We don't know. We have never heard of that.

Q. If you are going to make a parachute jump, at least how high should you be?

A. Three days of steady drinking should do it.

Q. Which of your five senses diminishes, as you get older?

A. Sense of decency.

Q. If you teach a child how to be polite and courteous are there any problems they can't handle when they become adults?

A. Yes, how to merge onto the freeway.

Q. I only have $12.15 to my name. How will I be able to live in retirement?

A. You have all the money you will ever need if you die by 4:30.

Q. What is a whack?

A. It is when something doesn't work right, like it is out of whack.

Q. I have dyslexia, can you help me to read?

A. Yes, just cross your eyes when you read.

Q. How many men does it take to open a beer?

A. None, it should already be opened when she brings it.

Q. Why is a Laundromat a bad place to pick up women?

A. Because, a woman who can't afford a washing machine probably can't support you.

Q. How do you fix a woman's watch?

A. You don't. There is a clock on the stove.

Q. If your dog is barking at the back door and your wife is yelling at the front door, who do you let in first?

A. The dog. He will shut up as soon as you let him in.

Q. What food will diminish a woman's sex drive by 90%.

A. Wedding cake.

Q. Do they sell perfume in South Carolina?

A. No, you will have to bring your own. People there don't stink.

Q. When the end of the world comes, where is the best place to be?

A. Arkansas, because everything happens in Arkansas about 20 years later than everywhere else in the world.

Q. Why is air like sex?

A. Because it's no big deal unless you're not getting any.

Q. Should I be afraid of getting wrinkles?

A. No, because they don't hurt.

Q. Could you describe friendship in a way that I can understand?

A. Friendship is like peeing your pants, everyone can see it, but only you can feel the true warmth.

Q. What's the difference between a northern fairy tale and a southern fairy tale?

A. A northern fairy tale starts off with "Once upon a time…." And a southern fairy tale begins with "Y'all ain't gonna believe this shit……."

Q. What is the hereafter?

A. It is your final destination, as in entering a room and saying "wonder what I'm here after."

Q. If 4 out of 5 people suffer from diarrhea, does that mean that one out of five enjoys it?

A. Absolutely, he's the one that made it to the toilet and laughs at the rest of you who didn't.

Q. How hard is it to get a 4.0 in college?

A. Not too hard. Many students achieve a 4.0 every Saturday night.

Q. How long is a minute?

A. It depends on which side of the door you are on.

Q. What is the oldest recorded writing about PMS?

A. It is found in Mathew 14 verse 94. "And Mary rode Joseph's ass all the way to Egypt."

Q. How could we discourage inbreeding?

A. Ban country music.

Q. What do you see when you watch the people at Wal-Mart?

A. That God has a sense of humor.

Q. What is the best way to handle stress?

A. Do what a dog would do. If you can't eat it or hump it, then piss on it and walk away.

Q. What's a good thing about a bad decision?

A. They make good stories.

Q. What should never be said while sitting on the toilet in a public rest room?

A. Uh oh, I knew I shouldn't put my lips on that.

Q. Is it true that I lose brain cells every time I get drunk?

A. Yes, but it appears that you replace them with fat cells.

Q. Can you name six animals that live specifically in the Arctic?

A. How about two polar bears and four seals.

Q. Do you think I should see a psychic?

A. Don't waste your money. Wait until you see the newspaper headline that reads: "Psychic Wins Lottery."

Q. Why is my wife so beautiful but so stupid?

A. God made her beautiful so you would be attracted to her. He also made her stupid so she would be attracted to you.

Q. What is the best way to die?

A. Like your grandmother, in her sleep. Not yelling and screaming like everyone else in her car.

Q. If my wife sits down next to me when I am flipping the channels and she asks, "What's on TV?" What should I tell her?

A. Anything, but don't say dust.

Q. My wife's birthday is next month and she hinted that she wants something shiny that goes from 0 to 150 in about 3 seconds. What should I get her?

A. A scale.

Q. What was the Pope's first miracle?

A. He made a lame man blind.

Q. Why does my dog bite people?

A. He doesn't like them.

Q. In what state was Abraham Lincoln born?

A. Naked and screaming just like everyone else.

Q. Restaurant rules - No Shirt, No Shoes, No Service. What if someone goes in with No Pants? Would the restaurant serve them?

A. According to the rules, yes. But the chair you sat in will have to be burned.

Q. Are eyebrows considered facial hair?

A. If they are on your face the answer is yes. If they are on your ass consider them pubic hair.

Q. If a woman wears thong underwear, will she whistle when she farts?

A. Yes, if she could whistle before she wore the thong.

Q. I overheard that Captain Scott said my brain was like the Bermuda Triangle. What does that mean?

A. All knowledge that goes into it is never found again.

Q. Can a cemetery raise its prices and blame it on the cost of living?

A. No it is the cost of dying that is going up. Just think how much money you can save by dying today. Hint.

Q. A soldier was overheard talking about Captain Scott in such a way that he said that there is no difference between him and the captain. Can you name just one difference between this soldier and Captain Scott?

A. Captain Scott does not scream when he pees.

Q. Do you yawn in your sleep?

A. Of course. Do a self-test. Sit up all night and see if you yawn.

Q. If someone with their nose pierced has a cold, and they take their nose ring out, does snot come out of the piercing hole when they sneeze?

A. Yes. There is a lot of pressure from a sneeze. Just don't pierce your butt cheek, could be messy.

Q. If there's a speed of sound and a speed of light, is there a speed of smell?

A. Yes. Smell travels at the speed of wind. Check out the speed of the men moving away from the campfire when someone breaks wind. Use a stopwatch to measure the time it takes to hear the rumble to the point where the men begin to move.

Q. If I can hear my own heartbeat, do I need to be concerned?

A. If you don't hear your own heartbeat you need to be concerned.

Q. If a fart smells bad, am I sick?

A. You better believe it. Do you really think smelling very bad is normal?

Q. Should I light a match to get rid of the fart smell?

A. Yes, you are the one to do that.

Q. Can you plan a surprise birthday party for a psychic?

A. Yes, but he will know that it's his party. To fool a psychic Captain Scott suggests that you hold a party for someone else and not on the psychic's birthday. Then tell the psychic happy birthday. When he says it is not his birthday just show him the calendar with today's date circled with his name in it. Then tell him, "If you're a psychic why didn't you tell me last week that it wasn't your birthday today when I marked the calendar?"

Q. What would happen to the sea's water level if every boat in the world is taken out of the water at the same time?

A. Simple physics would say that the water level would go down by the amount of water displaced by the removed boats. When your 275-pound body goes into a bathtub the water rises and when you get out, the water lowers back to the original level plus what you just peed in the water. The unknown factor is the amount of pee in the water which would be the flow of rivers into the seas. Another factor would be all of the sunken items in the seas represented by the "Baby Ruth" you left in the tub. (Baby Ruth? What?) Go rent Caddy Shack.

Q. Do all-boys schools have a girl's bathroom?

A. The answer is no. However, recently students can choose their own gender. A boy can now say he's a girl without showing he's nuts. (Or is that his nuts?) Rumor has it that the sergeant is a lesbian. Go figure.

Q. Do the English people eat English muffins, or are they just called muffins?

A. Yes, they eat English muffins no matter what you want to call them. Do the French eat French fries? Of course, even though they don't call them that. The English can call their food anything they want just like you do. All of the men ate donkey stew even though there was no donkey in it. But watch out for shit on a shingle because it just might be that.

Q. Why are dog's noses always wet?

A. Because they are unable to wipe their noses on their sleeves like you. Captain Scott suggests that you improve the well-being of dogs by wiping their noses for them. You should start with General Bragg's pit bull.

Q. Why don't women put pictures of their missing husbands on beer cans?

A. They would if they wanted him back.

Q. If a deaf person has to go to court, is it still called a hearing?

A. Yes, it is and that is why they stick that big horn in the deaf person's ear. If you are going to play the deaf card, we're going to play the "look stupid" card.

Q. If a clown farts, does it smell funny? (Various answers)

A. Aren't all farts funny? You don't have to be a clown to fart. Just look around the campfire.

A. I'm afraid of clowns, so if one farts I am afraid he will explode all over me.

A. It's only funny if it sounds juicy. Who wouldn't laugh at a clown with shitty pants.

A. If it is humor you want, Captain Scott suggests you all wear clown costumes around the campfire.

Q. What is the secret of life?

A. Everyone knows that there are four elements that make life possible. Captain Scott has watched the men during fatigue call and has a theory that not all men are given an equal amount of each element. Some men have more of the bad element and some have less. The elements are protons, neutrons, electrons and morons.

Q. If a bee is allergic to pollen would it get the hives?

A. Yes. If you were allergic to knowledge, would you be a moron?

Q. Will trying to stifle a fart make it louder?

A. Yes, and good luck with that.

Q. Can you cry under water?

A. Let's run a test. You go under water and someone will drop a brick on your head. When you come up let's see if you are crying.

Q. What do you call male ballerinas?

A. Sissies

Q. Why do they say "easy as pie"? Making a pie is not that easy.

A. True. But eating pie sure is easy.

Q. Do married people really live longer than single people?

A. No, it just seems longer

Q. Why aren't lawyers sworn in during trials?

A. Then they wouldn't be able to lie.

Q. Is it true that Captain Scott was once a world-class athlete? I heard that he was able to jump higher than a two-story building in Memphis. Is that true?

A. Yes, because buildings in Memphis can't jump.

Q. What is the difference between ignorance and innocence?

A. If you're 2 years old and you overturn your plate of spaghetti onto your head at a fine restaurant, its innocence. If you're 32 years old, it's ignorance. The reverse is the case for the person who took you there each time.

Q. Why is it that our high school experiences occupy such a prominent place in our memories?

A. During high school we develop the most vigorous bodies we will ever have. At the same time, we possess the least amount of sense we will ever have. This combination produces many memorable moments.

Q. What is a garbanzo bean?

A. The stuff on the bottom of your plate that you say looks like shit.

Q. Is it legal to name your kid "Anonymous"?

A. Of course. Several people have that name and I'll bet you don't know a single one of them.

Q. If you dig a hole in the South Pole are you digging up or down?

A. If the dirt begins to fall on top of you then you are digging up.

Q. How do you get off a nonstop flight?

A. The same way you got off the train to Louisville. Open the door and jump.

Q. What do you call a fart that sounds like someone stomped on a ketchup packet?

A. An overachiever; you better check your undies.

Q. When I put a sheet over my head for Halloween, am I a ghost?

A. No, you are a mattress, that's what sheets cover.

Q. Do illiterate people like alphabet soup?

A. Yes, but they don't get the full effect of the alphabet soup. Probably why you don't care for it that much since you think it is making fun of you.

CHAPTER 3

PUZZLES FOR WISE GUYS

OK wise guys- figure this out:

1. Everyone knows that New Year's Day traditionally follows Christmas Day by one week. For example, if Christmas is a Monday, then New Year's Day will be on a Monday one week later. So, what is the last year in which Christmas and New Year's Day fell on different days of the week?

2. Answer- This year. When you look at Christmas first, the two holidays are exactly a week apart, but in different years. If you look at the two holidays in the same year they are a little over 51 weeks apart and on different days.

Anyone old enough to know the answer to this one?

1. Quote: "The Ford dealer sold me the deluxe model for only a dollar more, and I often stop by the Ford dealership and get fuel for just five cents a pound." Unquote. What are we talking about here? You couldn't get this at a Chevrolet or Buick dealer. Don't even think about it at the Hyundai or Toyota dealer either.

2. Henry Ford was a cheapskate. To provide the wooden panels for his station wagons, he had his own lumberyard. He hated

to see scrap wasted so he had the leftovers made into charcoal briquettes. To create a market for them he forced Ford dealerships to sell backyard grills. It cost 2 dollars for the cheapo grill and 3 bucks for the deluxe model.

Let's see how lucky you are with this one.

1. You take your wife to the grocery store. She has purchased the following items: Filippo Olive Oil, a family size tube of Preparation H, chunky peanut butter, chlorine bleach, iceberg lettuce, a Butterfinger candy bar and cheez whiz. When you start the car, you realize that you are stuck on some ice. Which of the items is most likely to help?

2. Are you choosing something and hoping to get lucky? Captain Scott recently tested the chlorine bleach on Pvt. Fitzpatrick's Mini Cooper. After pouring the bleach over all of the tires the car moved off of the ice but got stuck on the pavement. The bleach softened the rubber of the tires and made it sticky. It also ruined the tires, so I think you made the wrong choice. Maybe you should have tried the peanut butter, but don't use the Butterfinger, that is your treat for waiting two hours in the car for your wife to buy all those groceries. And leave the Cheez Whiz alone, that's hers.

If you ever had a VW bug you should know what happened in this one:

1. Before Cpl. Sailhorst was in the army he had a VW Beetle. One day his car wouldn't run so here is what he did: He loosened three bolts, replaced something, and tightened the bolts. The car ran great for six weeks and then he took 4 of his buddies and decided to pick up some babes. Unfortunately, the car burst into flames. What had Sailhorst done?

2. Sailhorst replaced a battery which was located under the back seat, but he used the wrong battery- the terminals were too tall. When his buddy Lardbutt sat in back, the springs touched the battery and the seat caught on fire. A smoldering VW is not exactly a good babe magnet.

Do you know your wood?

1. Owen McGrath was recently in West Virginia and took a tour of a coal mine. He discovered that the timbers used in the mine were poplar. He wondered why they didn't use something stronger like oak or ash. He knew that poplar was best to use in a mine, do you?

2. When poplar begins to buckle from the weight above it, it cracks with a loud noise which provides a warning to those in the mine. Now you know why he got out of there in time to tell HQ. He didn't mention if his wife knew the answer. Hmmm?

Are you wise enough to solve this mystery?

1. It's a dark stormy might. A watchman is making his rounds in a warehouse. He turns a corner. On the other side of a closed door at the end of the hall he hears, "No Frank, don't shoot!" and then a bang. The watchman enters the room and there is a doctor, a lawyer and plumber standing over the dead body. The gun is on the floor. The watchman says to the plumber, "You are under arrest for murder." How does he know it is the plumber?

2. He knows it is the plumber because the doctor and lawyer are women, and neither is named Frank.

Only upper crust travelers know this term, do you?

1. When the British travelled to what was then called the colony of India they went by ship. If you had some pull you would ask for a cabin on the port, or left, side of the ship on the way to India. On the way home, you would ask for a starboard cabin. From this peculiar custom, a word was invented. What was that word? Clue: blimey, crumpet, knickers, cricket.

2. Did you fall for one of the clues? Of course, that was just to throw you off because the word is so obvious that only the wisest of you would get it. The word is posh. It stood for port out, starboard home. On the way to India, the hot afternoon sun is on the starboard side and on the way back it was on the port side. Travelers wanted the cooler side and not the sunny side.

More words of wisdom

1. If you ever changed spark plugs you know that you must keep any dirt from falling into the spark plug holes. You could use your shop-vac to suck out any dirt before putting in the new spark plugs. What would happen if you do that?

2. Captain Scott used Pvt. Long's 1986 Yugo to see what would happen. Pvt. Jackson smuggled the car keys out and then ran the shop-vac. The result was an immediate explosion caused by sucking some air and gasoline into the vacuum motor. Jackson is alright, just a little frazzled.

Just another trick question

1. A blind man enters the subway with his seeing eye dog. The dog takes him to a booth where the sign says "Tokens, 40 cents."

While the dog pees on the sign the man rummages through his pocket and hands the vendor a dollar. No words are spoken, no hand gestures, no notes, nothing. The vendor has never seen him before and it is doubtful that the blind man had have seen the vendor. The vendor hands him two tokens and 20 cents change. How did the vendor know he wanted two tokens and not one?

2. Obviously, he handed the vendor four quarters. If he only wanted one token he would have only given two quarters.

Here is another puzzle for the wise guys:

1. Three travelers stop at a motel and ask for the cheapest room. The clerk charges them $30 and gives them the key to the laundry room. Later the clerk feels guilty for over charging the travelers. So, he gives the bell hop $5 to give the three idiots in the laundry room. The bell hop knows they can't divide $5 three ways evenly so he keeps $2 and give the travelers $3. Each traveler paid $10 and got a dollar back. That's $9 each or a total of $27. The bell hop got $2. That's $29. Where is the other dollar? If you don't know this then you fail the wise guy test.

2. There is no missing dollar. The travelers paid $25 for the room, they got $3 back from the clerk and the bell hop got $2. That adds up to $30.

More wise guys

1. Here is a household task you might do every day. You ask for advice, "is 50 enough?" "How about 125? No, that's not enough either. Maybe you should try 90." What is the task? Clue, when isn't 125 more than 90?

2. When you punch in 9, 0- that is more than punching in 1, 2, 5 on the microwave.

This makes perfect sense. Let's see if you know this.

1. An American tourist was visiting in Europe when he decided to buy a motorcycle. The salesman asked if he was going to send it to America. He said yes. The salesman said that he would have to change something on the motorcycle when he gets to America but he does not have any to sell him in Europe. What will he have to change to make the motorcycle legal to drive in America?
2. He will have to change the headlight. He bought it in England where they drive on the left side of the road so the headlight points slightly to the left. When driving on the right side of the road it will blind oncoming traffic.

Take this you wise guys.

1. A man went to the store and went to a certain aisle and asked the salesperson, "How much does 1 cost?" The salesperson said, "One costs 99 cents." "OK, how about 12?" "oh, that will be 1 dollar and 98 cents." "OK, in that case I'll take 128." The cashier rang up the purchase and it came out to be 2 dollars and 97 cents. What is this person buying? Music sounds as you wise guys try to figure this out. Maybe we should have bought 5744 for $3.96 and brought up the battery wagon to haul it back to camp.
2. The person was buying house numbers and each one cost 99 cents. Duh!!

You old timers might know this

1. Years ago, tanker trucks carrying flammable liquids had large chains hanging from the undercarriage which went from the undercarriage to the ground. It often threw out sparks while the truck was moving. Why were they dragging these chains and why don't they do that anymore? (Hint- it has nothing to do with the chain crop.)

2. By dragging chains the truck was constantly discharging its static charge with a series of small sparks that were far enough away to prevent a fireball the size of, say Toledo. Today, trucks have a ground strap that they attach to the underground tank so when the nozzle goes into the tank we have by far singed fewer eyebrows than we used to.

Did you find a rare treasure?

1. Recently, Joe's grandfather died in Dearborn, Michigan and when he went through his belongings he discovered a letter written to Henry Ford and signed by President William McKinley. The letter said, "Dear Mr. Ford, thank you for your offer to present a gift of one two-cylinder, four-cycle gasoline engine-powered quadricycle that you have developed in your workshop in Detroit for the use of the president. I do not feel that can replace our carriages at the White House with your machine which may not have the proper safety and comfort the president needs. Sincerely, William McKinley." Joe took the letter to the Henry Ford Museum and offered it to the curator. The curator said, "This letter is a fake." How did he know that?

2. The president's house was not called the White House until Theodore Roosevelt became president. In 1898, it was called the Executive Mansion.

Who won the race?

1. Two identical cars are at a stop light and the drivers agree to have a race to the next light. Car A has the A/C on the stereo blasting and the windows up. Car B has the A/C off, a talk show on the radio and the windows down. Which car will win the race?

2. Based on this information, the winning car should be car B because the A/C will take a lot of power away from the engine from car A. However, the cars computer will shut down the A/C in car A once the driver floors the gas pedal. The open windows now produce enough drag in car B to allow car A to win.

Is this possible?

1. In 1992 Bill is 13 years old. In 1999 Bill is 6 years old. How can that be? (hint: Bill isn't his real name.)

2. This could only happen if we are looking at 1992 B.C. (or, if we are politically correct B.C.E.)

Do you know these men?

1. What do the following people have in common besides being deceased? Ulysses S. Grant, Rudyard Kipling, Woodrow Wilson, Grover Cleveland and Calvin Coolidge. (hint: they are not all presidents.)

2. They are best known by using their middle names. Grant dropped his first name, Hiram. This left him with his middle name Ulysses. He added the "S" for Simpson later in life, but often went by Sam, which he picked up at West Point. The others all swapped ordinary names for funkier middle names:

Joseph Rudyard Kipling, Thomas Woodrow Wilson, Stephen Grover Cleveland and John Calvin Coolidge.

A conversational mystery

1. A man and a woman are driving around town on a nice sunny day. Every time they stop for a red light, they turn toward each other and have a conversation. When the light turns green, the conversation abruptly ends and they drive down the road until the next red light. This continues until they reach their destination. The car is not excessively loud, there's no background noise, and they don't have the radio on. Why do they converse only at red lights?

2. Their conversation is limited to red lights because they are both using sign language.

Can you get exactly 2 gallons without measuring?

1. You are out camping with 30 of your friends (sound familiar?). You are going to make pancakes for everyone in the morning, so you check the label on the pancake mix and calculate that you will need 2 gallons of water to make the entire mix. So, you go to the well to get the water and you have no measuring devise. At the well, there are two jugs, one says 13 gallons and the other says 7 gallons. How do you come back with exactly 2 gallons without fetching another container or making any extra trips to the well?

2. First, fill the 7-gallon container, then pour it into the 13-gallon jug. Do it again. You now have one gallon left in the 7-gallon jug. Empty the 13-gallon jug and pour the one gallon into it. Now fill the 7-gallon jug and pour it into the 13-gallon jug.

Do this again. You now have 2 gallons of water in the 7-gallon jug. Got it?

Stranded on a deserted island.

1. You are stranded on a deserted island that is 10 miles long and 100 yards wide. It is completely covered with grass and an occasional palm tree. There is a sheer drop-off all around the island. It is 500 feet down onto sharp rocks and shark-infested waters. In the center of the island you discovered an abandoned grass hut with the following things in it: a case of canned Beany-weenies, a case of bottled water, a poster of Ginger from *Gilligan's Island*, a flashlight, a box of matches and a blanket. That first night, you are awakened by a loud clash of thunder. Lightning has struck the far end of the island, about 5 miles away, setting the grass on fire. A breeze is blowing toward you at a rate of 2 miles an hour. How do you save yourself?

2. Face away from the fire. Then take the matches and light up the poster of Ginger to start another fire that will burn away from you. After it has burned a mile or so, move the beanie-weenies and water to a burned-out area for your consumption while you use the flashlight to signal airplanes that will surely come to take pictures of the burning island. You better pray that it doesn't rain.

You'll never get this one without cheating or reading the answer before you guess an answer. Good luck.

1. Two Bedouins are crossing the desert on their camels. It's early in the morning when they come across a suitcase in the sand that is partially open. There are no tracks of any kind surrounding

it. They look at the suitcase and see western-style clothing, so they move on. A little while longer they find another suitcase in the sand. Same thing as before. It's open and clothes are strewn about and no tracks anywhere. A little while later they find a video camera. Later still they find shoes, hats, pants, shirts all scattered in the sand. Finally, they see a man in his underwear lying face down in the sand holding a piece of straw. Obviously, he is dead. What happened?

2. The man was part of a party that was trying to make a trip across the desert in a hot air balloon. As they began to lose altitude, they began to throw off their suitcases and everything else. Finally, they said, "We are going to crash; someone's got to go?" They stripped off a few pieces from the basket they were riding in, hastily pulled straws and this poor guy had the short straw and had to jump.

Do you know your bicycles?

1. Back in the 1800's, the common form of bicycle was called the ordinary. This bike had a huge front wheel and a small rear wheel and the rider sat quite high. The common accident of this bicycle was called the header. It sent the rider over the handlebars and could cause death. To popularize cycling, something called the Safety Bike was developed, which had two wheels of the same size, a chain drive and many features we see on bikes today. But the safety bike didn't catch on at first. It was considered ugly, inefficient and uncomfortable. What made the safety bike desirous to the general public was an invention of a veterinarian in Belfast, Ireland. He patented an accessary the made the Ordinary obsolete. What was the name of the veterinarian and what did he patent?

2. The problem with both the Ordinary and the Safety bicycles were the hard rubber tires that made the ride very rough and uncomfortable. The veterinarian's name was John Dunlop and he invented the pneumatic tire.

Let's try math again.

1. A man and a boy wearing baseball caps at the local McDonalds are writing some numbers on a napkin. They are 2.1, 4.2, 3.0, 3.2. Then it is totaled at 13.2. They leave McDonalds and leave the napkin on a table when you walk by on your way to get another fill-up on your soda. You, being the math whiz that you are, realize that the sum totals 12.5. You think those two were morons with the wrong answer. Actually, they were right. What kind of calculations were they doing?

2. The man and the boy were actually the coach and the pitcher of a little league team and they were counting up the amount of innings the boy had pitched. Since baseball innings are measured in thirds, 4.2 is four and two-thirds of an inning. Go ahead, recheck the math.

Building a better fan belt.

1. In 1936, Europe is on the brink of war. In a secret location, German officers are gathered around a table with the designers of a new personnel carrier. As they went over every detail one officer asks the engineer, "How long will the fan belt last?" The engineer said, "30- to 40-thousand kilometers." The officer said, "Not good enough, we need at least 60,000." The engineer said, "No problem, just take off the belt and flip it over to get 60,000." The officer says, "That's unacceptable, we can't

ask soldiers to change the fan belts on the battlefield." So, the engineers came up with a clever design. They don't alter the material of the belt in any way, yet they satisfy the new requirement. What did they do?

2. The engineers figured out how to run the belt on both sides. They lengthen the belt, twisted it into an 8. This allows it to run on the inside and outside at the same time and double the length of time before it needs to be replaced.

Try this trick to find your friends.

1. Jim Wood was at the airport where his wife just left on a flight to visit her mother. While having a drink at the bar he sees his old college room-mate going to catch a plane. He went to go see him but lost him in the crowd. He couldn't remember his name but wanted to at least say hello and find out how he is doing. Jim knew he lived somewhere in the south so he went to the kiosk to check on flights. That's when he had an idea. Two minutes later he was reunited with his friend. What did he do?

2. He went to the customer service desk and had himself paged. Two minutes later his old friend was there to say hello.

The greatest invention during WWII.

1. During World War II, a small group of British scientists worked in a secret laboratory. They made a discovery that will greatly aid the Allied efforts against the Germans. But they needed some money to develop this product but they could not get the British government to help. So, they left Britain and went to America and had to smuggle their invention into the U.S.

in their clothing to not arouse suspicion. What invention were they hiding?

2. One of the greatest causes of death during war is getting an infection from wounds. These scientists had invented reproducible penicillin. This strain of penicillin mold could be grown in a lab. So, they rubbed this into their clothes and after they arrived they scraped it off.

If you don't know this one, pay attention, it could be helpful someday.

1. Meck Polk was taking a flight to Timbuktu for a badly needed vacation. At the airport, he boards an old DC 3 and is a little confused about why this plane is still in service. After boarding the plane, he decides to befriend some of the passengers but soon realizes no one speaks English. After a 15 hour flight the plane finally lands in Timbuktu but it is past midnight and there is no one there to greet him. He tries to get a cab but no one speaks English. Then Meck sees a woman from the plane and he knows she speaks English. How did he know that?

2. The woman from the plane was not a passenger, Instead, she was the pilot, and all pilots who fly internationally must speak English.

Well wise guys, how's your math?

1. A landscaper came home one night and his wife said to him, "Did you have a rough day?" He said," Oh yah, I planted trees today: five rows of four trees each." She said, "Wow, that makes twenty trees, no wonder you look so tired." He said, "Oh no, it was only ten trees." OK wise guys, how did he plant ten trees

in five rows of four each. Music sounds as you wise guys grab your calculators. Hint, a calculator will not help.

2. You were tricked if you thought this was a simple math problem. It is actually a geometry problem. The landscaper planted the trees in the shape of a five-pointed star. Draw a star, then put a tree at the intersection of each line and one at each vertex. You get five rows of four trees each.

Did you find your hat?

1. At the end of the Little League season, the coach has a barbeque at his house and twenty-five kids show up. The coach says that nobody can wear their hat at the barbeque so twenty hats are thrown into a pile and the kids go about eating hotdogs and deep-fried Twinkies and have a good time. At the end of party, they all reach into the pile of hats and grab a hat at random and puts in on his head. What is the probability that 24 out of 25 of these kids get their original hat back?

2. The answer has to be zero because if 24 kids got the right hat, then the 25th kid as to get the right hat too.

The lady and the tiger.

1. A king designs a series of tests for men vying to marry his beautiful daughter. After a dozen contests the final challenge is to draw a slip of paper from a bucket. There are two slips of paper is the bucket: one says "the Lady" and the other says "The Tiger." If a suitor chooses the lady slip, he wins her hand. If he chooses the tiger slip, he is thrown into the tiger cage. Suiters come and go and the tiger gets fat. One day prince charming arrives. He dazzles the princess by completing all of the tests in

record fashion. It was now time to draw a slip from the bucket. The princess likes this young man so she tells him that her father is a cheater. She warns him that both pieces of paper say "The Tiger." The prince tells her not to worry. How does he win her hand without cheating or exposing the king's treachery?

2. The prince draws out a slip and declares that he has won the princess's hand. He then swallows the slip of paper. If challenged he can show that the remaining slip says "The Tiger." The king must accept the outcome because if he protests, he exposes his own treachery.

You're not as smart as you think?

1. As you drive through the parking lot at the movie theater looking for a place to park, you notice a car with an interesting license plate. It reads TAN 270. What is the make of this car?
2. TAN 270 refers to the tangent of 270, and the tangent of 270 is undefined or infinite. So, did you get it? Really? The car is an Infiniti.

Here' an easy one.

1. A lady brings her car into the car dealership and complains that a fuse in her car is blowing out repeatedly. A mechanic comes to look at the problem and when he opens the door of the car he knows immediately what the problem is. He sees something on the dashboard that explains the problem. What is on the dashboard? (clue- it is not a light or sign).
2. There is a compass on the dashboard. The short circuit is disturbing the surrounding electromagnetic field, causing the compass to spin wildly. There is a shorted wire in the dashboard near the compass.

What happened to this car?

1. Elijah Fawbusch bought a brand-new Toyota Camry and he went out and bought a few accessories. He bought a glue on digital clock, floor mats and fuzzy dice to hang from his rearview mirror. The next day the engine won't crank. After several attempts, he finally gets it going. This happens every time he tries to drive his car. So, he takes the car back to the dealer to complain. The dealer immediately realizes what is wrong. Which of the three items Fawbusch added to his car was responsible for the difficulty in starting the car?

2. Did you just guess one of the above? So, do you know why? If you picked the fuzzy dice, you need to get some help. The Camry has a manual shift, and like many stick shift cars it has a switch that disables the starter motor if you don't depress the clutch. Fawbusch had installed thick floor mats that slid around the clutch pedal and sometimes it was not depressed well enough to start the car. Now the floor mats are in the back seat where they belong.

This one will stump you?

1. When you have been asked a question, like many in this book, and you don't know the answer, have you ever said, "I'm stumped." Or "that one stumped me?" Where does this term come from?

2. Back in the early days of the founding of the United States, farmers often had to clear trees off their land so that they could plant their crops. After the trees were cut down the stumps had to be removed. The larger stumps were sometimes too difficult

to remove and were left in place and prevented growing crops there. What this did to the farmers literally stumped them.

Do you need a haircut?

1. You are in need of a haircut in a town that has only two barber shops. You go to the first shop and see the barber is unshaven, dirty and has a lousy haircut. So, you go to the second barber shop and see a nice clean shop and the barber has a great haircut. Which barber should you choose to give you a haircut?

2. You should have chosen the messy one. Since there are only two barbers in town the dirty barber gave the neat barber his stylish cut. And why is the other guy's shop so neat? Because he has no customers. The dirty barber is too busy to clean up his shop.

Can you make 5 feet long into 4 feet long?

1. A man is waiting at the bus stop with his brand new 5-foot-long fishing pole. When the bus arrives, the bus driver tells him he can't bring the fishing pole onto the bus because nothing longer than 4 feet is allowed. So, the man goes back to the store and without altering the rod, breaking it or collapsing it, he returns to catch the next bus. When the bus arrives, he gets right on and heads for home. What did he do to the fishing rod?

2. He bought a three foot by four feet box and put the fishing pole in the box diagonally. And you think you are wise.

Don't you love being so smart?

1. Albert Sailhorst finally got rid of that old pickup parked in front of his house. A junk dealer gave him $25 for it and then sent it to a crusher. It was turned into a 3-by-3-by-3-foot solid cube

of rust weighing 3000 pounds. It was shipped to Chicago and put on a barge with a hundred other cubes of rust. On the way across Lake Michigan this cube falls overboard. Assuming that water cannot escape from the lake, does the water level go up, go down or stay the same?

2. When the 3000-pound cube is in the barge, it's displacing its weight in water. A cubic foot of water weighs 62.4 pounds, so the barge displaces 48 cubic feet (3000 divided by 62.4 is about 48). When the cube sinks, it displaces an amount of water equal to its volume. Since it's a 3-foot cube, that's 27 cubic feet. So, the water level goes down about 21 cubic feet (48 minus 27 equals 21).

Did you know this?

1. Old broken-down cars are often called a Jalopy. So where did this term come from?

2. Back in the 1920's worn-out American cars were shipped to Mexico, a practice that still occurs today. The typical destination in Mexico was Jalapa which is pronounced ha-la-pa in Spanish. The longshoremen who were putting the junkers on the boats mispronounced the name of the town. That eventually turned into jalopy.

Flapping chickens

1. Eugene Sullivan is a chicken rancher. He has put 1000 pounds of chickens in his truck that weighs 2 tons (4,000 lbs.). The total weight of the truck is now 5000 pounds plus the 250 pounds that Sullivan weighs. He comes to a bridge with a sign that says "Maximum Weight 5000 Pounds." So, he revs up the engine,

bangs on the truck to get the chickens flying, thus making the truck lighter, and speeds across the bridge. Will he make it to the other side?

2. The downward air pressure exerted by the flapping wings of the chickens is at least equal to the weight of the chickens. Otherwise, how would they fly? So, he's not going to make.

Losing your marbles?

1. You have three cloth bags that have ten marbles in each bag. The bags are labeled "white", "black" and "mixed" but these labels are incorrect. How many marbles do you need to take out of any bag to figure out which bag is really the white bag, really the black bag and rally the mixed bag?

2. You only need to take out one marble from the mixed bag. If it is white, then you know this is the white bag. Since the other bags are labeled incorrectly, just reverse what each one says on the label.

CHAPTER 4

THE MEANINGS OF YOGI-ISMS

Q. What is a Yogi-ism?

A. Something Yogi Berra said that made perfect sense to him, but might not make sense to you.

Q. Why should we care what Yogi Berra said?

A. Here are some possible answers:

1. What he says is funny.
2. What he says is stupid.
3. Anyone named Yogi must have wisdom.
4. He is one of the great sages of history.

Q. Who is Yogi Berra?

A. Here is the Wikipedia answer:

Lawrence Peter "Yogi" Berra (May 12, 1925 – September 22, 2015) was an American professional **baseball catcher**, who later took on the roles of **manager** and **coach**. He played 19 seasons in **Major League Baseball** (MLB) (1946–1963, 1965), all but the last for the **New York Yankees**. He was an 18-time **All-Star** and won 10 **World Series** championships as a player—more than any other player in MLB history.

[2] Berra had a career **batting average** of .285, while hitting 358 **home runs** and 1,430 **runs batted in**. He is one of only six players to win the **American League Most Valuable Player Award** three times. He is widely regarded as one of the greatest catchers in baseball history,[3] and was elected to the **Baseball Hall of Fame** in **1972**.

Q. That's quite impressive, but what about the Yogi-isms?

A. Yogi was often asked questions by the press to various things about baseball or life in general. He said many profound things. Let's take a look at what he has said with what he really meant when he said it.

1. "You can observe a lot just by watching."
   Meaning: observing while sleeping has not worked out so well.

2. "The future ain't what it used to be."
   Meaning: some of that future is now the past and didn't turn out so well.

3. "Half the lies they tell about me aren't true."
   Meaning: but the other half of the lies are true.

4. "When you get to a fork in the road, take it." Meaning: Maybe there is a complete place setting up the road. Start collecting your dishes a few pieces at a time.

5. "Ninety percent of this game is half mental." Meaning: That makes the other half of the game ten percent physical. And statistics never lie half the time.

6. "I really didn't say everything I said."
   Meaning: some ventriloquist must have said it.

7. "We have a good time together, even when we're not together."
    Meaning: we have a better when we're not together.

8. "If you don't know where you're going, you might end up someplace else."
    Meaning: none needed, this is pure wisdom.

9. "It gets late early around here."
    Meaning: and in the morning, it gets early later too. Yogi seems to go to bed early and sleep in.

10. "A nickel ain't worth a dime anymore." Meaning: like today a dollar can't buy a nickels worth.

11. "I usually take a two-hour nap from one to four". Meaning: I'm such a restless sleeper when I nap so leave me alone.

12. "Slump? I ain't in no slump… I just ain't hitting." Meaning: Ah, Yogi, I hate to tell you, but, ah, not hitting is a slump.

13. "No one goes there nowadays, it's too crowded." Meaning: I won't go there nowadays because all of you are there.

14. "Always go to other people's funerals, otherwise they won't come to yours."
    Meaning: No one is coming to my funeral because all of my friends have died.

15. "We made too many wrong mistakes."
    Meaning: What we did right we did on purpose, what we did wrong was mistakes.

16. "How can you think and hit at the same time?"
Meaning: I obviously have a problem when you want me to think when I bat. So, stop asking me questions.

17. "All pitchers are liars or crybabies."
Meaning: According to you pitchers, you make the team win the games; when in reality it is the opposite.

18. "Even Napoleon had his Watergate."
Meaning: Every baseball player sometimes has a very bad day. He really didn't know his history very well.

19. "Bill Dickey is learning me his experience."
Meaning: Yogi was learning from Bill Dickey, just like you are learning from Yogi.

20. "It was impossible to get a conversation going, everybody was talking too much."
Meaning: Obviously Yogi didn't have anything important to say or they would have listened to him. I think they had already heard too many yogi-isms.

21. "I'm so ugly. I never saw anyone hit with his face."
Meaning: Apparently Yogi got his good looks by getting hit in the face with a baseball a few times.

22. (On the 1973 Mets) "We were overwhelming underdogs."
Meaning: Now think about this yogi-ism, think hard. He is saying they were a really bad team, really bad.

23. "The towels were so thick there I could hardly close my suitcase."
Meaning: The towels were so nice at this place I didn't have enough room in my suitcase to steel more than one, what a bummer.

24. "I'm not going to buy my kids an encyclopedia. Let them walk to school like I did."
    Meaning: As long as the kids have to walk to school, they will be able to get as smart as me. He probably didn't know how to ride an encyclopedia.

25. "In baseball, you don't know nothing."
    Meaning: Boy is that the truth, just look at the high intellectual bar placed on these yogi-isms.

26. "I never blame myself when I'm not hitting. I just blame the bat and if it keeps up, I change bats. After all, if I know it isn't my fault that I'm not hitting, how can I get mad at myself?"
    Meaning: We get it. Your logic is perfect.

27. "It ain't the heat, it's the humility."
    Meaning: It's not the heat or the humidity, it's the pressure from the fans that expect you to have more humility.

28. "I don't know (if they were men or women fans running naked across the field). They had bags over their heads."
    Meaning: Sure, that's where everyone's eyes were during the incident.

29. "I'm a lucky guy and I'm happy to be with the Yankees. And I want to thank everyone for making this night necessary.
    Meaning: Yogi, it wasn't necessary, we just wanted to show our respect.

30. "Pair up in threes."
    Meaning: Get into groups of three. He thinks any group of any size is a pair.

31. "We have deep depth."

    Meaning: We have three or more guys at every position. Maybe ten at every position.

32. "Congratulations. I knew the record would stand until it was broken."

    Meaning: Must have been an easy record to break. Next time make the record harder to break.

33. "Why buy good luggage, you only use it when you travel."

    Meaning: I'm not wasting money on expensive luggage unless I can get more towels in them.

34. "If the people don't want to come out to the ballpark, nobody's going to stop them."

    Meaning: It's not worth stopping people that aren't coming.

35. "If you ask me anything I don't know, I'm not going to answer."

    Meaning: That's a good idea.

36. "I wish everybody had the drive he (Joe DiMaggio) had. He never did anything wrong on the field. I'd never seen him dive for a ball, everything was a chest-high catch, and he never walked off the field."

    Meaning: He was lucky every ball was hit right at him. I've had to run all over the field, and sometimes dive at the ball, to make a catch because nobody ever hit right to me.

37. "Little League baseball is a very good thing because it keeps the parents off the streets."

    Meaning: Nothing worse than parents running all over the streets. They need to be with their kids.

38. "Mickey Mantle was a very good golfer, but we weren't allowed to play golf during the season; only at spring training."
Meaning: I wish we could have played golf in the off-season, but the management said we had to play golf between spring training games, what a bummer.

39. "You don't have to swing hard to hit a home run. If you got the timing, it'll go."
Meaning: I don't hit too many homeruns because I try to hit the ball to hard.

40. "Take it with a grin of salt."
Meaning: I always like smiling salt.

41. "He hits from both sides of the plate. He's amphibious."
Meaning: Are we talking baseball or frogs here? What did Mickey Mantle say about that?

42. "You better cut the pizza in four pieces because I'm not hungry enough to eat six."
Meaning: Yah, four slices is less than eating six. And I bet your diet is working well.

43. "You wouldn't have won if we'd beaten you."
Meaning: We lost because you won. But we never lose, we just get beat.

44. "I tell the kids, somebody's gotta win, somebody's gotta lose. Just don't fight about it. Just try to get better."
Meaning; Actually, some good advice. Way to go Yogi.

45. "Never answer an anonymous letter."
Meaning: Why not, don't you know where to send it?

46. "You've got to be very careful if you don't know where you are going, because you might not get there."
Meaning: If you don't know where you're going you won't ever get there.

47. "I can see how he (Sandy Koufax) won twenty-five games. What I don't understand is how he lost five."
Meaning: Simple math Yogi; the other team scored more runs in those 5 games.

48. "I'm lucky. Usually you're dead to get your own museum, but I'm still alive to see mine."
Meaning: Yes, you are lucky to live long enough to see all your stuff put in an organized collection.

49. "If the world were perfect, it wouldn't be."
Meaning: If the world were perfect, we would never have any yogi-isms.

50. "If I didn't make it in baseball, I won't have made it workin'. I didn't like to work."
Meaning: Good thing you liked baseball because we know you didn't like to work.

51. "It's like déjà vu all over again."
Meaning: That's what we thought as we read these yogi-isms.

52. "A lot of guys go, 'Hey, Yog, say a Yogi-ism.' I tell 'em, 'I don't know any.' They want me to make one up. I don't make 'em up. I don't even know when I say it. They're the truth. And it is the truth. I don't know."

Meaning: Yes, all yogi-isms are the truth.

CHAPTER 5

THE HEART OF THE ISSUE

Q. Who should I vote for? The guy who plays like he is poor but actually is a millionaire and owns three houses, or the dude who has billions of dollars and has a commercial on every TV show?

A. Ask two questions- 1. What do I get? And 2. What's does he get? If the answer to the first question is something you want, like world peace, but you are only going to get free food, look for a third choice. If they get power and more wealth instead of world peace, then look for a third choice. Intangible things are more valuable than free things. Besides if they want you to have free things, why don't they just buy them for you with their own money?

Q. Have we ever had a president who wasn't rich or became rich after being president?

A. Only one comes to my mind, Lincoln. I think his wife had something to do about that.

Q. What did you learn in kindergarten that is still true today?

A. That the dog next door was B-I-N-G-O and that the wheels on the bus did go round and round.

Q. Is time male or female?

A. Obviously it is female because it waits for no man.

Q. The doctor says that I need to drink more water. Does that mean that I need to drink less whiskey?
A. No, of course not. You are to add ice to your drinks.

Q. During Lent every fast food place is hustling fish sandwiches. So, who has the best sandwich?
A. It must be Culver's because they are the only one who have this guy in a boat catching them one by one.

Q. What object made by man first broke the sound barrier?
A. Some of you may think it was Chuck Yeager flying the X-15 or maybe how fast your mother slapped your brother the first time he used a cuss word. Both are wrong, but your mother may come in second. It was actually the whip. The crack you hear is the tip of the whip breaking the sound barrier.

Q. If the Wicked Witch of the West melts in water, how did she ever bathe?
A. She had to go to the dry cleaners.

Q. What three things would you bring to a deserted Island?
A. Only one thing really matters. Bring a boat.

Q. Is a fly without wings a walk?
A. No, more like a dive and a crash.

Q. When something fades in the sunlight, where did the colors go?
A. They are still there. Look deeper into the material or even onto the back where the colors should even be brighter. While you are there do some cleaning so we can see them better.

Q. Where are the germs that cause 'good' breath?
A. You don't have any.

Q. The sergeant told me I could go to town after dark. When is that, after sunset?
A. Don't be silly. After dark comes light, therefore it is after sunrise.

Q. Why do you need an appointment to see a psychic?
A. You don't, she knows when you're coming. She even knows you're going to give her a $50 tip. You better get going because your appointment is in an hour from now.

Q. Can you hear yourself think?
A. I can't but I am sure you can.

Q. What happens if you go on a survival course - and you don't pass?
A. You get a nice burial marker made of rocks.

Q. What happens when you swallow your pride?
A. Many people often choke on it. Some even die.

Q. What if someone died in the living room?
A. We could hold a wake without having to leave the room. Probably should put away the chicken wings that he died from.

Q. Why do fat chance and slim chance mean the same thing?
A. It is a play on words. Fat chance makes you think you have a better chance than a slim chance when in reality you have no chance in hell.

Q. What does no chance in hell mean?
A. It means that even if you die you won't win.

Q. If a person suffered from amnesia and then was cured would they remember that they forgot?

A. Yes. Your wisdom is so perfect.

Q. Why do they write, "May contain traces of peanuts or other kind of nuts" on peanut butter jars?

A. Because there may be traces of nuts in the peanut butter. This is not a problem. Be alert for jars that may say the following: "May contain traces of chicken feathers, mouse dung, toe nail clippings, beaver semen, fumunda cheese or bull shit."

Q. What is fumunda cheese?

A. That gooey substance found from under something. Example: that greenish substance found between your toes.

Q. Why is it so difficult to solve a redneck murder?

A. First of all, the DNA will be the same and there usually are no dental records.

Q. What four-letter word should never be said by a doctor during surgery?

A. OOPS.

Q. What is the rule of thumb?

A. Back in the middle ages there was a law that said you could not beat your wife with a stick thinker than your thumb. The sergeant uses this rule when you get your beef or pork ration. The HQ staff discards thicker portions so no one gets more than anyone else.

Q. What does the word "golf" mean?

A. Originally it was a Scottish game played only by men. The posting of GOLF, which means Gentlemen Only Ladies Forbidden, often appears in various city parks to signify that if you are not a gentleman you should stay out of the park. Please note your place when you see the word golf.

Q. Is it possible to lick your eyebrow?

A. No, but I can see that several of the men don't believe this and may be seen in camp trying to prove the answer wrong.

Q. Do the kings in a deck of cards represent anybody in history?

A. Yes, the spade is King David, the hearts is Charlemagne, the clubs is Alexander the Great and the diamonds is Julius Caesar.

Q. Who does the joker represent?

A. You.

Q. I think you just tried to lick your eyebrows.

A. Yes you did.

Q. If you multiply 111,111,111 X 111,111,111 what will you get?

A. This is something you really need to know. Most of you have already taken a calculator for the answer, which is 12,345,678,987,654,321.

Q. Statues of horses take many different poses. Is there a reason for that?

A. Yes, if the horse has both front legs in the air it means that the person on the horse died in battle. If the horse has one front leg in the air the person died as a result of wounds received in battle. If the horse has all four legs on the ground it means that the person died of natural causes. If the horse is lying down it means that the horse died in battle. Bird shit on the statue means this man is still disliked even today.

Q. Most boat owners name their boats. What is the most popular name for a boat?

A. Obsession.

Q. If you were to spell out numbers, how far would you have to go until you could find the letter "A"?

A. I can see you now, thinking through all the numbers as words. Did you get to one thousand yet?

Q. How many cars were wrecked in a single scene of the Blues Brothers movie?

A. 52, but maybe you should watch it again and do a recount.

Q. Where does the term honeymoon come from?

A. In ancient Babylon a bride's father was supposed to supply his son-in-law all the mead he could drink for the first month after the wedding. Mead is a beer made from honey. Apparently, women were ugly back then.

Q. What is so scary about living in a retirement facility?

A. All the old ladies running around with faded and sagging tattoos and pierced navels.

Q. When will I know that I am middle aged?

A. When you choose your cereal for the fiber and not the toy.

Q. Is it true that water contains E. coli?

A. Yes, E. coli is found in our feces as small amounts of it come from the water we drink. Be advised that any liquor, wine or beer does not have E. coli as it has been boiled, filtered and or fermented before it is bottled.

Q. What is better for me; wine or water?

A. Remember that wine equals health and water equals poop. Therefore, it is better to drink wine and talk stupid than to drink water and be full of shit.

Q. Is laughing good exercise?

A. Yes, it is like jogging on the inside.

Q. Should I be afraid of getting wrinkles?

A. No, because they don't hurt.

Q. What can a friend do for me when I am sad?

A. Help get you drunk and plot revenge against the sorry bastard that made you sad.

Q. Can kids in the back-seat cause accidents?

A. You have it backwards. Accidents in the backseat cause kids.

Q. Why don't people like the IRS?

A. When it comes to money, see what THE IRS spells.

Q. What happened to Preparation A through G?

A. No one was interested in a cream that causes itching, irritable bowels, anal leakage, hives, ulcers, lymphoma, leukemia, and in 40% of test trials, death.

Q. If cows laughed would milk come out of their noses?

A. Only if they were drinking milk. Since you have this problem, Captain Scott suggests that you clean out your nose by laughing and drinking soapy water.

Q. Why do they put pictures of criminals up in the Post Office?

A. Interesting point since the criminals probably stay away from the post office. It would be a better idea to put the criminal's pictures on the stamps so the mailman can look for them while he delivers the mail.

Q. Do Lipton Tea employees take coffee breaks?

A. You bet they do. Coffee helps get that nasty tea flavor out of your system.

Q. If lawyers are disbarred and clergymen are defrocked for breaking their oaths, do others suffer similar penalties?

A. Yes, electricians are delighted and dry cleaners are depressed.

Q. If it is true that we are here to help others, then what are others here for?

A. To piss us off with these stupid questions.

Q. If people from Poland are called Poles, then why aren't people from Holland called Holes?

A. Your logic is perfect. Ask some more questions so we can rate your I.Q. I think you are going to win a prize.

Q. Why do croutons come in airtight packages? Aren't they just stale bread to begin with?

A. Sure, but you want them fresh, don't you?

Q. What is life worth?

A. Life isn't worth much or you could trade it in for some needed cash. The labor of a life is worth more than life itself. In 1860 a strong field hand was worth $1000. Your labor is worth about 25 cents per day and your army pay is worth $11 a month. You should have asked, "What is death worth?"

Q. What is death worth?

A. Nothing unless you buy "life" insurance. Many policies pay over one million dollars. It isn't worth buying life insurance for yourself. Instead, buy several policies on your friends and then plan their deaths.

Q. How many things does a man have in the bathroom?

A. Six: toothbrush, toothpaste, shaving cream, razor, a bar of soap and a towel.

Q. How many things does a woman have in the bathroom?

A. The number varies but averages at about 337. A man would not be able to identify more than 20 of those.

Q. What is the best thing about being a man?

A. The world is your urinal.

Q. What is a planet?

A. A body of earth surrounded by a sky.

Q. What's worse than being in a rut?

A. Being in a grave. It's much deeper.

Q. My wife never lets me have the last word. What can I do?

A. You can get the last word in. Just apologize.

Q. Why haven't we heard about UFOs very much lately?

A. Today everyone has a camera in their phone.

Q. What advise can you give me on how to make ends meet?

A. You should forget about making ends meet. The problem is that someone is always moving the ends.

Q. Have you heard the question "Do these jeans make my butt look fat?

A. Yes, and jeans do not have the ability to make you look any worse than you already are.

Q. Where can men over the age of 60 find younger women who are interested in them?

A. Try a bookstore and look for the fiction section.

Q. What can a man do while his wife is going through menopause?

A. Keep busy. If you are handy with tools, you can finish the basement. When you're done you will have a place to live.

Q. How can I avoid elderly wrinkles?

A. Take off your glasses.

Q. Is it common for the elderly to have problems with short-term memory storage?

A. Storing memory is not the problem. Retrieving it is the problem.

Q. What is the leading cause of diminished sex drive among senior citizens?

A. Nudity.

Q. Do elderly people ever "get lucky?"

A. Sure. Sometimes they find their parked car at the first place they look.

Q. Is it possible to have sex with a prostitute against her will?

A. Yes, it is called shoplifting.

Q. What is cured ham?

A. Apparently it is the meat from a hog that was once sick.

Q. Why do some people park their $50,000 car in the driveway when they have a garage?

A. Because the garage is being used to store tons of useless junk. This junk has much more meaning to them because in a few years they will sell the car and still have a garage full of junk.

Q. When can you trespass on people's property, knock on their door and make a non-negotiable demand that they fulfill?

A. Between 5 and 8 pm. on Halloween.

Q. Do you know the politically correct term for being lazy?

A. Yes, a selective participator.

Q. What two words rhyme but have opposite meanings?

A. Getting thinner and having more dinner.

Q. Would you say that a cookie jar is half full or half empty?

A. I would want to know who ate half my cookies.

Q. What was the last challenge that you won?

A. For me it was completing a fourteen-day diet in just two hours and twelve minutes.

Q. What rule do they break on Old McDonald's farm?

A. The I before E rule.

Q. When I fix something with duct tape, how do I know when I have used enough tape?

A. When you hear someone say, "is that enough duct tape?"

Q. Has McDonalds done anything to reduce the number of calories in their meals?

A. Absolutely, to reduce the calories on your supersized Big Mac meal McDonalds suggests you order a diet Coke with that.

Q. I don't feel like saying "Good Morning" every day when I meet people. What would you suggest I say instead?

A. Try saying "Here we go again." It's worked for me.

Q. Before there were sports drinks, what did athletes drink when they got dehydrated and thirsty?

A. It's still available and very inexpensive. It's called the garden hose.

Q. When does a person realize that they are getting old?

A. When they sit on the floor and then need help getting up.

Q. I get confused when I read food packages and they say what a serving size is. What am I supposed to do? Measure everything before I eat it?

A. Silly you. That is only the recommended size. The real portion size is what you say it is.

Q. What is the most challenging thing about marriage?

A. Trying to find the things your spouse moved.

Q. What is the best way to wash my hands?

A. Pretend that you just ate a lot of buffalo wings and your about to put on a white wedding dress. (Rented tuxedo for you ruffians)

Q. Who was the scariest person you ever knew?

A. My grade school principal, she looked just like Nancy Pelosi.

Q. What would be an ideal amount of weight to lose so I won't feel so fat?

A. You know you are there when you are able to finally reach inside the Pringles can.

Q. Is it true that going to sleep on Sunday night causes Monday to occur?

A. Your logic is perfect, so the answer is yes. You might want to try staying up all night on Sunday to prevent Monday from occurring.

Q. Can you guess what I have discovered to be the easiest thing in the world to do?

A. yes, get fat.

Q. Have you ever met someone who has plenty of energy, high moral principles and wants to fight crime?

A. Yes, I have. It sounds like a four-year-old wearing a batman cape.

Q. Have you ever said something funny instead of the right answer?

A. Because of some of your stupid questions, the answer is yes.

Q. Have you ever met someone who is doing something they are not qualified for?

A. Now that you mention it, yes, it is you.

Q. When the store clerk asks if I want my milk in a bag, should I do that?

A. Don't do that. It is very messy. You should leave the milk in the carton.

Q. What is the correct spelling for this name: Tom Cruise, Ted Cruz or Terry Crews?

A. We don't have an opinion on this. Perhaps the three of them should settle this question with a cage match.

Q. My wife has been missing for over a week. The police said I better plan for the worst. What should I do?

A. See if you can get her clothes back from the Salvation Army.

Q. I'm looking for something fun to do that is different, inexpensive and will be a load of laughs. What might you suggest I do?

A. Tomorrow take two witnesses with you and dress in a blue shirt and tan pants and go to Best Buy. Ask for the manager and then tell him that you quit.

Q. I don't think I can do that, do you have any other ideas?

A. Sure, dress up in a red polo shirt and Khaki pants and take two friends with you to the nearest State Farm Insurance Agency and turn in your resignation?

Q. How is any of this funny?

A. When you take two friends with you they will tell the rest of us how successful you were quitting a job you don't have. We think that will be funny.

Q. I hear there is a coin shortage. What is the cause of that?

A. I'm not sure about where you live, but in my area, all of my friends decided to clean up our language and started swear buckets.

Q. I have concerns about the decisions the government makes. Is there anything I can do?

A. You obviously are voting for the wrong people. Have you ever considered sending the government something to guide their decisions? We suggest you send them a new Magic 8 ball.

Q. Where is the best place to get really good fresh produce?

A. Down the block in my neighbor's garden. Really good stuff and cheap too.

Q. When does a person become old?
A. When they stop lying about their age and begin bragging about it.

Q. How do you make holy water?
A. Boil the hell out of it.

Q. Did you ever have someone ruin your day?
A. No one can ruin your day without your permission.

Q. What is the best way to escape my problems?
A. You can either decide to solve them or get drunk.

Q. Where do I need to go to register my complaints?
A. Sorry, yesterday was the deadline for complaints.

Q. My wife always wants to argue with me. What can I do?
A. You don't have to attend every argument you're invited to.

Q. What is the best way to relax?
A. With an idle mind.

Q. Laugh and the whole world laughs with you, but what if I cry?
A. You will need a tissue to blow your nose.

Q. I went to the social security office to sign up for benefits and when I couldn't produce an ID the lady said, "show me your chest." I thought it was strange but complied and she saw my gray chest hair and finished the application. Is this common practice?
A. Yes, in fact if you had dropped your pants you might have gotten disability too.

Q. How do I know if there is a curse on my marriage?
A. If you have video of your wedding vows go back and watch them. See if the exact words of the curse are said: "I now pronounce you man and wife."

Q. My wife's doctor said he doesn't like the way my wife looks, should I get a second opinion?

A. It is not necessary if she is a good cook and will have sex with you.

Q. Unnamed soldier asked Lt. Marsh: "I didn't sleep with my wife before marriage, did you?"

A. Marsh replied: "I'm not sure. What was her maiden name?"

Q. Is it unhealthy to hold my farts in and not let them go?

A. Of course it is. Let them go and let the rest of your friends tell you about your health.

Q. Why do dogs retrieve a ball when you throw it?

A. Dogs think you like to throw balls and it amuses them.

Q. Which letter is silent in the word "scent," the S or the C?

A. The S is silent. It is always the first letter when 2 consonants are together at the beginning of a word. Example: pneumonia and psycho and philharmonic. The P is silent in every case.

Q. Do twins ever not like their twin?

A. Rarely, usually after finding out that one of them was not planned.

Q. Why is the letter W, in English, called a double U? Shouldn't it be a double V?

A. It's a double U because it is a vowel.

Q. What is the fastest land mammal in the world?

A. Recent studies indicate that it is a toddler who was just asked by his father "what's in your mouth?"

Q. Did you know there is not one canary on the Canary Islands?

A. Yes, it's the same with the Virgin Islands- not one canary there either.

Q. Have you noticed how fast a child can pick up dropped things?

A. Oh yah, now I have to decide if I need it anymore before I spend the effort to pick it up.

Q. Sometimes my eyes hurt after drinking coffee. What is the cause of that?

A. You forgot to take the spoon out of your cup.

Q. I have a hard time remembering what day it is. What advise do you have for me?

A. Arrange your underwear with the day of the week written on them and don't get dressed in the dark.

Q. Is it true that Illinois has a department called the Sandwich Police?

A. Yes, and the way you make sandwiches you better stay out of Sandwich, Illinois.

Q. What do you consider to be the most important technological innovation?

A. Most people would say the automobile or perhaps the miniaturization of the computer so you can wear it on your wrist like Dick Tracy. But for you it is the gravy boat. You can't live without it.

Q. What is one of the most enjoyable things about sitting around the campfire?

A. Seeing a bunch of 50+ year-olds pretend to have the body of a 28-year-old and have the mind of a 12-year-old.

Q. How can just one person, like myself, save ten trees.

A. Try using the receipts you get from fast-food, big box and drugstores in your fireplace this winter instead of wood. That's about 10 trees per year.

Q. Do you know what you will never hear anyone say at a pizza party?

A. For most people you will never hear anyone say the crust is the best part of the pizza, except for you.

Q. I've heard that cardiovascular exercise will help prolong your life. Is this true?

A. We have consulted the visiting Chinese Doctor at the prestigious University of Pidgeon Ridge Medical School, Dr. Chin Not Wong. Here is what he has to say about that: "Heart only good for so many beats, and that it. Don't waste on exercise. Everything wear out eventually. Speeding up heart not make you live longer; it like saying extend life of car by driving faster. Want to live longer? Take nap.

Q. Over the years, what has caused you the most pain?

A. The inability of the bed post and my right big toe to get along.

Q. Throughout your lifetime, have you had more accomplishments or stories to tell.

A. My biggest accomplishment has been to tell many true stories, most are sad but funny because I'm not very intelligent.

Q. Do you have any ideas how to keep burglars away from my house?

A. If you have kids in college, post the tuition bills on your front door.

Q. I saw a car with an elderly couple drive by with a sign in the window that said "just married." I think that was rather bold for elderly newlyweds. What do you think?

A. That couple has been married for 40 years, thus the sign of lost bliss.

Q. What should I do if I think someone is following me when I driving to the grocery store?

A. Drive like you are in a James Bond movie. That should get rid of them.

Q. My teenage son asked me to explain taxes. What would be a good way to show him what taxes are like.

A. Take him to Pancheros and make him pay for a burrito. Then you eat 41% of it and tell him he gets the rest.

Q. How do I know when I have enough money to be considered rich?

A. You know you are rich when your dog has a dog.

Q. What does it mean when a woman says "What."

A. She isn't asking you to repeat what you said, she is giving you a chance to change your response.

Q. Some of my friends say I am immature. I am 55 years old and think I am as mature as anyone else. What do you think?

A. Stop going to your friend's houses at night leaving pink flamingos in their yards.

Q. Some drivers seam to ignore my horn when I want to get their attention. What can I do?

A. Start carrying fireworks in your car. It has worked for me.

Q. How do I keep my kids from running out to the ice cream truck when it comes down my street?

A. Tell them that when the music is playing, they are out of ice cream.

Q. What is a newborn baby?

A. A redundant statement.

Q. What does a rodeo teach people about life?

A. That some people do stupid things with wild animals. Which of the things you see at a rodeo would you like to do? How about at a bull fight? If you chose an answer, I rest my case.

Q. In this digital age I think it is a good idea for students to learn how to write in cursive. Is there anything else that you think they should learn that is being forgotten?

A. Yes, how to use a rotary phone and how to read the hands on a clock. It also wouldn't hurt them to put away their video games and play a game of pong.

Q. Is there anything that still fits you that you haven't worn in ten years?

A. Only my hat.

Q. What would make a politician more interesting to watch?

A. If liars pants really did catch on fire.

Q. What is the cause of wind?

A. Recent research has determined that wind can be generated by eating a large helping of beans and cooked cabbage and wash it down with beer. Then wait 30 minutes or jump up and down for 10 minutes. There may be some rumbling before you hear the wind break.

Q. I don't understand the controversy over Roe v. Wade. Could you explain it to me?

A. It mainly has to do with whether you want to get your pants wet and how deep the water is. Deep water you will row and shallow water you will wade.

Q. Why is it that some people never seem to be embarrassed?

A. Because you can't be embarrassed if you don't care what people think.

Q. If a woman says "I'm not mad at you," what does she really mean?

A. It has the same meaning as the dentist saying "You won't feel a thing."

Q. My teenage son seems to be living in another world. What can I do?

A. Start recording the things that he does that seem alien to you. Here is an example of alien things you may observe: pouring milk into the bowl before the cereal, eating soft butter with a spoon like ice cream, thoroughly covering ice cream with pepper before eating it or refusing to eat at McDonalds because he prefers humus.

Q. What was the most pleasurable trip you ever took?

A. The last time I took my mother-in-law to the airport.

Q. I heard that you have been in love with the same woman for 50 years. What is your secret to this long relationship?

A. My wife has never found out about it.

Q. What are the three words a woman never wants to hear when she is making love?

A. Honey, I'm Home.

Q. My wife lost her credit card and I decided not to tell the credit card company. Do you know why?

A. I have a pretty good idea. The thief probably spends less than your wife.

Q. I always see you at the shopping mall holding hands with your wife. That's so sweet. Why do you always do that?

A. Because if I let go of her hand she will go shopping.

Q. My wife spent two hours at the Beauty Shop and came home with nothing being done. What was she doing there for two hours?

A. I suppose she was just getting an estimate.

Q. I heard that a doctor gave a man six months to live and then in six months he gave him another six months to live. What happened with this?

A. The man didn't pay his bill in the first six months.

Q. Why do football players put black lines under their eyes?

A. The official answer given by football players is that eye black is a grease or strip applied under the eyes to reduce glare. However, no study has conclusively proven this. It is a form of functional makeup. Our own study has determined that the players actually think it looks cool. Players who don't wear this makeup are often considered pussies thus everyone wears it because it looks cool. The butterfly tattoo on a certain quarterback's ass looks cool too.

Q. How much sanitizer should I use each time I enter a new environment?

A. We've seen your hands, we suggest three large pumps.

Q. Is there such a thing as a quick question?

A. No. But there is such a thing as a quick answer.

Q. What would happen if all of the bumpy roads suddenly all became very smooth roads?

A. All of the travel stories would suddenly become boring.

Q. A child asked his grandfather this question: "Papa, what do you remember to be the best part of your childhood?"

A. We had lots of fun playing outside in all seasons, building things from scraps, exploring all of the neighborhoods, meeting new friends and we played cards and tried to do magic tricks. Then social media took over.

Q. What was the theme of President Biden's inaugural address?

A. We aren't sure about that, but we are sure that Garth Brooks had new hair plugs when he sang "Amazing Grace" at the inauguration.

Q. Some people have magnets of religious icons on their refrigerators. If God had a refrigerator what magnet would he have?

A. A picture of Chuck Norris.

Q. I have a house, a car, a job and make good money. My immature video game playing son hits me up for money all the time. So, when he scored an 88 on his biology exam, I also took it to teach him a lesson. I got a score of 61. What does that mean?

A. You need to turn over your car, house and money to him since he can obviously invest it wiser than you. You better keep your job though, in case your son needs a bigger bankroll.

Q. My wife thinks I should stop yelling at my son. How do I convince her that yelling at him is necessary?

A. Tell her it is a technique used by experts to motivate selective listeners.

Q. Do you know why I talk to myself?

A. Sometimes you need expert advice.

Q. I've heard that football players last season saw a rise in concussions. What was the cause of that?

A. It appears to be head butting each other after a touchdown.

Q. I was wondering if yoga would be good for exercise. Is it?

A. You won't even bend over to pick up a coin on the floor so I don't think you will like yoga

Q. Why can't teenagers manage their time?

A. Research has shown that they have the management skills of a carrot.

Q. I am tired of exercising to get rid of my excess weight. How can I look slimmer without all of the exercise stuff?

A. We recommend you try to learn photo-shop and work on your photos.

Q. I lost a contact lens. What should I do?

A. Announce to everyone nearby that you lost your contact lens and a lot of people will help you find it. Haven't you noticed; people love to look for them.

Q. I am afraid of germs. Is there anything I can do to break my fear of germs?

A. Of course. Use a porta-podi until you no longer fear the germs.

Q. When will I know that I have enough money to retire?

A. When you no longer complain about the cost of airport food.

Q. I see eating six large mozzarella cheese sticks as disgusting. What do you think?

A. If you are eating them to stop diarrhea, that is fine. But eating six mozzarella breadsticks as an appetizer for $8, now that is disgusting.

Q. Have you ever heard the phrase "If you love something, you must set it free?"

A. Sure, I follow that advise whenever I come across a distressed pie.

Q. What do you think about kids nowadays watching cartoons like Sponge Bob Square Pants?

A. We think they will become sissies and snowflakes. They need to see some real powerful cartoons like Yosemite Sam and Foghorn Leghorn. Those guys were real problem solvers.

Q. I want to be important even after I die. Where is that possible?

A. Chicago, you can still vote there after you die.

Q. As I get older my eye sight seems to be getting poorer. Is there any advantage to having poor eye sight?

A. Some people have found that older age and poor eye sight allows them to see through some people.

Q. What are the three symptoms of laziness?

A. Going to bed early, sleeping in every morning and taking long naps.

Q. Do we all have that one friend that we greet with a swear word insult?

A. No, just you.

Q. What is the opposite of irony?

A. For you it is wrinkly.

Q. Why is there a handle inside the car above the passenger front seat?

A. That is for your use when you teach a teenager how to drive.

Q. Have you ever heard the term "getting too big for your britches?"

A. Yes, when you were little it meant that you were getting into trouble, now it means that you are getting fat.

Q. What is one of the strongest scientific theories in the world?

A. For every male action there is a stronger female reaction.

Q. What happened to the man that went before the judge for drinking too much?

A. When the judge told him he was there for drinking he said, "ok, then, let's get stated."

Q. Why do Jewish mothers make great parole officers?

A. They never let anyone finish their sentences.

Q. Why do so many women order Won Ton at a Chinese restaurant?

A. Because Won Ton spelled backwards is Not Now.

Q. What is the best advice to give to a young bride?

A. Never underestimate the number of times your husband will do things wrong.

Q. What is the secret to keeping friends?

A. Never tell anyone that you had a good night's sleep.

Q. Now that Biden is president, have we ever heard who won the Democratic caucus in Iowa?

A. No, but we know it wasn't Joe. However, we will know the winner some day since Iowa can't have another caucus until they complete the tabulation of the previous one.

Q. What happened to the politicians promise to end kids going to bed hungry?

A. They spent $100 million getting elected instead.

Q. Could you list everything that people don't argue about on Facebook?

A. Sure, here it is: (crickets)

Q. I just got a subscription to Ancestry.com. I bet you $5000 that you can't guess what I just discovered about my ancestry.

A. We'll take that bet. After some discussion, the staff has figured that you have traced your ancestry back 62 generations and discovered that your ancestor was a prostitute in ancient Rome and may have had an affair with Julius Caesar. This would explain your receding hair line, the way you walk with a slight limp, your hunched shoulders, club foot, the six fingers on your left hand and the disfigurement of your face before your accident. Were we right?

Q. How did you know that and will you take a check?

A. Lucky guess and no, cash or gold only.

Q. Why do I forget things?

A. Because your brain doesn't want you to remember. Your brain is the smart part of yourself so if it doesn't want you to find your car keys, I'm sure it has a good reason, like it is afraid to ride in the car with you.

Q. What is a score?

A. You may think that it is the results of last night's game. Your team lost 108 to 4. But a score is also an amount. Just like eggs are counted by the dozen, that is 12. Your whiskey consumption is counted by the score, that is 20.

Q. Do you know what a piffle is?

A. First you must say it four times out loud very fast. I'll wait..
Now don't you feel better? You just did a piffle, that is you just did trivial nonsense.

Stories in Minnesota often revolve around the Norwegian immigrant couple, Ole and Lena. Much has been written about this couple but we offer here a sample of Minnesota humor as well as discovering some more truth. Just as we don't judge a book by its cover, we don't judge immigrants from looking at Ole and Lena. This is just pure Minnesota.

Direct from Minnesota

The toilet seat was invented by a Norwegian in Minnesota. Twenty years later a North Dakotan improved it by putting a hole in the middle.

OUTHOUSE PROBLEM

When Ole accidentally lost 50 cents in the outhouse, he immediately threw in his watch and billfold. He explained, 'I'm not going down dere yust for 50 cents!'

VE COULDN'T AFFORD MORE

Two Norwegians from Minnesota went fishing in Canada and returned with one fish. 'The way I figger it, dat fish cost us $400' said the first fellow. 'Vell,' said the other, 'At dat price it's a good ting ve only caught one!'

THE RELATIONS

Ole and Lena were getting on in years. Ole was 92 and Lena was 89. One evening they were sitting on the porch in their rockers and Ole reached over and patted Lena on her knee. 'Lena, vat ever happened tew our sex relations?'

He asked.

'Vell, Ole, I yust don't know,' replied Lena.

'I don't tink ve even got a card from dem last Christmas'

MUSIC SOLUTION

Ole bought Lena a piano for her birthday. A few weeks later, Lars inquired how she was doing with-it.

'Oh,' said Ole, 'I persvaded her to svitch to a clarinet.'

'How come?' asked Lars.

'Vell,' Ole answered, 'because vith a clarinet, she can't sing.'

THE PRANK CALL

The phone rings in the middle of the night when Ole and Lena are in bed and Ole answers.

'Vell how da hell should I know, dats two tousand miles from here' he says and hangs up.

'Who vas dat?' asks Lena. 'I donno, some fool vanting to know if da coast vas clear.'

HONEYMOON TRIP

On their honeymoon trip, they were nearing Minneapolis when Ole put his hand on Lena's knee.

Giggling, Lena said, 'Ole, you can go farther dan dat if you vant to'.

So Ole drove to Duluth.

DA PARTY

Ole was arrested one night while walking bare naked down the streets of the little town of

Alexandria, Minnesota. The policeman, who was a good friend of Ole's said,'Ole..What in the world are you doing? Where are your clothes?

You're naked.'

'Yah, I know,' said Ole. 'You see, I vas over to dat 'playboy' Swen's for his birthday party. Dere vas about ten of us. Der vas boys and girls.'

'Is that right?', his policeman friend asked.

'Yah, Yah, anyvay, dat Swen, he says, 'Everybody get into the bedroom!'

'So vee all go into the bedroom.... where den he yells, 'Everybody git naked!'

'Vel, vee all got undressed. Den he yells, 'Everybody go to town!'

I guess I'm the first one here!'

We know, truth isn't always pleasant.

CHAPTER 7

ANSWERS TO COVID-19 QUESTIONS

In the year 2020 the world was hit with a very serious pandemic that was named Covid-19. Covid comes from the name of a Coronavirus that was first discovered in late 2019. If you lived through this time you will understand the answers to the covid questions since parts of the government went overboard with solutions that many times were not solutions at all. If you were too young or born after the event just enjoy what we thought of those times. The questions and answers found below were written in 2020 during the crisis.

Some Covid-19 Tips

1. In case you struggle with social distancing accuracy, remember that six feet is the average length of a Walmart receipt.
2. Stay away from anyone who says "Ciao."
3. Stay away from stationary bikes. There has been an increase in road rage from stationary bike users.
4. We will know when the government is really serious when they fire Dr. Fauci and replace him with Chuck Norris.
5. Covid-19 is noticeable if you see anyone dipping French fries in milk shakes. Get them to the ER.

Wise guys on Covid-19

Q. Can you tell me a good way to avoid the coronavirus?

A. Don't listen to Justin Bieber music. It has worked for me.

Q. Everyone is buying up the toilet paper around here. I don't have very much left at my house. What should I do?

A. You need to reduce the number of times you go to the bathroom to poo to make your toilet paper last longer. Eat an eight-ounce block of cheese every day should help.

Q. With COVID-19 out there now, when can I expect to see "normal?"

A. Last time we checked, you can still find normal on your washing machine.

Q. We've had a shortage of toilet paper and bottled water, what will be the next item in short supply?

A. We checked the garbage collected in your neighborhood the past month and figure there will soon be a run on Jack Daniels No. 7 and Captain Morgan rum.

Q. My wife is having a birthday soon. What should I get her that will be inexpensive now but in six months should be worth ten times what is costs today?

A. We suggest getting her a barrel of crude oil. Get a dozen if you have room in your garage.

Q. I have a $50 gift card for J.C. Penny, when will I be able to use it?

A. You may have lost the chance to use it at the store. You might want to put in in a frame and hang it on the wall in your home as a collector's item. You should be able to recoup your $50 in about 72 years.

Q. What is your biggest concern about being quarantined in your home?

A. Trying to decide when it's too late for coffee or too early for alcohol.

Q. I keep hearing people say "in these uncertain times." What do they mean by that?

A. Before the present day we always knew what was going to happen.

Q. If people knew what was going to happen, then did they know the South would lose the Civil War?

A. According to the people who use the term "in these uncertain times" the answer is yes.

Q. How do you like working at home?

A. I didn't work at work so what makes you think I'm working at home.

Q. During the quarantine I got my wife a 1000-piece puzzle to keep her busy. What do you think she got me?

A. A list of nursing homes for you to choose from.

Q. Do you think things will change after the covid-19 thing is over?

A. No, you're still going to jail.

Q. I love the Big-Mac and could eat one every day for ever. Is there anything you could get from eating at McDonald's every day?

A. Yes, a stomachache.

Q. They say that when I have stress, I should go to my happy place. Where is your happy place?

A. That's a no brainer, Dairy Queen.

Q. Are you afraid of murder hornets?

A. If you live along the Mississippi River you have a problem with shadflies not murder hornets. I dare these murder hornets to take on the shadflies.

Q. My bathroom scale says I have gained 15 pounds since I began wearing a facemask in public. How can that be?

A. Sure, blame the facemask for you getting fat. You should wear your facemask in the house every time you enter the kitchen.

Q. What is your biggest fear during the Covid-19 pandemic?

A. That the CDC will outlaw buffets.

Q. My favorite chicken wing place doesn't have home delivery. What can I do?

A. Nothing, because Hooters doesn't deliver for the reason that you want them to deliver.

Q. Why does the quarantine make this year seem so long?

A. Because 2020 is a leap year with 29 days in February, 300 days in March and 5 years in May.

Q. I seem to be eating more and gaining weight during the covid-19 self-quarantine. Do I need to do more exercise?

A. No, you need to wear your mask indoors.

Q. I heard that a child could cure the covid-19 pandemic. Who is this child?

A. He is known to have found solutions to many medical problems in less than thirty minutes. His name is Doogie Howser.

Q. I heard we could have been preparing for Covid-19 as early as 1985. Why didn't we start preparing 35 years ago?

A. Doc and Marty didn't set the flux capacitor in their De Lorean for 2020.

Q. I'm afraid that NFL games will be played without any fans in the stadium. Will it still feel like the games I remember?

A. Yes, the TV people will be dubbing in crowd noise and showing old footage of the fans in the stands. It will be just like the old days.

Q. Is there a way to get the experience of a totalitarian state without the danger of being put in jail?

A. Sure, during the covid-19 quarantine, people from Vermont would slip into New York to see what it was like. They never stayed long since there was nothing to buy and nothing to do.

Q. For years I didn't have time to thoroughly clean my house. Then I was quarantined and still didn't clean my house. Can you help me?

A. Lack of time was not the reason you didn't clean your house, laziness was the reason. The answer is no.

Q. What was the worst thing that ever happened to you?

A. Just last week I got a murder hornet caught in my facemask as I was driving to my favorite sit-down restaurant to get some carry out food. I thought I was going to die.

Q. During the Covid-19 quarantine several businesses have gone under. Can you explain why Spencer's Gifts is not one of them?

A. Sure, they are one of the few stores that sells the things people really want.

Q. They say we live in unprecedented times. What did they call the time period before the unprecedented times?

A. My grandfather remembers as a child that his father called the life he was living as prece- dented times.

Q. During the recent quarantine I started drinking more alcohol to relieve my anxiety about staying home. Is there something else that I could drink with less alcohol and would make me be glad I was staying home?

A. We suggest that you have a daily drink of colonoscopy prep.

Q. What was the best thing about pizza delivery in the "good old days?"

A. Today they leave the pizza on your door step, in the "good old days" if they took longer than 30 minutes to deliver it, it was free.

Q. Do you know someone who should not be notified when the quarantine is over?

A. Just one, you.

Q. What do you hate about the grocery stores rules we have today?

A. The one-way tape in the aisles. The can of beans I need is just 2 steps up the aisle the wrong way. Then the stock boy came running up and wrote me a ticket. I had to pay an extra $5 at the checkout for a fine. I'm never going to eat beans again.

Q. What is one of the biggest changes you have seen about men and women since we started the quarantine?

A. We've noticed that more women are going to therapy but men start podcasts.

Q. Did you notice that kids don't get snow days anymore?

A. Yes, remote learning took care of that. Besides, the kids don't play in the snow anymore.

Q. Do I need to wear a mask when I go outside?

A. According to Dr. Fauci, the answer is no. Then the answer is yes. Then the answer is one mask is not enough.

Q. How many masks should I wear?

A. Every expert has a different answer. So, the best thing to do is wear each type of mask that the experts recommend. That means you should wear about 6 masks.

ANSWERS TO STUPID QUESTIONS

Q. What is the fastest land mammal in the world?

A. Recent studies indicate that it is a toddler who was just asked by his father "what's in your mouth?"

Q. Did you know there is not one canary on the Canary Islands?

A. Yes, it's the same with the Virgin Islands- not one canary there either.

Q. Have you noticed how fast a child can pick up dropped things?

A. Oh yah, now I have to decide if I need it anymore before I spend the effort to pick it up.

Q. Sometimes my eyes hurt after drinking coffee. What is the cause of that?

A. You forgot to take the spoon out of your cup.

Q. I have a hard time remembering what day it is. What advise do you have for me?

A. Arrange your underwear with the day of the week written on them and don't get dressed in the dark.

Q. Is it true that Illinois has a department called the Sandwich Police?

A. Yes, and the way you make sandwiches you better stay out of Sandwich, Illinois.

Q. What should I do if I think someone is following me when I driving to the grocery store?

A. Drive like you are in a James Bond movie. That should get rid of them.

Q. My teenage son asked me to explain taxes. What would be a good way to show him what taxes are like.

A. Take him to Poncheros and make him pay for a burrito. Then you eat 41% of it and tell him he gets the rest.

Q. How do I know when I have enough money to be considered rich?

A. You know you are rich when your dog has a dog.

Q. What does it mean when a woman says "What?"

A. She isn't asking you to repeat what you said, she is giving you a chance to change your response.

Q. Some of my friends say I am immature. I am 55 years old and think I am as mature as anyone else. What do you think?

A. Stop going to your friend's houses at night leaving pink flamingos in their yards.

Q. Some drivers seam to ignore my horn when I want to get their attention. What can I do?

A. Start carrying fireworks in your car. It has worked for me.

Q. I'm looking for something fun to do that is different, inexpensive and will be a load of laughs. What might you suggest I do?

A. Tomorrow take two witnesses with you and dress in a blue shirt and tan pants and go to Best Buy. Ask for the manager and then tell him that you quit.

Q. I don't think I can do that, do you have any other ideas?

A. Sure, dress up in a red polo shirt and Khaki pants and take two friends with you to the nearest State Farm Insurance Agency and turn in your resignation?

Q. How is any of this funny?

A. When you take two friends with you they will tell the rest of us how successful you were quitting a job you don't have. We think that will be funny.

Q. They say we live in unprecedented times. What did they call the time period before the unprecedented times?

A. Captain Scott remembers as a child that his father called the life he was living as precedented times.

Q. What was the best thing about pizza delivery in the "good old days?"

A. Today they leave the pizza on your door step, in the "good old days" if they took longer than 30 minutes to deliver it, it was free.

Q. I hear there is a coin shortage. What is the cause of that?

A. I'm not sure about where you live, but in my area, all of my friends decided to clean up our language and started swear buckets.

Q. I have concerns about the decisions the government makes. Is there anything I can do?

A. You obviously are voting for the wrong people. Have you ever considered sending the government something to guide their decisions? We suggest you send them a new Magic 8 ball.

Q. Where is the best place to get really good fresh produce?

A. Down the block in my neighbor's garden. Really good stuff and cheap too.

Q. What do you consider to be the most important technological innovation?

A. Most people would say the automobile or perhaps the miniaturization of the computer so you can wear it on your wrist like Dick Tracy. But for you it is the gravy boat. You can't live without it.

Q. What is one of the most enjoyable things about sitting around the campfire?

A. Seeing a bunch of 50+ year-olds pretend to have the body of a 28-year-old and have the mind of a 12-year-old.

Q. How can just one person, like myself, save ten trees.

A. Try using the receipts you get from fast-food, big box and drugstores in your fireplace this winter instead of wood. That's about 10 trees per year.

Q. Do you know what you will never hear anyone say at a pizza party?

A. For most people you will never hear anyone say the crust is the best part of the pizza, except for you.

Q. I was in the liquor store the other day and I heard the whistle from the theme of "The Good, the Bad and the Ugly." What was that all about?

A. Nothing to fret about. It came from the beer section where Albert Sailhorst was answering his cell phone call from his beer bookie.

Q. I've heard that cardiovascular exercise will help prolong your life. Is this true?

A. We have consulted the visiting Chinese Doctor at the prestigious University of Pidgeon Ridge Medical School, Dr. Chin Not Wong.

Here is what he has to say about that: "Heart only good for so many beats, and that it. Don't waste on exercise. Everything wear out eventually. Speeding up heart not make you live longer; it like saying extend life of car by driving faster. Want to live longer? Take nap.

Q. Over the years, what has caused you the most pain?
A. The inability of the bed post and my right big toe to get along.

Q. Throughout your lifetime, have you had more accomplishments or stories to tell.
A. My biggest accomplishment has been to tell many true stories, most are sad but funny because I'm not very intelligent.

Q. Do you have any ideas how to keep burglars away from my house?
A. If you have kids in college, post the tuition bills on your front door.

Q. I saw a car with an elderly couple drive by with a sign in the window that said "just married." I think that was rather bold for elderly newlyweds. What do you think?
A. That couple has been married for 40 years, thus the sign of lost bliss.

Q. How do I keep my kids from running out to the ice cream truck when it comes down my street?
A. Tell them that when the music is playing, they are out of ice cream.

Q. What is a newborn baby?
A. A redundant statement.

Q. What does a rodeo teach people about life?
A. That some people do stupid things with wild animals. Which of the things you see at a rodeo would you like to do? How about at a bull fight? If you chose an answer, I rest my case.

Q. In this digital age I think it is a good idea for students to learn how to write in cursive. Is there anything else that you think they should learn that is being forgotten?

A. Yes, how to use a rotary phone and how to read the hands on a clock. It also wouldn't hurt them to put away their video games and play a game of pong.

Q. Is there anything that still fits you that you haven't worn in ten years?

A. Only my hat.

Q. What would make a politician more interesting to watch?

A. If liars pants really did catch on fire.

Q. What is the cause of wind?

A. Recent research has determined that wind can be generated by eating a large helping of beans and cooked cabbage and wash it down with beer. Then wait 30 minutes or jump up and down for 10 minutes. There may be some rumbling before you hear the wind break.

Q. What comes before maybe?

A. April A.

Q. What comes after maybe?

A. If you think June C comes after maybe, boy are you gullible. What comes after maybe depends on what was offered such as a bribe of cash or favors. Then, what comes after maybe is yes.

Q. I don't understand the controversy over Roe v. Wade. Could you explain it to me?

A. It mainly has to do with whether you want to get your pants wet and how deep the water is. Deep water you will row and shallow water you will wade.

Q. Why is it that some people never seem to be embarrassed?

A. Because you can't be embarrassed if you don't care what people think.

Q. If a woman says "I'm not mad at you," what does she really mean?

A. It has the same meaning as the dentist saying "You won't feel a thing."

Q. My teenage son seems to be living in another world. What can I do?

A. Start recording the things that he does that seem alien to you. Here is an example of alien things you may observe: pouring milk into the bowl before the cereal, eating soft butter with a spoon like ice cream, thoroughly covering ice cream with pepper before eating it or refusing to eat at McDonalds because he prefers humus.

Q. I heard that you have been in love with the same woman for 50 years. What is your secret to this long relationship?

A. My wife has never found out about it.

Q. What are the three words a woman never wants to hear when she is making love?

A. Honey, I'm Home.

Q. My wife lost her credit card and I decided not to tell the credit card company. Do you know why?

A. I have a pretty good idea. The thief probably spends less than your wife.

Q. I always see you at the shopping mall holding hands with your wife. That's so sweet. Why do you always do that?

A. Because if I let go of her hand she will go shopping.

Q. My wife spent two hours at the Beauty Shop and came home with nothing being done. What was she doing there for two hours?

A. I suppose she was just getting an estimate.

Q. What was the theme of President Biden's inaugural address?

A. We aren't sure about that, but we are sure that Garth Brooks had new hair plugs when he sang "Amazing Grace" at the inauguration.

Q. What is one of the biggest changes you have seen about men and women since we started the quarantine?

A. We've noticed that more women are going to therapy but men start podcasts.

Q. I heard that a doctor gave a man six months to live and then in six months he gave him another six months to live. What happened with this?

A. The man didn't pay his bill in the first six months.

Q. Why do football players put black lines under their eyes?

A. The official answer given by football players is that eye black is a grease or strip applied under the eyes to reduce glare. However, no study has conclusively proven this. It is a form of functional makeup. Our own study has determined that the players actually think it looks cool. Players who don't wear this makeup are often considered pussies thus everyone wears it because it looks cool. The butterfly tattoo on a certain quarterback's ass looks cool too.

Q. How much sanitizer should I use each time I enter a new environment?

A. We've seen your hands, we suggest three large pumps.

Q. Is there such a thing as a quick question?

A. No. But there is such a thing as a quick answer.

Q. What would happen if all of the bumpy roads suddenly all became very smooth roads?

A. All of the travel stories would suddenly become boring.

Q. A child asked his grandfather this question: "Papa, what do you remember to be the best part of your childhood?"

A. We had lots of fun playing outside in all seasons, building things from scraps, exploring all of the neighborhoods, meeting new friends and we played cards and tried to do magic tricks. Then social media took over.

Q. Did you notice that kids don't get snow days anymore?

A. Yes, remote learning took care of that. Besides, the kids don't play in the snow anymore.

Q. When will I know that I have enough money to retire?

A. When you no longer complain about the cost of airport food.

Q. What is the best advice to give to a young bride?

A. Never underestimate the number of times your husband will do things wrong.

Q. What is the secret to keeping friends?

A. Never tell anyone that you had a good night's sleep.

Q. Now that Biden is president, have we ever heard who won the Democratic caucus in Iowa?

A. No, but we know it wasn't Joe. However, we will know the winner some day since Iowa can't have another caucus until they complete the tabulation of the previous one.

Q. What happened to the politicians promise to end kids going to bed hungry?

A. They spent $100 million getting elected instead.

Q. Could you list everything that people don't argue about on Facebook?

A. Sure, here it is: (crickets)

Q. Should I tell my parents I'm adopted?

A. Don't do it. That would ruin your inheritance.

Q. If I eat myself will I get twice as big or disappear completely?

A. This is new territory for the command staff. You will have to set up a date for us to watch you. Then we will know the true answer.

Q. Does it take 18 months for twins to be born?

A. That's right, nine months each. And if your mother delivers quintuplets, she will be pregnant for eight years.

Q. Hey wise guys, help me understand why the CDC said that people who are fully vaccinated for covid-19 now must wear a face mask both indoors and outdoors. Aren't fully vaccinated people safe from the virus without wearing a mask?

A. The CDC has changed its position several times. They have now developed a new plan that will not ever change, it is called the extra precaution plan. The CDC is reviewing all health issues and will make new protocols in every area. Expect the new seatbelt protocol to require wearing seatbelts even when out of your car.

Q. How can I wear a seatbelt when not in my car?

A. A new company in Dover, Delaware now makes the out of car seatbelt. We have no further information at this time although we have contacted the company and are awaiting a reply from the company CEO Hunter Biden.

Q. Do you think NASA invented thunderstorms to cover up the sound of space battles?

A. It's not the question that we are concerned about, but why you might think this is true. Before NASA existed, it was believed that the gods were doing battle. That is still the answer and NASA is lying.

Q. I swallowed an ice cube whole, and I haven't pooped it out. Need I be concerned?

A. Be sure to wait at least three days. If it still hasn't come out, drink a gallon of hot water. That will dislodge it.

Q. How big is the specific ocean?

A. Really big. You can't even see across it to the other side.

Q. How am I sure I'm the real mom of my kid?

A. Just look at him; big nose, droopy eyes, ugly complexion and all those warts. It's yours.

Q. Is there a pill that'll make me gay?

A. Don't worry about it, we slipped it into your coffee last year.

Q. How do I ask a question on Yahoo Answers? (This was asked on Yahoo! Answers.)

A. There are two ways to do this. The slow way is to send it to google questions. The faster way is to ask Captain Scott.

Q. Why are the holes in cat's fur always in the right places for their eyes?

A. It's just pure luck. Some cats have to have the hair shaved around their eyes or they keep bumping into things.

Q. What does a quarter till 4 mean? like, why is it called that?! cause a quarter is worth 25 cents, so why is it 15 min?!

A. It's true that a quarter is worth 25 cents but with inflation the way it is, it is only worth 15 minutes on a clock.

Q. Are chickens considered animals or birds?

A. They can be considered for breakfast, lunch or dinner.

Q. Is it possible for tattoos to get passed on genetically from parent to child?

A. Yes of course. That's why there are many sailing ship tattoos but not very many aircraft carriers. You should probably have that butterfly tattoo on your ass removed, it was alright on your grandmother.

Q. If I shave my golden retriever like a lion, will the other dogs respect him more?

A. Yes, of course. You should do that right away to improve your dog's self-esteem.

Q. Can your baby get pregnant if you have sex while pregnant?

A. That's why you should never have sex during pregnancy. You and your wife should switch to vegetables like everyone else during pregnancy.

Q. Where do lost socks go when they go missing?

A. Where do your pants go when they go missing? That's where the socks went.

Q. What happens to the people born on Feb. 29? Do they stay one until 4 years pass?

A. Your question assumes that something happens to people born on Feb. 29. If you know what happens to people born on your birthday then you know the answer. The second part of your question asks if they stay one for four years? Did you? If you did, so did they.

Q. Does looking at a picture of the sun hurt your eyes?
A. Nope. Everyone on the staff tried it. It must be just you.

Q. I lost my child in Home Depot. Where should I go to look for him?
A. If that is the kid that called an elderly gentleman an "old fart" go check the red LG in the dryer section.

Q. What do you know about me that I have never told anyone?
A. Based on some of the questions that you have asked the wise guys, we know that your fourth favorite color is aqua.

Q. How do I know if someone is using my Netflix account?
A. Change the password and see who calls you.

Q. What if I don't want to be a good example for other people?
A. Then at least be a good warning on what not to be.

Q. Should I be concerned about people wanting social justice?
A. Yes, because people wanting social justice are disguising their real intention and that is that they really want revenge.

Q. I'm concerned that in this woke world others will feel offended about the things I might say or do. What should I do?
A. Nothing. Just because someone is offended does not mean they are right.

Q. What was the biggest disappointment you had this week?
A. I decided to unfriend you on Facebook only to find out that you beat me to it.

Q. There are a lot of new sports added to the Olympics this year. Are there any other sports you think that would attract more athletes as well as spectators?

A. Only one comes to mind: belly flops.

Q. Why do sharks attack people at the beach?

A. You would be angry too if a bunch of guys in speedos showed up at your house.

Q. I have a problem when the doctor tells me to drink eight glasses of water each day. What should I do?

A. You didn't seem to have a problem with eight glasses of beer last night. See if the doctor will approve of substituting beer for water. It has water in it.

Q. At what age does a boy's period start?

A. The same as a girl's period. At the end of the first sentence.

Q. Why doesn't the Earth fall down?

A. It can't fall down, but the sky can. Just ask Chicken Little.

Q. If Batman's parents are dead, then how was he born?

A. The same way all children are born. Do we need to draw you a picture?

Q. Yes, will you draw me a picture?

A. No, you pervert.

Q. I keep hearing the saying, "Let's go Brandon." What does that mean?

A. It is not a cheer for NASCAR driver Brandon Johnson. President Bidden is Brandon. It is actually a derogatory statement criticizing every bad thing that Biden has done. "Let's go" also could mean F U.

Q. What is a grawlix?

A. This is a grawlix: &%#@$. When it is used in a sentence the grawlix is a substitute for your favorite cuss word. "Let's Go Brandon" is technically a grawlix.

Q. What does F U mean?

A. It means &%#@$ You.

Q. Why is it called 'shipping' if it goes by truck?

A. Years ago, all packages were sent on ships. Today many packages are now sent by the trucking industry. We suggest you stop shipping packages and instead have them trucked.

Q. How do bankruptcy attorneys make any money?

A. Just like all of the other attorneys, they gouge you for their services.

Q. If animals could talk, which would be the rudest?

A. It is already you. The human animal. The others don't stand a chance.

Q. Is cereal soup?

A. Only after you pour on the milk. Before that it is considered candy.

Q. How many chickens would it take to kill an elephant?

A. Just the last one. The other 115,000 chickens are accessories to the fact.

Q. What does it mean when a restaurant advertises new menu items?

A. It means they just raised the prices on everything.

Q. When I tell a joke and the person not laughing says, "you're funny," what does that mean?

A. It means you are not funny.

Q. What do you think about a person that eats ribs with a knife and fork?

A. This person cannot be trusted. It also applies to eating fried chicken.

Q. What sport would be the funniest to add a mandatory amount of alcohol to?

A. Gymnastics comes to mind. A bunch of people jumping and twirling on the rings is just like the drunks at the campfire. Probably will be more puking.

Q. Would you rather have no nose, or no arms?

A. I would rather have my nose and arms and watch you picking up things without arms.

Q. What is your spirit animal?

A. Mine is the fox, able to sneak around the chicken house. Yours is the jack-ass and I think you know why.

Q. Which sport do you think they'll invent next?

A. Probably roller bowling. On a rink the size of a hockey rink, ten players on each side try to knock down pins or skaters. Any skater who falls down is out of the game. Once a team is out of players the score is tallied like bowling plus 10 points per player knocked over.

Q. Do you think cavemen had nightmares about cavewomen?

A. Sure, because I know you still do.

Q. What's the most useless word?

A. Using the word like to describe something. Example, I ate a sandwich like it was good, like I would eat it again, like you know, I liked it. So, what kind of sandwich was it?

Q. What sound would be the scariest if you could hear it?

A. The screaming of the Banshee when she is coming for you.

Q. What is the coolest sound?

A. The sound of rippling water is soothing unlike that awful snoring you make.

Q. What would you rather have; an arm that regenerates every month, or legs that grows back in every month?

A. Give it a rest. Who told you to send in this question? Toland?

Q. What is the most useful invention of all time?

A. I know you think it is the gravy boat but give some thought to electrical generating. If you think of something that requires electricity, then we rest our case.

Q. What is your favorite holiday?

A. Nothing can beat Festivus.

Q. What do you do in your spare time?

A. Recently I spent some time answering these stupid questions. Only thing worse than this was you writing them.

Q. Which smells better, fresh cut grass or bread baking in the oven?

A. Here is a test to determine the answer. Someone will drive you blindfolded to a hog farm where you will smell fresh bread and grass clippings and tell the driver the answer.

Q. What would be your dream job?

A. Getting a paycheck from the Publishers Clearing House sounds good, But, you actually have to work at a job. You look like you should unclog drains at the sewage treatment plant.

Q. If you could be any type of plant or animal, what would you be?

A. We suspect that you would want to be a stinkweed or a skunk.

Q. What would be the hardest thing to give up?

A. You don't want to give up having a bowel movement.

Q. What word is spelled incorrectly in every single dictionary?

A. The word is Incorrectly.

Q. What goes up and down but can't move?

A. We thought it was you that time you got stuck in that pickle barrel, but on second thought it's a staircase.

Q. What goes up but never down?

A. We bet that you are so smart that you wouldn't say it was your age.

Q. What will you give up, brushing your teeth or wiping your butt.

A. What a choice; you either get rotten teeth and bad breath or an unending desire to scratch your ass. Swamp ass is so miserable, I'll give up brushing my teeth and start chewing gum.

Q. Crime doesn't pay... does that mean my job is a crime?

A. Yes, because your job performance is so bad no one will pay you.

Q. Do fish ever get thirsty?

A. Only when you pull them out of the water. They tend to then get dry mouth and begin to smell a little fishy.

Q. Do hummingbirds hum because they don't know the words?

A. Of course, they can't talk so they can't sing.

Q. Do pilots take crash-courses?

A. Yes they do. When this is about to happen, the pilot will put on his parachute and jump out the pilot's door. If you see a parachute go past your window on your next flight then you will know that a crash is imminent.

Q. Do you think that when they asked George Washington for ID that he just whipped out a coin?

A. It seems that you think Washington was on the quarter when he was still alive. But then we are assuming that you meant a quarter but you might have meant a penny. Actually, we should be discussing if coins are an acceptable form of ID. Glue some picture of yourself onto a quarter and use that for an ID next time you buy some beer. Let's see how that turns out for you.

Q. Why doesn't glue stick to the inside of the bottle?

A. It does. Leave the lid off of the glue bottle and let the glue dry. It might take a few days. If it's Elmer's glue, it dries clear, so put a photo in the glue to create a nice picture inside of a blob.

Q. Does a man-eating shark eat women, too?

A. You are such a sexist. Sharks aren't and will even eat you.

Q. How can you tell when it is time to tune your bagpipes?

A. Obviously you don't understand musical instruments. You tune the bagpipes when they sound out of tune. We're guessing.

Q. How do you know if honesty is the best policy unless you've tried some of the others?

A. So true. Did you notice we lied in the answer to one of the last six questions? Or maybe we didn't and we are lying now.

Q. How do you write zero in Roman numerals?

A. There is no zero in Roman numerals because the Romans believed that no numeral could represent nothing, the value of zero. However, the Romans could write zero in the Latin alphabet as follows: ZERO.

Q. If you have a cold hot pocket, is it just a pocket?

A. No, it is still a hot pocket because that is the name of it.

Q. Why is it said that an alarm clock is going off when really, it's coming on?

A. Your logic is perfect. Don't confuse the clock with the alarm function. The clock should always be on and the alarm should always be off. Turn the alarm function on to a set time, like 4:01 am. If you want your alarm clock to go off, pull out the plug from the outlet.

Q. What are imitation rhinestones?

A. Here is how you can make your own imitation rhinestones. Take a lens out of your sunglasses. Then throw it onto the sidewalk and stomp on it with you size 13 FFFF wide shoe. Then put on your sunglasses and examine your imitation rhinestones.

Q. What do batteries run on?

A. A light electrical charge. Here is how to test your battery to check if it has any power in it. Pop it into your mouth. You will now know if it has a charge.

Q. What do chickens think we taste like?

A. Because chickens can't talk we will make a guess. Chickens think you taste like humans.

Q. What do you call a bedroom with no bed in it?

A. Just because you can't afford a bed doesn't mean we change the name of the room to the clothes pile room. It's still the bedroom. Lucky for you.

Q. How come people tell you not to stand in front of an emergency exit, if there was an emergency surely you would not stay standing there?

A. You are not to stand in front of the emergency exit because you are not to be the first person to use the exit in case of an emergency. People who are more important than you are always to go first so you should get out of the way until it is your turn.

Q. In libraries, do they put the bible in the fiction or non-fiction section?

A. There is a special section in the library for religious books. You should have asked earlier so you wouldn't have spent so much time in the fiction and nonfiction sections.

Q. Why are both of Sponge Bob's parents round like sea sponges while he is square?

A. Sponge Bob doesn't look like his parents just like you don't look like your parents. We know they claim you were adopted because they can't explain why you look different from them. We think Sponge Bob had bad genes.

Q. Why do they call it 'chili' if it's hot?

A. It's to trick your brain because your brain doesn't like hot foods.

Q. Why do they call it 'life' insurance?

A. It is actually death insurance, but that isn't correct either. You don't buy insurance for your death but for your life. You don't buy insurance for your car after it crashes but before it crashes. Thus, you buy the insurance before you die. Looking at your health we suggest you buy a large life insurance policy. We see a big payday for you soon.

Q. Why do they make cars go so fast it's illegal?

A. Nobody wants to buy a car that only goes 55 mph downhill with a 30-mph tailwind. That's why that Mini Cooper you drive goes from 0 to 100 in 3.2 seconds. Why else would you buy that?

Q. Why do we call them restrooms when no one goes there to rest?

A. You are wrong. Many people go to the rest room to rest. We suggest you should stop moving, that is rest, while you pee instead of that pacing you do. Your wet pants make you look sloppy.

Q. Why do we have hot water heaters when hot water doesn't need to be heated?

A. I suppose boiling water doesn't need to be placed on the stove either. Where do you think the hot water came from? The river warmed by the sun? The water heater is called a hot water heater so it is not confused with your beer cooler. I suppose a beer cooler doesn't need to be cooled.

Q. Do they call a fortune teller who can't see a "blind seer"?

A. As redundant as that sounds the answer is yes.

Q. Why do you give your two cents worth when it's only a penny for your thoughts?

A. Because what I am thinking for one cent will be worth double when I let you have it.

Q. Why do we need training bras? What can we teach them?

A. I won't tell you what we can teach them. When you grow up you will know.

Q. Why do your feet smell and your nose runs?

A. Your feet smell because they stink and your nose runs because you are sick.

Q. How did Walt Disney figure out how to make people pay to stand in lines all day and then come back for more the next day?

A. People do that for a thrill. Come to my house tonight at 8 pm and I'll give you a thrill for free and no lines.

Q. Why do sleeping pills have warning labels that state: Caution - May Cause Drowsiness?

A. Because that is what they do. Would you take them it they said 'Caution, may cause diarrhea?

Q. What happened to Old Zealand?

A. Everyone left Old Zealand and moved to New Zealand. Now no one remembers where Old Zealand is. Do you?

Q. Which is the other side of the street?

A. Stand where you are and don't move. Now look at the street. Can you see the other side? Now you know where the other side of the street is and strangely that's where you live.

Q. Who opened that first 'oyster' and said "My, my, my. Now doesn't 'this' look yummy!"

A. We couldn't find anyone in history who ever said that and for obvious reasons. Then we realized that you said that and for obvious reasons.

Q. Why are cigarettes sold in gas stations when smoking is prohibited there?

A. That is so people can't sample them before they buy them. Take them off the premises and there is no refund.

Q. Why are highways built so close to the ground?

A. Some highways are built under ground in tunnels. Some are built above ground on pillars called viaducts. Those built on the ground are the cheapest to make. The answer is purely economics.

Q. Why are there flotation devices under plane seats instead of parachutes?

A. That is to prevent people from jumping out of the plane before landing or crashing. Would you jump out of a plane holding on to a rubber inner tube? I didn't think so.

Q. Why are they called "stands" when they're made for sitting?

A. They are made for sitting when there is no action on the field. But once the game begins everyone will stand to watch the game until halftime when they will sit again.

Q. Why do they call someone "late" if they died early?

A. After someone dies they will always be late for every event they are invited to. So late they don't even show up.

Q. Why are the adjectives 'fast as' and 'slow as' often used in conjunction with hell? Is hell slow or fast?

A. Good observation. Since you will be visiting there soon, perhaps you could send us a report.

Q. Why is chess considered a sport?

A. Apparently you have only observed amateur chess that is sometimes so slow that it would be more fun to watch paint dry. Put a chess clock in the professional chess match with a three-minute time for each player. Now the game must end in six minutes and the player's minds and arms will be moving so fast that they will break a sweat and hit the showers after the match just like in the WWE.

Q. Why is it that when you are sleeping it's called drool but when you are awake it's called spit?

A. You are fooling yourself. Your spit is just controlled drool. Drool is drool.

Q. Why don't they call mustaches "mouth brows?"

A. You can call them that. Start a new trend and show everyone how intelligent you are.

Q. If a teacher were to teach a younger grade than they were teaching before, would they be "degraded"?

A. No it is demoted. Teachers look for promotions to higher grades just like the students. Unfortunately, some teachers never get out of kindergarten.

Q. How come people tell you to stay a kid for as long as you can. Yet the moment you do anything childish or immature they tell you to grow up.

A. That never happens to any of us. Maybe you should seek professional help.

Q. How do mermaids make babies?

A. We are not going to describe graphic sex of mermaids, you pervert. Use your imagination.

Q. If Fed Ex and UPS were to merge, would they call the resulting company Fed UP?

A. Probably, it makes perfect sense.

Q. Why are elderly people often called "old people" but children are never called "new people"?

A. That's because the new people are the ones that moved into the house next to yours and have been borrowing things out of your garage.

Q. Do one-legged ducks swim in circles?

A. Where did you see these one-legged ducks, next to the one winged ducks? No, they don't fly in circles and neither do the one-legged ducks. They swim where they want to. If they are swimming in circles it's because that is what they want to do. Do one-legged people walk in circles? I hope you get the point.

Q. Why do you get on a bus and a train but get into a car?

A. Because that is what you do. Go ahead get on a car and see if you can hang on while someone drives you to the store.

Q. If marbles are not made of marble, why are they called marbles?

A. Those round glass spheres known as marbles are called that because they make the same noise if you shake a bag of marbles as you do when you shake your head.

Q. Why is it called lipstick if you can still move your lips?

A. Try the lipstick again. You're not putting enough on.

Q. Why is it called tourist season if we can't shoot at them?

A. It is illegal to shoot a tourist without a license. You need to go to the sheriff's office and tell the deputy that you want to shoot tourists. He'll take care of it for you.

Q. What happens if you get a paper cut from a Get-Well card?

A. You will get more get-well cards.

Q. Can you read a picture book?

A. Sure. Apparently, you can't.

Q. Why are dandelions considered weeds when daisies are considered flowers?

A. A connoisseur does not consider dandelions as weeds. Dandelions can be made into a fine wine and you could make some money harvesting those yellow flowers in your yard. Unfortunately, you are not a connoisseur and as far as flowers go, you could be described as a pansy.

Q. Why do people seem to read the Bible a whole lot more as they get older.

A. They're cramming for their final exam.

Q. Why whenever you start to sing, you automatically sing in a higher voice than you talk?

A. That doesn't happen to everyone. If it happens to you, you need to remove your jockey shorts before singing.

Q. If you called the police station to talk to an officer and he is not there, would that be considered a cop out?

A. Yes, you are such a genius.

Q. Can a school teacher give a homeless child homework?

A. Yes, it would be embarrassing to call it cardboard box work.

Q. Why do mattresses have designs on them when they're always covered with sheets?

A. The designs help camouflage those yellow stains.

Q. If a person suffered from amnesia and then was cured would they remember that they forgot?

A. Put yourself in this situation. You don't have amnesia and you can't remember what you forgot. The answer is no.

Q. What hair color do they put on the driver's license of a bald man?

A. If this is your situation, be prepared to tell them the color of your pubic hair.

Q. What happens if you take No-Doze and wash it down with Nyquil?

A. You will probably get sick from this. If you take the antidote at the same time you won't want to sleep. The antidote is a large dose of laxatives.

Q. What happens when you swallow your pride?

A. You will choke on your self-esteem.

Q. What if someone died in the living room?

A. What if they did? It is not an issue but before you call the coroner you should hide the chicken wings.

Q. The label on a package says "Open here". What is the protocol if the package says, "Open somewhere else"?

A. Then open it somewhere else, probably outside.

Q. Where did Webster look up the definitions when he wrote the dictionary?

A. He just made things up like we do here.

Q. Why is it when two planes almost hit each other it is called a "near miss"?

A. That is what happened. They almost hit each other but missed. What do you want to call it, "Chicken?"

Q. Why is it called 'after dark', when it is really after light?

A. Remember, as far as the movement of the sun goes, after dark comes light, and after light comes dark in a continuous cycle. If you come home after dark then it is already light.

Q. Why is it called a TV "set" when you only get one?

A. You get one TV but you should also get two chairs. If you buy a TV set then you get two chairs with that. Be sure to ask the salesman for your chairs the next time you buy a TV set. Some stores are now selling the TV without the set, so if you pay for the set, demand your chairs.

Q. Why is a women's prison called a penal colony?

A. It has something to do you your perverted mind. You can sign up at the local penal colony to be a conjugal volunteer. Probably something you should do as your civic duty.

Q. Why is a person who plays the piano called a pianist, but a person who drives a race car not called a racist?

A. Who said the race car driver isn't a racist? He drives a race car, doesn't he?

Q. Why do you need an appointment to see a psychic?

A. You need an appointment so you know when to go. The psychic already knows you are coming.

Q. Why does a grapefruit look nothing like a grape?

A. Because grapefruit grows on a tree and grapes grow on a vine. They have nothing in common except they both taste the same.

Q. How can there be "self-help GROUPS"?

A. If you are reading all of these questions and answers it is obvious that you need help and if you provided some of the questions it may be too late for you. The groups meet periodically at various campfires to share their intelligence. Good luck and don't be shy.

Q. If you saw a heat wave, would you wave back?
A. No, but I am sure you would.

Q. If you're born again, do you have two bellybuttons?
A. No, bellybuttons are reusable just like your sphincter.

Q. Is a sleeping bull, a bull-dozer?
A. You are very clever, of course it is.

Q. Is a small pig called a hamlet?
A. Yes, and the small pig jowls are very tender and should be eaten with a nice merlot wine sauce with garlic. We know you are tempted to use ketchup but don't do it, it will spoil the atmosphere.

Q. Is an oxymoron a really dumb bovine?
A. Sure, and if you drop the oxy we have you.

Q. What is a refried bean? Why do they have to fry it twice?
A. "Refried" doesn't mean the beans have been fried twice. The word comes from the Spanish name for the dish—frijoles refritos. In Spanish "refritos" means "well fried." But if your beans are English, then you have to fry them twice to get the best flavor.

Q. What is shaved ice? Did it have hair on it before it was shaved?
A. Yes, your logic is perfect to qualify to be a contestant on Jeopardy.

Q. Can atheists get insurance for acts of God?
A. Sure, someone will sell you an insurance policy on anything. I'm still holding a policy of your life insurance. I have a feeling I will get a payoff soon.

Q. What do you call a male ladybird?

A. A gay bird.

Q. What would you use to dilute water?

A. Typically for each gallon of water add a quart of dehydrated H2O.

Q. If you're in hell, get mad at someone, where do you tell them to go?

A. You may not understand this answer so be sure to think long about it. You tell them to go to the devil's pitchfork.

Q. Why do grocery stores buy so many checkout line registers if they only keep 3 or 4 open?

A. Sometimes a register burns out from over use, so you go to the extra registers.

Q. Why do mattresses have springs, if they aren't made for jumping on?

A. You have been misinformed. Who said they weren't for jumping on?

Q. Why do people tell you when they are speechless?

A. They are letting you know that they have nothing to say. What do you want speechless people to do? Just stand there in silence?

Q. Why do the signs that say "Slow Children" have a picture of a running child?

A. You know children will do the opposite of what they are told to do. Be sure to tell your children to run across street so they will do what the sign says.

Q. If the speed of movement is slower than the speed of light - how fast is a moving light?

A. Check the headlights of a moving car. No matter how fast or slow the car moves the light gets out farther than the car every time. There is your proof that light moves faster than movement.

Q. If electricity comes from electrons, does morality come from morons?

A. That's right and you are a fine example, I might add.

Q. If you fed a bee nothing but oranges, would it make marmalade?

A. This is the perfect example that you should not believe everything you read on the internet.

Q. How come thaw and unthaw mean the same thing?

A. They don't. Unthaw means to refreeze the object.

Q. If I melt dry ice, can I take a bath without getting wet?

A. In theory yes, in reality you will want to wear a lot of heavy clothing while bathing in dry ice because it is very cold.

Q. If the product says "Do not use if seal is broken", how are you supposed to open it and use it?

A. You must open it from the other end.

Q. If time heals all wounds, how come bellybuttons don't fill in?

A. Silly you, your bellybutton is not a wound, it is your birth dimple.

Q. If work is so terrific, how come they have to pay you to do it?

A. They don't have to pay you, you can refuse to be paid and just enjoy the terrific job. You will need to pick up some lousy part-time work to pay the bills.

Q. Is a hot car cool or is a cool car hot?

A. Yes to both questions. The terms hot and cool mean the same thing when talking about cars. They mean opposite things when talking about the stew you just made.

Q. Is a man full of wonder a wonderful man?

A. Typically this would be true as there are many fine examples. However, in your case, we can tell by some of your questions that you wonder about some strange things so we reserve the right to call you wonderful. Just look at the next question that you recently sent in.

Q. Is a duck's Hiney waterproof?

A. Really, this is what you wonder about? Have you seen ducks sinking by taking on water through their hiney? How about yourself? Drinking through your hiney, although possible its really only for experienced hiney drinkers. You may need help to practice this and I know a few guys who would be happy to help you.

Q. How can you hear yourself think?

A. Turn off any devise that makes noise, TV, stereo, cell phone, then plug your ears with plenty of cotton. Now think about your next question you will be sending us. See, it works.

Q. How can you chop down a tree and then chop it up?

A. Let's say the tree is 30 feet tall and you chop it down and it falls to the ground. Now you chop it into firewood and neatly stack behind your garage in a pile that is 8 feet tall and 20 feet long. Now it is chopped up.

Q. If Americans throw rice at weddings, do the Chinese throw hamburgers?

A. Have you seen this? Does everyone bring a bag of hamburgers to the wedding? This is so ridiculous that we won't tell you that they really through French fries.

Q. What's the difference between a wise man and a wise guy?

A. Finally an important question. A wise man is very smart and you would be right to follow his advice. A wise guy will give you advice about some stupid question that you should not follow.

Q. What would happen if an Irresistible Force met an Immovable Object?

A. This is the big bang theory. It creates a new world.

Q. Where in the nursery rhyme does it say humpty dumpty is an egg?

A. It doesn't. You are the one who says he is. Maybe he was a Lego figure.

Q. Why do they say "getting my dog fixed" if afterwards it doesn't work anymore?

A. We didn't want the dog to get over rambunkuous so we fixed that. Now he is a lazy dog like his master.

Q. Why do you click on start to exit Microsoft Windows?

A. That is where you will find the exit button. Go ahead, see if you can find it somewhere else.

Q. If there's an exception to every rule, is there an exception to that rule?

A. Yes, this rule is solid and exceptional.

Q. Is a sleeping bag a nap sack?

A. It sure can, if you want to nap there?

Q. Why is the blackboard green?

A. Original blackboards were black, but later green ones were developed but the name didn't change. Now schools have whiteboards. Soon you will see them in other colors but probably never black.

Q. On the periodic table, why do some elements have symbols with letters that aren't even in the word?

A. This has something to do with language. Not all elements come from the English language so if it came from German the German word and symbol is used instead of English.

Q. If you try to fail and succeed, what did you just do?

A. It is true that most people who want to fail have actually succeeded.

Q. Is the opposite of "out of whack" "in whack"?

A. Yes.

Q. Why are toe nail clippers bigger than finger nail clippers when your toe nails are smaller than your finger nails?

A. Just because you have little feet doesn't mean some people won't need those big clippers. Ask someone with a size 15 shoe if you can see his toe nails.

Q. If Practice makes perfect, and nobody's perfect, then why practice?

A. That's why you're not very good at anything. With that attitude, you will never improve. Are you still seeing your barber to fix your teeth?

Q. What's the opposite of opposite?

A. The opposite of opposite is the same. If white is the opposite of black, then white is the same as white.

Q. Can good looking Eskimo girls be called hot?

A. The one's we've seen are. You need to stop looking for Eskimo girls at the fish market.

Q. Why do people never say "it's only a game" when they're winning?

A. As you know, when you are losing you don't want to put too much into that fact. Next time you play checkers bet your car keys that you will win. Then see if it's only a game.

Q. If somebody vanished without a trace, how do people know they are missing?

A. They are missing, so they are gone. Where did they go? You say without a trace; therefore, they must have vanished.

Q. Can you sentence a homeless man to house arrest?

A. Yes, and it's your turn to use your house.

Q. What do people in China call their good plates?

A. The clean plates. What do you call yours, paper chinette?

Q. If you stole a pen from a bank is it a bank robbery?

A. Yes it is. Next time you are in the bank, slip that pen back onto the counter. You're looking at up to 20 years.

Q. Why are Softballs hard?

A. Original softballs were actually softer than they are today. No one could hit the softball very far so they had to make it hard so it could be hit farther. That's our answer and we're sticking to it.

Q. In France do people just ask for toast and get French toast? Do they have to ask for American toast?

A. It's not French toast in France but fried toast in an egg batter. And nobody asks for American toast. I think you know why.

Q. What do you call a female daddy long legs?

A. We'd like to say a mommy long legs but how can you tell the males from the females. The jury is still out on this one.

Q. Why is the word "dictionary" in the dictionary?

A. All words are in the dictionary so we know what they mean. I suppose you don't know what a dictionary is. Just google it and you will know.

Q. Why are they called stairs inside but steps outside?

A. It is a matter of elegance. The stairs are nice and maybe even carpeted. The steps are out in the weather and are either made of boards or concrete. And the way to your upstairs apartment is called the ladder.

Q. If you mated a bull dog and a shiatsu, would it be called a bullshit?

A. Your logic is so obtuse that we will say yes. We won't waste time with semantics.

Q. How fast do hotcakes sell?

A. That depends on the price and the quality. Really good hotcakes at 25 cents each sell fast as "hotcakes." But your hotcakes made in fatback grease without water at $2 each aren't worth looking at.

Q. How do they get those boats in those glass bottles?

A. Steady hands and long tweezers are necessary and don't glob the glue on the small parts.

Q. What is the name of the phobia for the fear of long words.

A. Hippopotomonstrosesquippedaliophobia?

Q. Why is it that we have the weight of the world on our shoulders but we have to get it off our chests?

A. You have that right. Keep the weight on your shoulders and get things off of your chest. This is how you carry your burdens without hurting yourself. Just don't lose your footing or the burdens will crush you.

Q. If you decide that you're indecisive, which one are you?

A. You are uncertain.

Q. If an anarchist group attained political power, would they by principle have to dissolve their own government?

A. Absolutely, and you better guard your stuff because they think it is now there's.

Q. If Luke took a bath, would the water be lukewarm?

A. Only after he peed in it.

Q. Why do they call the angel of death an angel if all it does is bring pain and suffering?

A. Oh you of little faith; Lucifer is a fallen angel and so is the angel of death. You might want to have a confidential conference with a priest.

Q. Can blind people be dyslexic when they read Braille?

A. Our studies have determined that this can happen when a right handed blind person reads braille with their left hand.

Q. Why do we say "bye bye" but not "hi hi"?

A. "Bye bye" is how we said good bye to babies and small children. If you are still doing this with adults you probably should stop that. We cannot find anyone who ever said "hi hi" except you. You should probably stop that too.

Q. Why do we feel blue?

A. This means that you feel sad. We call it blue because that color is soothing and somewhat melancholy.

Q. What color does a smurf feel when he is down?

A. Tan.

Q. If the universe is expanding, what is it expanding into?

A. Space. It is like knowledge moving into your brain. It displaces space. Space is an invisible nothing.

Q. If you were on a plane going the speed of sound and walked from the back of the plane to the front, would you be walking faster than the speed of sound?

A. Yes, but only a couple feet per second more. We don't recommend jumping up off the plane floor at that speed. Could be painful.

Q. Why are things typed up but written down?

A. When you type, or use your computer, the words are placed above (or up from) the keyboard. When you write by hand you place the paper down (or on a table) to write your message. If you can reverse this trend, you can start a new trend and people will call you a genius. I wouldn't put much hope into this happening.

Q. Why do old men have hair in their ears?

A. Everyone has hair in their ears. Most people have small, thin and light-colored hair that is difficult to see without getting up close. Some men have darker hair and as they age it becomes a bit coarser and easier to see. We recommend you test this idea with a magnifying glass. In a large gathering come up behind people and use your magnifying glass to look into people's ears. We will wait for your report.

Q. If it is a 50 mph per hour wind and you drive your car at 50mph downwind, if you stick your head outside would you feel the wind?

A. According to your logic, no. Now toss a balloon out the window and watch it move next to your car. It looks like it isn't moving but it is actually moving 50 mph. You are so smart.

Q. If water spins clockwise when it drains in the northern hemisphere and water spins counterclockwise when it drains in the southern hemisphere...which way does it spin at the equator?

A. There is no spin, the water just flushes strait down but it has to be exactly on the equator or there will be spin.

Q. Have you ever thought what life would be like if your name was Anonymous? Can you get credit for everything nobody wanted credit for?

A. Nope, we don't know anyone who ever thought about being named anonymous except you. As far as credit goes, you can go for it. Good luck.

Q. Do Siamese twins pay for one ticket or two tickets when they go to movies and concerts?

A. The ticket you buy is for a seat. If you sit in two seats, you need two tickets. If you take five friends to the movies you will only need to buy one ticket if you all sit on each other's lap.

Q. Why did Superman wear his briefs on the outside of his tights?

A. To prevent getting brown stains on his briefs.

Q. Do sheep get static cling when they rub against one another?

A. Of course, that is why they literally stick together in a herd.

Q. Is an alcoholic a drunk that's scared of a hangover?

A. Of course not. An alcoholic is someone who just likes to drink.

Q. Can anybody who has a job go in the "employees only" doors at restaurants?

A. This is the kind of wisdom that makes some people stand out in a crowd. After you go through the "employees only" door stop at the sink and wash a few dishes, then tell the bus boy that you are going home and want to know where the tip jar is. This could make a pretty good story. Be sure to tell us how this worked out.

Q. Why are you IN a movie, but you are ON TV?

A. If you appear IN the movie you actually were at the film making several months ago, but the TV has to be turned ON to watch anything including the movie you are IN.

Q. If the weather man says "it's a 50% chance of rain" does that mean he has no idea if it's going to rain or not?

A. Yes.

Q. Why do they call him a Skipper when he just stands there?

A. It doesn't matter if he is standing, sitting or skipping; he is still the skipper. If you don't think so, just tell him you don't think he is the skipper and see what happens. I hope you can swim.

Q. If dessert before dinner ruins your appetite for dinner won't eating dinner before dessert ruin your appetite for dessert?

A. This is what the wise guys have been saying for years. Remember, life is uncertain, eat your dessert first.

Q. What do you mean when you say "Life is uncertain, eat your dessert first?"

A. Eat the pie before the chicken. If you choke on a chicken bone someone else will get your pie.

Q. When lightning strikes the ocean why don't all the fish die?

A. That would have to be very strong lightning to kill all of the fish. Certainly a few nearby fish will be zapped.

Q. Why is it when we ask for the check in a restaurant they bring us a bill?

A. Good point, I think you are on to something.

Q. Do people with big eyes see at a wider range than people with smaller eyes?

A. You appeared to be wise in the previous question and now this question is short on vision. Actually, people with big eyes see everything bigger than people with small eyes.

Q. What happens when you say "hi" to your friend on an airplane whose name is Jack?

A. You will get jumped by a bunch of sky marshals. We suggest you say "Hello, Jack."

Q. Why are women and men's shoe sizes different?

A. Because their feet are different sizes.

Q. Why isn't the word 'gullible' in the dictionary?

A. It is in the dictionary and the definition describes you very well. Here is the definition: To be gullible is a failure of social intelligence in which a person is easily tricked or manipulated into an ill-advised course of action.

Q. Why are there pictures of the sun wearing sunglasses when the purpose of sunglasses is to protect your eyes from the sun?

A. If the sun had eyes it would definitely need the sunglasses.

Q. Does it really count in court when an atheist is sworn in under oath using a Bible?

A. The Bible is only used for Christians and Jews because if they lie under oath God will punish them. Atheists just swear an oath that they promise not to lie. We guess that they think God can't punish them if they don't believe in God. We suspect they may already be punished and if they lie there will be more punishment.

Q. How do they get the air inside the bubble wrap?

A. The air isn't under pressure. When the bubble wrap is manufactured they just capture air as each bubble is sealed. You, on the other hand, pop the bubble by forcing the air out of the bubble by squeezing the bubble. This obviously gives you much amusement.

Q. Can crop circles be square?

A. No circles cannot be squares. You may need a little remedial geometry refresher.

Q. Can you blow a balloon up under water?

A. Yes, but if you are doing this with your mouth you probably need to come up for air each time you blow into the balloon.

Q. Why is it that when we are humming and then we plug our nose, our humming stops? Do people really hum through their nose, or their mouths?

A. The interesting thing is that everyone who just read the question hummed and plugged their nose. More interesting is that the humming did stop, but you can start humming again with your mouth open. You need air to hum and more exactly you need to exhale air to hum. Now try humming while inhaling.

Q. Why would Dodge make a car called Ram?

A. That is the car we all wish we had some times particularly when following a slow driver. Now we can actually own one.

Q. What do vegetarians feed their dogs?

A. Our first guess is dog food. If you are thinking their dogs should eat radishes, cucumbers and asparagus try it out on your dog and tell us how that turned out. Probably should run that through the blender.

Q. If the day before a holiday is called Christmas Eve, is the day after Christmas Adam?

A. No, Adam came before Eve. Therefore, using your logic, Christmas Adam is the day before Christmas Eve.

Q. Do stuttering people stutter when they're thinking to themselves and does it take just as long?

A. Of course, unless they are a speed thinker. Can you speed think?

Q. Why do dogs walk around in circles before lying down?

A. They are just making sure no other dog is about to sneak up behind them and grab their spot. Probably something you should do before you lay down.

Q. Why do most people put more effort into their wedding than their actual marriage?

A. Because it is the last thing the parents are going to pay for, so gouge the hell out of them because you can't afford the stuff you want after the wedding.

Q. Why is it that on the back of a medicine bottle it says "adult" is 12 and above, but the adult age in reality is 18?

A. We are talking drugs here. It is ok to take adult drugs but not adult liquor. Go figure.

Q. If there is a rule that states "i" before "e" except after "c", wouldn't "science" be spelled wrong?

A. Yes, but don't forget there are exceptions to every rule and this is one of them.

Q. Who makes up these spelling rules and who can break them?

A. Somebody told your English teachers and they told you. That's where the rules come from. Everyone can break the spelling rules except when you are spelling things for your English teacher.

Q. If a mirror reverses right and left, why doesn't it reverse up and down?

A. It will if you turn the mirror on its side.

Q. If all the nations in the world are in debt, where did all the money go?

A. For cars, boats, houses and many useless items. For you it went for gum, candy and a paddle ball game.

Q. Did you just turn a mirror on its side?

A. You really should read more nonfiction.

Q. Why is it considered necessary to nail down the lid of a coffin?

A. Just in case the pall bearers drop the coffin, you don't want the body to fall out onto the floor.

Q. Why is it that only adults have difficulty with childproof bottles?

A. No, children have difficulty too.

Q. Why isn't there a special name for the tops of your feet?

A. There is, it's called the dorsal. The bottom of your feet is the plantar surface.

Q. Why do people say PIN number when that truly means Personal Identification Number?

A. You answered your own question. Dah!

Q. Why do people call it an ATM machine, but they know it's really saying Automated Teller Machine?

A. Really, you did it again. And you send these questions to the wise guys because you don't know this.

Q. Why get even, when you can get odd?

A. It's just a 50/50 choice. You probably prefer to get odd.

Q. Why is a carrot more orange than an orange?

A. Are you looking at them in the store? Those are all cleaned up and polished to make them look better. It also means that they cost more. To save money we suggest raiding your neighbor's garden or fruit trees. If you want fruit and vegetables to look nice, then buy them at the store.

Q. Why is it when we laugh in school the teachers say do you find something funny? When obviously we do?

A. Your teacher is making sure you are not laughing at him. Next time, instead of laughing, slip him a note that his zipper is down.

Q. Don't accept candy from strangers, yet on Halloween, its encouraged! Why is that?

A. In the first place the stranger may be a kidnapper. On Halloween, the kidnappers lay low because there are so many kids out that could be a witness.

Q. Just what was the "Baby On Board" sign for? Did it help us decide which car not to hit in case of an accident?

A. That is exactly the point. Try putting a sign in your car that says, "Moron on Board," and see what happens.

Q. When a boy is named after his dad, he is called 'Junior,' but what do you call a girl that is named after her mother?

A. She is also "Junior." The word junior is genderless. However, if a girl is called junior and she has a brother who is also a junior we have a strange family. To tell each other apart we would need to create nicknames, which is what the children should have been named in the first place.

Q. How important does a person have to be before they are considered assassinated instead of just murdered?

A. They have to be considered important to be assassinated. You don't need to worry because no one will assassinate you. You might want to hide that special $20 bill you keep in the back of your wallet that you have told everyone that you keep it for emergencies. Someone might murder you for it.

Q. If you can wave a fan, and you can wave a club, can you wave a fan club?

A. You silly play on words guy! The only thing you can do with a fan club is wave at them since they will never let you be a member.

Q. If you can't drink and drive, why do bars have parking lots?

A. That is so you will know where to get your car after you sober up in some alley three miles away.

Q. If you get into a taxi cab, and ask the driver to drive backwards to your destination, will the cab driver owe you money?

A. You have it all wrong. If he drives backwards you should owe him double. But really, that is not what a taxi driver is paid to do. He drives you to destinations, not do stunt tricks for pay.

Q. If you jog backwards, will you gain weight?

A. Only if you are eating a super-sized big mac, a large chocolate cake and a box of donuts and don't drop anything.

Q. Why is Donkey Kong called "DONKEY" Kong if he's a monkey?

A. He is not the King Kong that you think he is. Have you ever noticed that he would lose every game he is in if you didn't help him? Without help, he is as smart as a donkey.

Q. Why do we teach kids that violence is not the answer and then have them read about wars in school that solved problems?

A. Look deeper into your thought. How many people were killed, how much money was wasted? Could there have been a better answer to the problem besides going to war? Learn from history instead of criticizing history.

Q. How come you pay extra to get something put on your hamburger but they don't take off the price if you get something taken off?

A. You are right. I think you should demand a discount for holding the lettuce and removing the pickle. If they say it is included in the price, then demand they give them to you separately from the hamburger.

Q. Did Noah have woodpeckers on the ark? If he did, where did he keep them?

A. Locked in a cage until he felt it was the right time to let them go. Do you think Noah allowed all the birds and animals to just wonder around the ark?

Q. What happens if your snot freezes in your nose?

A. Well it is going to be there until you get inside and allow it to thaw. You could pick at it but that might pull off your skin. Or ask someone to pick it for you. It is always great to share.

Q. Why does Donald Duck wear a towel when he comes out of the shower, when he doesn't usually wear any pants?

A. He has a towel to dry off his feathers from the shower. He doesn't wear pants because he doesn't have a pecker, chickens do.

Q. If mars had earthquakes would they be called mars quakes?

A. Of course, the earth can't quake on Mars.

Q. Why do all superheroes wear spandex?

A. Sponsors paid for their costumes.

Q. If heat rises, then shouldn't hell be cold?

A. Where do you think the heat came from?

Q. Can a stupid person be a smart-ass?

A. Congratulations. You have asked a question about yourself and I am sure you already know the answer.

Q. Why is chopsticks one of the easiest songs to play on the piano, but the hardest thing to eat with?

A. Over a billion people in China eat with chopsticks but can't play chopsticks on the piano. Your question is not based on facts but on your own biased opinion.

Q. What happens if you put this side up face down while popping microwave popcorn?

A. All of the popcorn will pop upside down.

Q. Isn't it funny how the word 'politics' is made up of the words 'poli' meaning 'many' in Latin, and 'tics' as in 'bloodsucking creatures'?

A. Funny but true. Politics tends to turn good meaning people into the bloodsucking creatures that they ran for office to stop.

Q. Why is clear considered a color?

A. We checked our 256-color box of Crayola Crayons and could not find clear. It is either invisible or you are wrong.

Q. Have you ever noticed that if you rearranged the letters in mother in law, they come out as Woman Hitler?

A. You better behave, her oven might not just be for baking.

Q. If it is illegal to park in a handicapped parking space is it also illegal to use a handicapped toilet?

A. Yes, a $250 fine in each case. Might be worth paying the fine when you have that diarrhea urge at Wal-Mart.

Q. Why did Yankee Doodle name the feather in his hat Macaroni?

A. Macaroni was the name of his horse.

Q. What is the speed of dark?

A. Zero. Dark does not move, only light moves and it moves into dark.

Q. When dog food is new and improved tasting, who tests it?

A. You can volunteer your dog Fido to test dog food, but the best way for you to be sure it is new and improved is to sample it yourself. We suggest that you purchase multiple brands and then you and Fido blind sample them together. Could be fun.

Q. If athletes get athlete's foot, do astronauts get mistletoe?

A. Very funny. If we say yes, that will account for you having small cox.

Q. If everything is part of a whole, what is the whole part of?

A. It is part of the sum.

Q. What if you were to ask a genie to grant you more than three wishes for one of you wishes?

A. You are a genius. For your first wish ask for unlimited wishes. For your second wish ask for your enemy to get double of anything you wish for. Then wish for 20 beautiful women to fall in love with you. For your next wish, wish for your sex drive to be cut in half. That should be enough for the first day.

Q. Are you telling the truth if you lie in bed?

A. Of course not, you couldn't tell the truth if you were standing in bed.

Q. Are you breaking the law if you drive past those road signs that say "Do Not Pass"?

A. You are confusing the word passed with past. The road sign has nothing to do with the past except if you passed someone after the sign.

Q. Is a lightning rod on top of church a lack of faith?

A. No, it does 2 things. First it keeps the building insurance rate down. Second, it protects the church if God gets angry at anyone sinning in the congregation.

Q. How come only your fingers and toes get wrinkly in water and nothing else does?

A. I think you should look a little closer. See if there are any wrinkles inside of your swim trunks.

Q. A pack of gum says 10 calories per piece, is that amount for chewing it or for swallowing it?

A. That is a swallow answer. You can have an entire chocolate cake at zero calories if you chew it, don't swallow and spit it out.

Q. How many questions in this book did you get right?

A. If you got more than 50% of the answers correctly you are a possible candidate to be a true wise guy.

ABOUT THE AUTHOR

Bruce R. Kindig is a retired teacher from the Davenport Community School district where he taught various history classes. He also taught American History as an adjunct professor at Scott Community College. He has a B.A. and M.A. degree in history from the University of Northern Iowa and 46 years of teaching experience. As an accomplished author, with several book review awards, he stays active with writing projects. All of his books can be found on Amazon.com.

His latest book is: **The Evil Party.** This is a primer of the origins of the United States Declaration of Independence, Constitution and the Bill of Rights. Drawing from Judeo-Christian traditions, ancient Greece and the Roman Republic and the founding of this country we see a struggle between good and evil. Those who practice evil do it for their own growth of wealth and power at the expense of various minority groups. The Democratic Party is seen as the evil party both in the reason for its founding and in the practices it used in the past and still uses today. This is explored in its history of favoring slavery, segregation and white supremacy. The policies of Presidents Jackson, Van Buren, Wilson, F. Roosevelt, Lyndon Johnson, Clinton and Obama are harmful to minorities and now critical race theory, political correctness and white privilege is used to push a socialist agenda. This book is about the evil the Democratic Party has pushed for its own wealth and power.

His first book was a Civil War regimental history called ***Courage and Devotion: A History of Bankhead's/Scott's Tennessee Battery***. This book has received several book review awards and is known for its focus on detail.

He has written his own autobiography entitled: ***A Good Time to Live***. Here he focuses on the last half of the 20th century from a socio-economic perspective with details on his genealogy and family.

Focusing on a teenage audience his book, ***George Washington Starts a War***, is a primer on the French and Indian War with a focus on George Washington who has the distinction of starting a war in his youth and ending a war in his maturity.

The Origins of Military Theory in World War I is a scholarly look at a subject every history student has studied. The focus is not the typical diplomatic approach but instead an evaluation of military theorists from Clausewitz to Foch.

Peace Proposals of the First World War, is about the little know diplomatic attempts at peace from 1914 through the Treaty of Brest-Litovsk. It discusses why peace could not be negotiated and why; in spite of the seriousness of those who wanted a just peace.

Essays in Military Leaders is a collection of three essays. The first essay is about Hannibal and Scipio Africanus and the development of Roman tactics in the Second Punic War. With Julius Caesar, we develop his philosophy of war by examining the strategy and tactics of the Gallic Wars. Finally, we examine the philosophy of history from the author of *On War*, Carl von Clausewitz. The descriptions are all in their own words.

Finally, Bruce R. Kindig has written a non-historical work. Combining good advice with humor he writes under the pen name John H. Marsh, ***Words of Wisdom from Anonymous Wise Guys***. Through a question format he answers the dumb questions people often ask like "what are two things you should never ask in bed"? It is the prequel to this book.

www.ingramcontent.com/pod-product-compliance
Lightning Source LLC
Chambersburg PA
CBHW020843150726
48196CB00002B/188

MEDITERRANEAN MOTHERS

masters

of

guilt

MEDITERRANEAN MOTHERS

masters

of

guilt

MARIA ORLANDO & NICK PAPPAS

atmosphere press

This book is dedicated to our moms and
aunts, who showed us how to use guilt as an
art form – but we love you – Maria and Nick

CONTENTS

PROLOGUE

With all due respect to other nationalities and ethnicities who may have claimed to have a monopoly on guilt, their version of it pales before the passion and fear which is a staple in the handbook of an Italian or Greek mother...

"GROWING OLD IS A CURSE;
HAVING KIDS MAKES IT WORSE"

Mediterranean Island Saying....

CHAPTER ONE

Your Kids Never Listen

"Maria, come in here. You gotta see this movie with us. What are you doing in there? Maria, do you hear me?" Shaking her head, she turns to her sister to make a point: "Liz, they never listen. Your children never listen."

Elizabeth somehow nods her head and shakes it at the same time.

"Mare, you are preaching to the choir. Don't I know it! It's the truth, the absolute truth." She crosses herself and keeps shaking her head.

The speakers? Sisters, two Italian(Sicilian) mothers, both around sixtyish, give or take. The place is Marie's house in a quiet town in New Jersey. She and her older sister are about to watch *MARTY*, starring Ernest Borgnine.

The younger of the two, Marie, is Maria's mother. The age difference between her and her sister Elizabeth is almost exactly seven years. They rarely use their full given names when speaking with each other, but rather "Liz" and "Mare." They are both "old school" Italian mothers when it comes to their perspective on their children, but Marie, the younger sister, fancies herself just a bit more "with it" than Liz, who really couldn't care less about the latest trends in fashion, language, or just about anything else.

"Maria, come watch this with us. Why don't you ever listen to me?"

"Ma, I've seen this movie a dozen times."

"It's a great movie. It's about Italians, like us. It's about Italian mothers whose children won't listen to them. They have no respect for their mothers. It's a sin. Look, it's starting. MARIA!"

Maria knows when she is beaten, so rather than buck her mother some more, she decides to come in from the dining room and watch the movie. It is, after all, one of her favorites, and she figures she can put off her work for an hour or so, and hopefully the minutes invested with her mom and aunt will give her some time to herself on the other side.

"OK, mother, just a minute. I just want to organize my papers here before I come in with you. They're just running the credits now anyway."

"Good. Hurry up. And bring us something to snack on, would you? Something sweet, OK? Maria....(louder) OK?? And don't roll your eyes at us!"

"Ma, you can't see me. How would you know if I rolled my eyes." Maria rolls her eyes again, then gathers her stuff together, and organizes it as efficiently and quickly as she can,, all the while cursing profusely under her breath.

Her mother turns to Elizabeth.

"You see, my daughter had to go to college and become an English teacher. She thinks she's so damn smart. I tell her – just pass all the kids. Who cares? Nobody cared about her when she was going to school. Now she spends all her time correcting all those papers, and she got no time for her mother."

"I know, I know, Mare. When they're small, they need you and they obey most of the time. Now when they're grown, they couldn't care less."

Elizabeth is sitting in a rocking chair, and the louder and quicker the conversation, the faster she rocks. This particular chair used to be her grandmother's in Sicily, and it creaks and squeaks like an old barn door that has never been oiled. It seemed to be held together by masking tape, and it's a wonder someone, namely Liz, hadn't broken her neck on it. But it was almost like a member of the family, and it would have been almost sacrilege not to use it....

"Hey, Liz, , Be careful. You gonna fall..."

"Don't worry for me. This gets out all my worries. You talk, I rock. It's like when we were little and we went on the swings. You stayed low and talked, I went way up in the air."

"Yeah, and you fell out at least once every day. And who brought you in the house and bandaged you up? I did Listen, if you fall you patch yourself up on your own. I want to watch MARTY. It's gonna start any second.. Where's Maria? Maria, come on, you're gonna miss the beginning. And don't forget our snack."

The beleaguered Maria was toying with the idea of throwing all her work into her bag, then jumping into her car and making a break for it. She loved her mother, and her aunt, but some days they were harder to take than usual, and the "usual" was quite intolerable in its own right. But, as she told herself many times, they were getting older and she had to cut them some slack – but God almighty, they were getting worse and worse with each passing year...Actually each passing day. Oh well, she figured she would just bite her tongue and play the dutiful daughter and niece for the afternoon. She did like the movie, and hopefully, she could get back to her stuff afterwards. Although she would probably wind up taking them out for dinner, and that would blow the whole day. Trapped again!

It seemed to Maria that she was always running somewhere for something and usually at the behest of someone else. "Maria, do this. Maria do that. Maria, where are those grades. Maria, get us something to eat." When she was with her mom or her aunt, it seemed she was more of a personal valet than a daughter or a niece. Now, she had some autonomy in school, since in her classroom she was more or less in charge. But the red tape and bureaucratic regulations seemed to have increased exponentially over her thirty years of teaching. Trapped in school, controlled at home. How did things wind up this way? She had always wanted to be a writer — more specifically a travel journalist — but life got In the way, and she wound up teaching English, mostly in New Jersey, but there was also that sojourn in California.

Was she ever really there? It seemed like yesterday and at the same time a hundred years ago...For that matter, was she really here? "Here" being her mother's house where she grew up. It's hard to believe her mother was still living in the same house. The mother of all sighs — infused with years of exasperation — escaped despite her valiant attempt to keep it inside.

"Maria, did you say something?" her mom exclaimed from the living room.

Jesus, there was certainly nothing wrong with her hearing.

"No, Ma, just yawning. Be right there."

"You work too damn hard. Just give them all A's. Who's gonna know?"

Maria almost bit through her tongue so she would not reply. Her mother must have said that to her a hundred times. A hundred times in the last few days. She wondered if all mothers got like that, or if it were just "Mediterranean Mothers," like her mom, her aunt, and the women in the movie. She made a mental note to ask Nick about his mother. That would be Nick Pappas, her lunch duty partner, a full-blooded Greek with all the flaws and emotional excesses of that particular ethnic group. Or was it a separate species? Why in the hell did she ever agree to write a book with him? No, not this book, a book chronicling their sixty-five years of teaching. Well, in all fairness, it *was* a good idea, but she really didn't need another obligation she didn't have time for. Lord!

All these things went racing through her mind as she opened up a package of biscotti and a bottle of Pellegrino for the matinee in the next room. What was the name of that song Nick sent her...*Forgotten Dreams?* That summarized her life in two words. How did he know she would like it — which she did? Even though she and Nick had known each other only a short time, he seemed to "get" who she was. What a scary thought. Meanwhile, she was not as quick with the snacks as she should have been...

"Maria, come on! Where are you?"

"Coming, mother."

She almost took a header on a settee that had no business being where it was, but she managed to steady herself and then navigate the rest of the room without an Incident. She put the biscotti and mineral water on the table. Of course, there was a problem.

"Maria, don't put the cold bottle on my good table. What's the matter with you? You know I have that table for fifty years. Put something under it. You didn't bring any jam for the biscotti? Something to make them sweet?"

Maria only half heard her mother. She had already sat down and was busy ungluing herself from the clear, plastic furniture covers that apparently were required of any household whose owners could trace their roots to the northern shores of the Mediterranean Sea. Why the hell had she worn a dress? They were sticky and hot and gross and as she tried to move one way, her skin seemed not only to be transfixed, but to be moving in the opposite direction, not only defying the laws of physics but causing extreme discomfort.

"For God's sake, Ma, when are you going to get rid of these

damn plastic covers?"

"Well, they have been a lifesaver. They have protected all this furniture for thirty years, and they're still in good shape."

"They've protected it because people don't want to sit on it. Ah, OK, it's your house, I'm sorry I yelled. YEOW...." Maria concluded. Her mother and aunt quickly turned their heads with the same scornful looks.

"That was pain, Mom, pain," she explained, as she finally managed to pull her thigh loose. "Pain!"

It was moments like this when she thought of her friends, most of whom would have taken a shot or two before continuing. But that was not an option, so what would would be the best thing to do? Somehow find a way to calm herself down or smash everything and go home? When she got passionate or angry, Maria's eyes took on a life of their own, and at the moment they were on fire. All this took place in a millisecond, and while pondering her next move her glance fell on a bottle of red wine on the breakfront in the corner of the room. It made her think of Nick, and his incredulity when he found out she didn't drink.

"How the hell can you be a Sicilian and not like – at the very least – red wine?"

"Didn't you tell me that your former writing partner didn't like red wine? And he was Italian, right?"

That shut him up for the moment, but Nick had a nonstop mouth and could be very irritating from time to time – more often than not, actually – but thinking of this little exchange between the two of them calmed her down, and a hint of a smile began to emerge. She considered emailing him later and thanking him, but then she thought better of it. It would just get his damn Greek ego up and running again just as she was beginning the monumental task of toning it down.

So, without missing a beat, Maria turned both her mood and countenance around one hundred eighty degrees.

"Sorry, ma. I'm just edgy from work," she said with a grin. "You put whatever torturous covering you want on your furniture. I'll get some jam for you."

"I told you that you work too hard. It's OK. But don't go yet..first watch this part where the mother gets upset with her children. You can learn something from this.. Go back during the commercial."

"OK, Ma."

Another colleague came to mind. He was also a history teacher and his favorite expression was, "No good deed goes unpunished." Jesus, was he ever right!

CHAPTER TWO

Italians On and Off The Screen

MARTY was Ernest Borgnine's Oscar-winning role, and if you were Italian, or a mother, or both, it was like *your* signature role. It told the story of an Italian, unmarried butcher in the Bronx of the 1950s. He was a pleasant, hard-working guy who was harried by all the older Italian women in the neighborhood because all his siblings were married, which begged the question, "When you gonna get married, Marty?" something he heard many times on any given day. Of course, the person who repeated it the most was his own mother, who also always mentioned the ethnicity of the girl he should find: "Why don't you find nice Italian girl, Marty? There are plenty of nice Italian girls."

Getting Marty married off was only one part of the equation his mother had to solve. She was a widow in her sixties, and worried not only about her son, but about her own future. She had a sister, Catherine, who did not get along with her daughter-in-law, who, along with her husband and young baby, lived with Catherine. Talk about a recipe for disaster! Well, Marie and Elizabeth were also widows in their sixties, and while they didn't have to worry about marrying off their kids or anyone living with them, they could very easily have portrayed these roles on the screen because they saw themselves as playing them out in their own heads and their own lives. This was especially true with regard to listening to your mother, which seemed to be a universal problem among those who traced their heritage to somewhere along the Mediterranean. This movie had been a universal hit and deserved all the accolades it and its star received, and while you didn't have to be Italian (or Greek) to love it, it did seem to resonate more with these two groups, which is fortunate because that is essentially the backstory of this book.

Maria finally got things settled to the satisfaction of the finicky ladies. Two kinds of biscotti and jam had been brought out, and there was a coaster for the bottle of Pellegrino, and there was some dark Turkish coffee, complete with a folded-over tablecloth for protection. Plenty to go around – food, drink, and guilt. On the TV the two sisters were talking about their situation in life, and the buzzwords were "curse" and "old," neatly tucked into the phrase "It's a curse to be old," which was repeated several times in the movie, and then reprised at least a dozen times in the living room.

"You see, Maria! Those two women are right. It is a curse to get old, it's a curse. No one cares about you, everyone thinks you're good for nothing, and your kids grow up and leave you. And you know what's the worst thing? They don't listen to you. You give birth to them and feed them and raise them, and then they spit on you. You sacrifice the best years of your life, and they don't call, and they don't care. I could be dead and buried and no one would ever know. Right, Liz?"

Elizabeth had been rocking faster and faster, and when her sister posed the question she appeared to be approaching the speed of sound, which would have made her the first Italian woman to reach that velocity in recorded history. She put her legs straight down and came to a screeching halt.

"You're damn right, Marie. You wake up one day and you see an old woman in the mirror, just like that Catherine says in the movie. And it's a curse to be a widow. See, she's gonna say it right now – listen." Sure enough, Marty's Aunt Catherine said her lines right on cue: "These are the worst years. I see an old lady in the mirror. It's a curse to be a widow."

Maria couldn't hold her laugh in. Her aunt and her mom knew the lines from the movie the way some people know the lines from *The Honeymooners* – actually, the way she and Nick did. What was also both ironic and "laugh-worthy" was the "sainthood" Italian widows often bestowed on their late husbands, who were considered to be good-for-nothing, arrogant, bossy, and abusive bums when they were alive. Well, everybody's personal stock does seem to go up when they're no longer around. But her frivolity drew cold stares from the two women, and it took quite a bit of explaining to extricate herself from their wrath. Of course, she'd been dealing with this her whole life, but to use a sports analogy, ballplayers slow down as they age, these ladies were getting quicker and more combative as the years progressed. Maria couldn't imagine what they might be like in the future, but right now her problem was calming them down and smoothing out the cornucopia of guilt they were unfolding.

Elizabeth just shook her head and whispered to her sister an upcoming line from Catherine to her sister in the movie about "college girls – one step from the street." Maria pretended not to hear it. What else could she do? She didn't want to start a big hubbub, and to tell the truth she was glad her mother made her watch the movie. It was a nice break from school and from editing what Nick had written for their book. *MARTY* ends happily, as he finds a girl he loves and decides to pursue her, even though his mother doesn't approve because she's not Italian. Nobody's perfect, right?

"Maria, you wanna stay and eat with us? Your husband is

on a business trip, right? So you stay and eat with us."

Translation: "let's go out to eat."

Marie had quit cooking quite a while ago, a decision commemorated by a gift from her daughter – a plaque: KITCHEN CLOSED – THIS CHICK HAS HAD IT!

Now, Maria had no problem having dinner with her mom and aunt, as long as they let her pick the place. That way she could be sure the food was OK and the ladies would like the accouterments. She figured they may as well go to a diner. As far as getting any work done, the day was pretty well shot, and it was good to get them out of the house, especially this house, the same house where Maria grew up and where her mother had lived for the better part of five decades.

CHAPTER THREE

"Nobody Bothers Me Here"

Ah, the house. Maria and her two siblings had grown up here. There were holidays, and birthdays, happy, carefree days, and sad days, like when her father died. There seemed to be a memory in every room, and, while life does go on and change is indeed a necessary part of it, just as the ladies in the movie, her mother was used to living there and took offense at any suggestion to the contrary. Guilt trips notwithstanding, Maria was a fairly regular visitor, and there was always something that had to be addressed or looked into or argued over. Always. It was a stately, impressive looking home, built in a neighborhood of similarly traditional but unique structures, in what had been an area that, while not exclusive, showed that the families who lived here had done pretty well for themselves.

The inside was welcoming and familiar, a place that had served the family well for almost fifty years. The decor was more or less Italian, with its mixture of art and stone, paintings, sofas and tables of all sorts, and scores and scores of family pictures. Even with the "super glue" plastic on the upholstered chairs, everything seemed to echo the words "come and sit and visit." Her mother always kept it up nicely, but now that she was getting older, neatness was no longer a priority and there were piles of things in various places, and chairs set up where no one would ever sit. The neighborhood was also different, as people raised their families and moved, so her mother really didn't know the people around her anymore. Maria had talked to her about this many times, but it was always the same answer: "Nobody bothers me."

"Mom, you have bars on your windows."

"So what? This neighborhood is safe. I feel *comfortable* here. Nobody bothers me."

My God, Maria would often think to herself, it's no wonder she likes that damn movie so much. There are crazy Italian women in it who think their kids are trying to take their houses from them. Even though her mother said she felt comfortable there – "as long as nobody bothers me" – the location of their home was never *completely* worry-free, even when Maria was growing up there. But her mother was who she was and wasn't about to change on a dime or anytime, actually. "Change" was not part of her vocabulary. She would often say that In Sicily people would often live their lives and die in the same house where they were born. Reminding her that they were not *in* Sicily, and that she was born here in the States never caused her to change her mind even just a little. "Nobody bothers me here."

So, harking back to one of her favorite quotes from Shakespeare about "discretion being the better part of valor," Maria decided not to bring the house up today. There were however a couple of other things she wanted to talk about as long as she was here. But first, they had to settle on dinner plans. It was no easy feat discussing *anything* with the two of them, but the sooner the meal was settled the better it would be.

"Hey, Mom, Aunt Elizabeth, I know a great place we can go for dinner. My treat."

The two sisters had been waiting for that statement, but, of course, they couldn't let it stand as it was.

"Well, all right, Maria. But you don't pay. We split it. You don't make no money in that damn job of yours."

A smile crossed Elizabeth's face as she snuck a look at Maria.

"We'll figure out the money, Ma, don't worry about it. And I know a real good place, but I got to talk to you about something first."

"I'm not moving. I'm comfortable here."

"It's not about moving, Ma. But you have a lot of stuff here. If you sorted it out, it would be easier to take care of this place. I mean, look at those chairs – chairs nobody sits in. Do you really need all those chairs? And what about all the things in your attic? It's like a museum up there. You're never gonna use *any* of those things. Why do you insist on keeping them?"

"Maria, you never know when you're gonna need them. And they're all in good condition."

Of course, what her mother neglected to say is that the reason so many of them are in such good condition is that a lot of them have never been opened. A prime example is a cell phone she bought twenty-five (yes, that's 25) years ago. It's still in the box it came in. Untouched, like a collector's item. But this idiosyncrasy is limited to things smaller than a breadbox. No sir. There are stories about cars that are hard to believe, unless, of course, if you know Marie.

For a long time, she had two cars. Two cars – one driver. When asked about the rationale for this, the lady's reply was simple and, to her, very logical: "What if my car breaks down? This way I have another one I can use." Maria begged and begged her mother to sell it, and she finally did. Well, it was actually Maria who sold it, though the process was so laborious and tortuous that it almost defied not only logic but reality. What should have taken a few days took weeks that seemed like years. "Put the price up high, you can always come down" was the strategy her mom advised. Miraculously, a boy from New York wanted it, and she haggled with him and his father for days over two hundred dollars – never mind that with maintenance and insurance she was wasting FAR more than that.

Most people have seen on TV the oft-used story about the little old lady whose car was in perfect condition because she kept it in the garage and drove it only to church on Sundays. Marie was one better than that. She bought a new car and hardly *ever* drove it at all – five years, less than 3,000 miles. Five years! When asked why she didn't drive it more, Marie evoked the same response she used when she had two cars: "What if it breaks down?" EWWWWWWW....the screech going through Maria's head could have competed with the shot heard round the world in intensity and duration. Competed? It would have won! Whenever the subject of change came up, whether it was a car, furniture, an appliance, or the house itself, Marie would put on the same "record" she had been playing for decades. It was always the same, and Maria pretty much knew it by heart. But it wasn't just the context that touched or aggravated the listener (depending on who was listening), it was the passion and emotion with which it was delivered that filled the air and everyone there with GUILT. Everyone, distant relative, neighbor, delivery man, or DAUGHTER. Once, in an ill-advised moment when she was much younger, Maria was about to say to her mother that if she could bottle and sell the guilt she was peddling the whole family could retire to a villa somewhere in the Adriatic and live there comfortably for the rest of their lives. Somehow, luckily, she had stopped herself after saying "Ma, if you could..." or this book would probably neverhave been even started, since Marie would still be sobbing her rebuttal. Maria often thought of that potential disaster when the "change" soliloquy was about to start.

"Maria, we've been here fifty years. You were a year old when we moved in. I raised three kids here. I know it's big and things have changed, but I'm comfortable here. Nobody bothers me. And I know I have a lot of stuff, but I keep it in case I need it. If I didn't keep those chairs, suppose someone comes over: where they gonna sit? It happened so many times. I throw something out, the next day I need it. So, if I don't throw it out, when I need it, I have it! And - I have this house. There were a lot of years, here, and a lot of people...."

There was no use getting into an argument over an attitude that wouldn't be changed without an act of God. Or perhaps even *with* an act of God, so Maria simply changed the subject.

"Ma, listen, I want you to stay here as long as you want to. As long as you feel comfortable. OK? Now, let's go out and get something good to eat."

Elizabeth gave a definitive nod, but Marie had a rather questioning look on her face, something Maria had seen all too often.

"What's the matter Ma? Why the frown?"

"What about my doctor next week. You gonna take me?"

"I said I would."

The conversation had taken a sharp turn, and Maria wanted to get off this road, and on the road, as soon as she could. She *always* took her mother to the doctor, and she *always* saw to her medicines and her general well-being. But none of this would be of any value if at least *some* guilt weren't thrown into the mix, so she figured she'd let her mom play a hand or two of "woe are Italian mothers," but not an entire game.

"Ma, you know you're my lady."

That usually did the trick, and it worked like a charm again.

"I know Maria, I know," she said with a warm smile. "I know."

That would have been the ideal time to turn their thoughts towards food and a place to get some, but there was something else which had to be addressed, and Maria reluctantly brought it up.

"Mom, just one more thing."

"Oh, no. Is it something bad? Is someone sick? Did someone die? You know, Linder has been very sick."

"Who?"

"My friend Linder. You know who she is."

Who the hell was she talking about? Was that a first name or a last name?

Elizabeth had just returned from the bathroom and caught the tail end of their discussion, and of course felt obligated to jump in.

"Marie, was she the daughter or the mother?"

"Who, Lindner?"

"Yes."

"She worked so hard she killed her mother. That's what she did. That's how much that Lindner cared about her mother."

Maria realized that there was no easy way out of this labyrinth her mother had led them into, but at least she figured out that the name – "Lindner" was really "Linda." But was she the mother or the daughter? It didn't really matter, because neither she nor her aunt or most probably her mom…knew who the hell she was. She quickly made a quick turn and steered the subject back to the doctor's appointment and away from "Lindner."

"OK, Mom, now don't forget to call me to double-check what time you want me to pick you up, all right?"

"For what, Maria?"

"For your doctor's appointment."

"You know that Lindner never took her mother to the doctor. She killed that poor old lady. Oh, and by the way I am having trouble using the phone you gave me I don't know my password."

"Ma, you don't need a password. But, if you're having trouble, you can just text me. You know how to text me, right?"

Her mom had a puzzled look on her face, and Maria at first thought she'd better back off, but the doctor's appointment was Wednesday, she had already taken the day, off, and if anything went wrong, it would most certainly turn out to be her fault. So, it was probably best to get it straightened out tonight. Her sanity depended on it.

"OK, Mom, now you have my phone number, right? But if it is easier, like I said, just text me. Or call me. Or don't do anything. I will be here Wednesday morning. All right?"

The puzzled look slowly changed into a smile.

"OK, Maria. I know you'll bc here to get me. Thank you."

"Hey, Ma, you're my lady, right? Right! Let's go eat."

CHAPTER FOUR

Beware Of Greeks Running Diners….

They piled into Maria's car bound for "parts unknown," which was Mom's assessment of the trip, being that they hadn't really talked about where they were going to go to eat. But of course, there was a more immediate problem. Maria's car was a medium-sized Honda, perfect for going back and forth to Burns High School, but was also, according to her mom and aunt, the smallest car ever made in the hundred and twenty-five-year history of the internal combustion engine.

"You know Maria, this car might be OK for you when you're by yourself, but it got no room when you have somebody else in the car, don't you think? I can barely move. Tell that damn school to pay you more so you get bigger car."

Now, being Sicilian, Maria had some of the same blood coursing through her veins as her mother, and her aunt, for that matter. And at the moment it was starting to boil. She was about to ask her mother why it was that if the car had been good enough to take her to all her appointments at various doctors and agencies over the past five years, why wasn't it adequate enough for the three of them to take tonight? But if there was one thing she had learned over her many years teaching high school it was that sometimes you can't win. Taking a beat and cooling your jets often proves to be the best course of action, so she bit her already blistered tongue and just turned on the radio.

"I don't like this song, Maria. Most of these people just have one song. Not like Sinatra or Dean Martin. One song. And I don't like it anyway."

"Well, Mom, this is Bon Jovi. He's no one-hit wonder!"

"Oh, yeah, I know him. I know Stevie Wonder."

Maria just gently shook her head. You had to laugh, really, to keep at least some of your sanity. But it wasn't quite over.

"And where are we going for dinner?"

Her aunt had been quiet the whole time, and it startled Maria to hear someone speaking from the back seat.

"Yeah, I don't care about your car or your songs, but I am kind of hungry. Is this place close by?"

"We'll be there in about ten minutes, Aunt Elizabeth." Maria wished she were Elizabeth Montgomery so she could twitch her nose and be at their destination instantly, because she knew what was coming: 'the tapping' – as opposed to but just as disturbing as *The Shining"!* Both sisters had long, polished fingernails, which they used in a staccato-like cacophony of clicks upon the windows. And with every series of taps there appeared to be a recollection of some past catastrophe.

"Isn't that where Bill had that bad accident? Or was that Paul who had it?"

"Look at that car. That was the same car Lindner used to drive. isn't it? Didn't she crash it somewhere around here?"

The thoughts were totally random, and rarely, if ever, completed. Were these real events or just emotionally charged memories that actually never happened? Maria had long ago given up trying to figure out the answer to that question, and to hold onto what was left of her mental equanimity, she thought it best not to tackle it tonight.

She almost ran the red light, or perhaps it was red when she went through it, but no jury would have convicted her. They were there....!!

"We're here!" Maria exclaimed as she exhaled a day's worth of frustration.

They pulled into the parking lot of the Starling House Diner, which, from all appearances, looked like a good place to eat. The outside was framed by about a dozen tall and arching trees, and there were flowers and bushes in a beautiful arrangement which complimented the shiny and well lit edifice they were about to enter. There was a double parking lot, and it looked like they did a brisk business.

"This good place, Maria?"

"Would I take my mother and my aunt to a place that was no good? Would I? A lot of the teachers eat here."

Elizabeth cut to the chase, "As long as they have food and a bathroom, it's good enough for me. Let's go in!"

They walked up the short, sloping incline that led to the front door. A couple was just walking out, and they were saying how full they were and appeared to have a take home box with them They smiled and held the door for the three ladies.

"See that, Mom, they ate all they wanted and then had left overs to take home."

"Maybe they didn't like it and were just taking it out so they didn't have to eat it."

They went in, her mom and aunt talking and Maria just shaking her head.

The diner was crowded, but not jammed, and there seemed to be both booths and tables free in various locations.

"Now Maria, let's make sure we get a good place to sit. It's too cold right here; I can feel the air conditioner right on my head."

"Mother, we're standing at the entrance to the diner. They have to keep it cool; and don't worry, they won't make us sit on the floor."

They were greeted by a pleasant young man, about twenty five or so. He was clean shaven and neatly dressed in a pair of slacks and shirt. He could have been one of Maria's former students..

"Welcome, ladies. Would you like a booth or a table? We have both."

"Maybe a booth," Maria answered.

"Good idea, Maria. People can't kick the back of your chair when you're in a booth," Elizabeth chimed in.

"Yes, but we don't want one of those tight booths where you can't get in or out," said Marie. "Right, Liz?"

"Correct! And we don't want to bc too close to the bathrooms. Phew! Sometimes the odor is too much."

"But we don't want to be too far away either, in case one of us has to go."

"Well said, Mare."

The young greeter, who seemed to have aged about ten years during his brief encounter with the sisters, stopped short right in the middle of the restaurant. He still had his smile, but as he glanced over his shoulder, he could see other people waiting to be seated, and he had to bring this to some sort of conclusion.

"Ladies, we stopped here so you could look around and find the perfect spot to enjoy your dinner."

Luckily, the "perfect spot" seemed to be right where they were standing. There was what appeared to be an adequately sized booth available, not close to – but not far from – the restrooms. However, there was still a problem: directly overhead was an air conditioning vent, and though it was really on the quiet side, and it wasn't particularly cold, the two ladies reacted as if they had been dumped in northern Alaska in December with a Texas tornado imported to circulate the freezing air.

"Oh, no, that air is coming right down on my head. It's freezing. Can't we sit somewhere else?" Marie exclaimed.

The host noticed the foursome near the door just getting up. He suggested that spot as an alternative.

"No, no, not there either. There is always a terrible draft when you sit near the entrance. Am I right, Liz."

"Yes, Mare. We can't eat with the wind blowing on us."

The young man spotted another couple about to leave what looked like a potential eating place, but the sisters had already spotted it and were shaking their heads. Marie started to cough.

"Oh, Liz, I can smell the food from here," quipped Marie, as she started to cough. "If we go closer to the kitchen, it will kill me; it's no good for my cough." Elizabeth nodded in solemn agreement.

Somehow, miraculously, they managed to find a booth. It wasn't a "perfect" place, but apparently it would do. The two sisters were nodding in acquiescence and Maria suppressed a scream. She told herself that she should be used to this because it happened every time – but no matter how many times you bang your shin, the pain is still there. And tonight had all the makings of one of their signature performances!

As the two sisters settled into their seats, their heads were swiveling as they took in the immediate surroundings, perhaps looking to see if some other negative feature may have been surreptitiously planted to spoil the ambiance Maria pulled the young man aside.

"My companions are my mother and my aunt. Do you know who our waiter will be?"

"It's probably going to be my father, the owner. We're a bit short tonight, and he likes to pitch in and meet his customers at the same time. Why?"

"Well, I usually talk directly to the waiter, but maybe you can tell him for me. I love these ladies, but they can be – how should I put it – a bit uh..."

"Eccentric?" the young man volunteered.

"Crazy!" Maria responded. "It will take them quite a while to decide on their selection, and I usually make it up to the waiter dollar-wise. Get it?"

"Got it! I'll tell my dad, but I think he'll be OK!" He then turned to the sisters. "Here are your menus, ladies. Your waiter will be here momentarily. Enjoy your dinner."

Marie and Elizabeth were just beginning to scan their menus when another gentleman appeared. He was about fifty, swarthy and dignified looking, with a mustache and casually but neatly dressed.

"Good evening, ladies. My name is Stavros, and it will be my pleasure to wait on you tonight. Actually, my wife and I own this place, but we're a little short of help, so I'm doing a little of this, a little of that. If there's anything you need, just let me know. I see you have your menus; would you like a little time to look them over?"

Raising her eyebrows just a bit, Maria answered, "yeah, that might be best."

Stavros gave an understated nod indicating he had been given a scouting report by his son. "Just let me know when you are ready," he uttered politely as he walked away a step or two.

"Well, Stavros, huh. Must be Greek with a name like that."

"Ma, you know as well as I do that every diner in Jersey is owned by a Greek."

"I was just making conversation. They usually have pretty good food, but you gotta watch them. You know what I mean, Maria? Although this one did seem nice. He did seem nice."

"Yeah, Ma, he did. But could we get back to your dinner selection?" Maria uttered desperately.

"My goodness, there are so many things to choose from!

What are you gonna have, Liz?"

"I don't know," her sister replied. "It's such a hard choice."

"Why don't we ask the waiter what he recommends," Marie suggested. "Hey, Stavros, come here," she shouted as she pointed to the owner.

Stavros, was at that moment was balancing a tray full of food for the table across the aisle. He nodded to indicate he would be right over – and he was.

"Well, are we all set?"

"Uh, not quite," Maria deadpanned.

"We thought you could suggest something," Liz replied hopefully.. "You have so much on the menu!"

"OK, what are you in the mood for? How about roast beef?"

"No, that repeats on me," Marie responded, putting her hand to her stomach. "And I don't like to see the blood.... eww...." as she moved her hand to cover her eyes.

"Our chicken is tasty and easy on the stomach," was Stavros' next suggestion.

"No, I had chicken this week," was Liz's counter.

Of course Maria had been through this all too many times – in fact, it was the same show *every time* they went out to eat. She marveled at the restraint that Stavros was showing.

Meantime, Elizabeth had to use the ladies room, so she told Maria to just get her a cup of minestrone and a grilled cheese and tomato sandwich. .

In the middle of the great dinner decision, Stavros seemed to get somewhat of a quizzical look on his face, and what followed was typical of a Greek and predictable of Marie – at least that's the way Maria felt!

"Excuse me if this seems forward, but are you two sisters? You are both so lovely and look so much alike."

Maria couldn't help laughing and shaking her head – the goddamn Greeks are all alike, she thought almost out loud.

Her mother, on the other hand, ate the hyperbole up, as she played one of her hole cards, a demur and flirtatious blush that enveloped her whole countenance.

"Oh, aren't you sweet? This is my daughter. But what a nice thing to say."

"Oh, I am sorry. But I can see where her good looks come from!"

"Well, if you say so!! You;re not so bad yourself!"

Stavros just nodded slightly as an acknowledgement. Maria was exercising all the self control she could muster as she matter of factly asked her mother if they could just order. So she did, both for herself and her aunt, who had not yet returned. Now it was center stage for mom, something that would always prove to be humorous and memorable, yet at the same time reminiscent of a TV sitcom..

"OK, hon, give me the matzo ball soup, but not too much chicken.and Yeah" – Her mother continued while looking downward at the imaginary soup – "Do you have any crackers?" Marie remained animated this whole time, as she then began to simulate breaking crackers up in the bowl of soup. Stavros was doing his best to suppress a grin, and Maria was just shaking her head with a gentle smile, as she quietly and matter-of-factly ordered lentil soup and a salad for yourself. But her Mom wasn't quite done.

"Oh, and hon, I like lots of butter. Make sure you bring the butter. Oh, and yeah, make sure you bring the crackers, too."

"Your wish is my command, fair lady," said Stavros, with such a genuine demeanor that even Maria was impressed. He took the menus with a flourish and promised to be right back with the soups.

"What a sweet man, Greek or no Greek."

"You're impossible, mother. Just awful!"

"Hey, the man knows a beautiful woman...excuse me...women...when he sees them."

Stavros was as good as his word, and was back in a flash with the minestrone, matzo balls, and lentils. Quite a trifecta..

"Do you want me to keep the minestrone hot till the other lady gets back?"

"You are soooo thoughtful, Stavros. *She* is my sister, and she'll be back in a minute. You can just leave it."

"All right, call me if you need anything else before the main course is ready, the owner offered as he walked away.

Marie had already begun to attack her soup, as she put the spoon into it and twirled around all the chicken pieces she really didn't want..

"They never get this right. Too much chicken, and not enough crackers! They're so cheap. What's the matter with that guy Stavros, or whatever his name is. He must be a new owner."

Maria finally had to say something....."Hey Mom, if they were CHEAP, wouldn't they be cheap with the chicken, and not with the crackers? Huh? Hold on; I'll get you some more."

"No one needs to order for me," her mother shouted, as she pointed toward Stavros with a gesture that would have made General Patton blush. She caught his eye almost literally – "Sir, sir, I want some more crackers."

Maria had this battle with her mother time and time again, but to no avail.

"Mom, haven't I told you that pointing is rude and aggressive body language?"

"Say what you want, but I know what I have to do," her mother stated triumphantly as the owner promptly arrived with an overflowing basket of crackers..

Stavros and the crackers arrived at the same time as Elizabeth, and as she scooted in to sit down she called Maria by name when asking if she could move just a little bit. Maria had inadvertently left a small Burns High School pad in her purse as she had packed her stuff in the hustle to leave her mother's house, and it fell out as she moved. It caught Stavros' attention.

"Excuse me for interrupting your dinner, ladies, but is that a Burns High School insignia?"

Maria nodded.

"And your name is Maria?"

Maria nodded again. This was getting interesting, especially for her mother, who took time out from "crackering" her soup to look up with a very intense grimace on her face.

"Then you must be *the* Maria. The Maria that teaches English and works with Nick.! So glad to meet you! I've heard so much about you, and here you are in person. You teach with Nick, right? He told me you were very smart – and very beautiful."

"Efharisto," Maria answered in her best Greek.

"You speak Greek so well. But Nick said you were."

"SICILIAN," her mother shouted.

Stavros didn't miss a beat.

"Hey, Greeks, Sicilians....it's all good!" Stavros laughed with a genuine tone that made it hard not to like the guy. Hard, but not impossible.

Stavros was still chuckling. "You're probably wondering how I know all these things. Well, Nick and I go way back. He used to work here with Mario when they were writing musicals. . So when he got a new writing partner, he told me all about you. Oh, and your money is no good here tonight. Enjoy!" Stavros walked over to his son and was still smiling as he apparently was filling him in on their newly found celebrity.

Maria's mother turned toward her with a reproachful look that could only mean an ill wind was blowing and about to turn in her direction.

"So, you have a writing partner? His name is Nick? It seems that everyone but your mother knows about it. Who is this 'Nick'? Nick what? And what are you writing?"

She turned to her sister.

"See, strangers know more about your kids' lives than their mothers. Just like in *MARTY*."

Elizabeth nodded so hard her head almost hit the table. Luckily they were in a booth or she probably would have rocked herself out of the diner.

"Ma, I told you about him. You just didn't remember. Nick. Nick Pappas."

"Pappas? Pappas? He's a damn Greek, too?. Believe me, I would remember that. And he works with you?"

"Yes, we have lunch duty together."

"What is that, lunch duty?"

"Well, we watch the kids while they eat lunch."

"Where you watch them from?"

"Well, we sit at a table. That's how we got started writing the book. We have a lot of the same ideas."

"You can bet he's got ideas, and they got nothing to do with the book. You saw this guy, this Stavros, when we came in. They're all like that. They're all after one thing."

"But you didn't get mad when Stavros gave you a compliment!"

"That's different, I will never see him again. Ever. You see this guy every day! And he sits next to you! He knows you're married?"

"He knows. He's married, too. And he has lots of kids."

"See!!, They can't keep their hands off women."

"He ever tells you that you look nice? He told this Stavros guy that you are beautiful."

"It's just a compliment, Ma. That's all. You know what, he took piano lessons on our street."

"Our street? Where the house is?"

"It was many years ago, Mom."

"Mmmmmm," was all her mother uttered with her mouth,

but the wink and the shaking of her head and finger said it all.

"He's not a bad guy, Ma."

"Yeah, well, now that he knows, I bet he still drives by. Just watch your step. And don't wear any more dresses to that 'lunch duty,' you hear me?"

The "tennis match" between Maria and Marie was thankfully interrupted by the main course, brought by the apparently always smiling Stavros.

"Enjoy. And just call me if there's anything else you need."

When Elizabeth saw what her sister was having, she was beside herself.

"Oh, no, I didn't know you could order French toast!"

CHAPTER FIVE

Lunch Duty ...

Nick got to lunch duty first, so he settled in at the table occupied by the lunch duty teachers and yelled at a few kids just to keep his timing. The room was huge and had been constructed only ten years before when the school had undergone massive – and expensive – renovations. Several doors opened to the outside, which featured some picnic tables and a glorious view of the teachers' parking lot. The teachers' lunch room was at the far end and was a separate facility unto itself. It was a pleasant enough and spacious area in which to eat, but very few of the seventy odd teachers actually ate their lunch there since it was almost in a different zip code from the rest of the school. Some staff members would come by to grab a sandwich, but they would usually go back to their rooms to eat, so it was basically just Nick and Maria as far as teachers went. Speaking of Maria, where was she? Something must be up, Nick thought, and it was, as Maria came in with that all too familiar look on her face that meant he'd better tread lightly. She slammed her pile of stuff down on the table and uttered one of her infamous "ehhhh" sighs that could mean any number of things, but the bottom line was that she had something on her mind, and it wasn't the agenda for today's faculty meeting.

She turned and stared at Nick with a look that would have made Medusa envious. He said a quick silent prayer that her wrath wasn't directed at him. It wasn't.

"I just got a call from my mother. She was so proud of herself that she was able to get through"

"Well, that's good right? You had said she was having a problem with her phone."

"Yeah, but I was probably better off when she couldn't get me."

Nick knew that he shouldn't ask what he was about to, but he wanted it to look like he cared – which he did. How could he put this so it didn't look like he was prying, and at the same time not appear his query was just perfunctory.

"Maria, what's up?"

His partner was shocked at the directness and simplicity of his question. Usually, if ten words were adequate, Nick would use a hundred. But this time he would have put a mime to shame.

"Silent Cal would be proud, Nick.

"Huh?" replied the dumbfounded Greek. Perhaps just "dumb" would have been enough. "What?"

Aggravated as she was, Maria could not suppress a laugh.

"Usually you go on and on and on. You got right to the point, just as Coolidge used to do. I'm proud of you."

Nick sighed a big "whew" under his breath. He really liked Maria, but he was also just a bit – actually quite a bit – afraid of her, and she was one person you did not want to get mad at you. But it looked as if the storm clouds were receding a little..

She turned to face him, which was good unless she were yelling because her eyes were something else.

"Didn't mean to blow a gasket. It's just frustrating dealing with my mother. I told you I was taking a day Wednesday so I can take her to the doctor, right?" She didn't wait for an answer.

"So I told her to call me if there was a problem about anything."

Thinking that she was going to keep on rolling, Nick was caught flatfooted, and managed just a half uttered "So...?."

"So – she calls me this morning just as my class is starting, and like an idiot, I think It's an emergency and answer the damn phone. Guess what? She just wanted to talk. I've been teaching thirty years and my mother still can't get it through her head that I can't just put things on hold to listen to her day. Geees..."

"Been there, still doing that," Nick exclaimed. "They don't understand what we do or what the constraints are when we are in front of a class."

They high-fived!

"Oh, and by the way, Nick."

Nick broke out in a big grin.

"I knew there had to be a 'by the way' in here somewhere," he chuckled, quoting one of their favorite Jackie Gleason lines from *THE HONEYMOONERS,* a show both of them loved. The two of them started laughing so hard they were getting quizzical looks from several of the students passing by, as well as from the principal, who always bought his lunch during this period.

But for once Nick was ready, as he looked up with a grin and said..."Yeah, Mr. Morgan; we're working on a really funny part of the curriculum."

The head man just shook his head and kept on walking. Nick had had his share of battles with him, and so had Maria, but this looked like just another puzzle Morgan would have to leave in the box.

"Now, 'dear,' what were you going to tell me?" Nick inquired, still laughing uncontrollably.

"Not a big deal...I promised Stavros I'd tell you Hi."

"Stavros? Oh, Stavros at the diner! Did you eat there over the weekend?"

"No – I ran into this random guy on the street and asked him if his name happened to be Stavros. He said yes and so then I asked him if he knew you. And he said to say 'Hi.'"

Nick had been caught flat-footed...again.

"Of course I went to the diner, you idiot."

He could never keep up with Maria, so he just bowed his head in defeat.

"Nice place, huh, Maria?"

"Nice if you're going by yourself or with normal people. A trip to hell if you're going with your mother and your aunt. And, my lunch duty colleague, what exactly did you tell him about me?? Hmmm??"

"I told him that we were working together on a book about all our years teaching."

"And?"

"And that you were very bright."

Maria kept the glare on full.

"And, well, that you were easy on the eyes....actually, I think I used the word 'beautiful.' Was there a problem?" he asked with trepidation and a cringe embedded in his face.

"Well, not really a 'problem,' more like a hornet's nest. My mother found out we were working together, and that you used to take piano on our street....and that you're Greek At the very least she thinks you are stalking me; I'll stop there."

"Sorry, Maria."

"Well, for once it's not really your fault. Let me ask you a question: is your mother like that?"

"Not only my mother, but my aunt as well. Ironically, they are about seven years apart, and my Aunt Mable is the older one. Pretty close to your situation. And let me tell you something: from all the stories you've told me, they could be the same people."

Nick was getting somewhat of a glazed look over his eyes, as he started to daydream and talk through his thoughts. "Yeah, it sounds as if they're pretty much the same people. Not easy to deal with as they're getting older – or ever. You should have experienced what it was like growing up with the two of them shadowing my every move. I'm lucky I made it this far."

"My aunt is a past master at jokes, especially at someone else's expense. Not to mention guilt trips. Oh, Lord, I could tell you some stories about her!"

"And your mother?"

"Don't get me started," Nick replied. "They are both good at what they do, which was to get you to do what they wanted you to do, but their styles are completely different. Mable would come with a Sunday punch, sort of like your mom, while my mother would wear you out with her footwork and then jab you into submission. And they're still going strong. My mom has tucked away grudges and guilt for decades – literally. I could tell you stories that would make you cringe.

Just then the fire alarm rang, and they had to herd two hundred students out into the parking lot.

"I'll take a rain check on those stories, Greek," Maria exclaimed as Nick was busy clearing out some reluctant seniors, who apparently felt that the school rules no longer applied to them.

"You got it Maria. Hey, you know what, this might make a good book. I mean a second book, all about our moms and aunts. Whadayathink?"

Before she could answer the principal re-appeared, vigorously waving his hand in a rapid circular motion to indicate they needed to get the kids out quicker. Nick was about to say something when Maria shot him a deadly reprimand with her now blazing eyes.

She was right. Nick buried his comment inside - expletives not deleted.

CHAPTER SIX

"Is That Asking Too Much?

Nick was on his way home from school and decided to stop at his mother's to see how things were and to see if perhaps she needed something at the store. He tried to stop there once a week just to check in on her, and he would call her every couple of days just to be sure she was doing OK. Of course, she wanted him to call her every day, but he had decided long ago that would not be a good idea. He needed a bit of space between them, and besides, if he had gotten in the habit of calling every day, a missed day would be cause for concern – and guilt.

She was glad to see him and had the grocery list all ready.

"When do you need the stuff, Ma?"

"No rush, a day or two would be fine. Just be sure to get everything I want, and be sure you buy the brands and sizes I indicated. OK?"

Of all the regular "duties" Nick had to do, going food shopping for his mother headed the list when it came to stress. He was used to buying large sizes for his own family, and for the most part, one brand was as good as another. His mother was finicky when it came to *everything,* but there had to be an asterisk next to food shopping because she was the most precise and had zero tolerance when it came to her food supplies. Nick looked at the list: about fourteen items. It would have taken him about twenty minutes at the outside to shop and get checked out if he were doing his own shopping. But this was different. It took him about twenty minutes just to go over the damn list, and he could feel the stress as he looked over the things once he had gotten back into his car. Nothing out of the ordinary, just the usual stuff: tuna fish, peanut butter, bread, eggs, cream cheese. A grown man really should not be scared of a shopping list, but just looking at it brought out a bevy of fears and pressures.

Of course, Nick had two strikes against him. First of all, the supermarket near his mother's house was not the one he usually shopped at. And there was no real order to the list he was intently looking at. Nick's lists, which were actually just visualizations, had the items in close proximity to each other in the store and also near each other on his "list." He wasn't sure how his mother's shopping list was put together, but if he ever got the wrong thing, or worse yet, forgot one, there would be more than hell to pay.

Nick pulled up to the store, grabbed his jacket and his keys, and strode in, mumbling a thing or two which cannot be printed here. He tried to give himself a pep talk, but his heart wasn't in it. So he settled on just taking one item at a time and getting it right. If it took two hours, so be it. Of course, it would have helped had he not left the damn list in the car! His loud and clear "goddamnit" resonated across the parking lot as he marched out to his small SUV. He uttered one more expletive as he unlocked the vehicle, grabbed the paper, and then slammed the door so hard it sounded like a shot, causing the guy in the next parking space to nearly jump out of his seat. After flashing the man the dirtiest of looks, Nick headed back into the store, determined to get out before it got dark.

Meanwhile, in another galaxy....just a few miles away..... "Mom, what is it you want me to get you? I never seem to buy the right thing. What is the problem?"

"If you paid attention to what I was saying, we wouldn't have to have this conversation every time you go shopping. It's the least you could do for me. I gave birth to you, you know. Without me, there would be no you. Did I ever tell you that?"

"Only a few thousand times, only a few thousand times."

"There's no need to get fresh. Someday you will miss me and be sorry you didn't treat me better. Now, are you listening?"

"Yes, Ma, I'm listening. Go ahead."

"OK, it's actually very simple, Maria. I just need you to get me some food. It shouldn't be that hard. I don't eat that much. Is that asking too much?"

Maria took a breath. She and her mother had this same conversation many times before, and there was no use getting aggravated. It was just the way things were, so she put on her game face, paused, and as calmly as she could, answered in very measured tones.

"I always do your shopping for you. Just tell me what you need."

"My cereal, I need my cereal. It isn't that heavy. And you know what else I eat, right? You can get everything I need. But don't go getting those store brands. They are terrible. And you know my arm hurts. I can't really pick things up very well."

Despite her practice over the years, Maria couldn't help a slight grimace as she cringed a bit to keep from losing her temper. It was tough enough going shopping when she had a list. The line "you know what else I need" was a lose-lose situation. And sometimes the store brands were the only ones that fit what was needed. Good Lord. Her mother noticed the slight change in her daughter's demeanor, and, of course, had to make a comment.

"What's the matter, Maria, why are you so fresh to me? Just like everybody else. My friend hasn't called me in days. He doesn't care if I'm dead or alive. I think he's bipolar or something. He doesn't even want to see if I'm still alive. He's got some kind of mental condition."

"Ma, listen. He'll call. He always does. And he cares about you. If someone doesn't touch base with you every thirty seconds you think they've forgotten you. Just like with me. I call and come over as often as I can. And he's not bipolar!"

"Maria, why do you always take everyone else's side against your mother? Can't you agree with me one time? Just once I'd like to hear you say: 'Yeah, Mom, you're right, I know just what you mean.' Couldn't you do that, just one time? Did you hear me?"

There was really nothing her dutiful daughter could say that would have appeased her mother when she went in that direction, so Maria basically threw in the towel with a subdued "Yes, Ma, yes." But her mom was not quite finished.

"Can they deliver the food? Make sure you don't get the store brands. Did I ever tell you about Linder? She used to live around the corner from us. There's a story on every corner. Every corner. What happened to her?"

At just about the same time, Nick was going up and down the aisles in the food store trying to find the particular deodorant – brand and size – that his mother wanted. There must have been a hundred different smell protectors, as he often called them, but not the one she wanted. Wait, was that it, buried among the travel choices, all about thumbnail size?

Nick grabbed it and looked at the specifications which he could barely read. : It was two ounces more than what his mother had indicated. Well, close enough for government work as he used to say in high school. He grabbed the Secret, threw it in his cart, and started for the registers. He counted the items, fourteen, then double-checked the number on the list – fifteen. How was that possible? He did a quick inventory – Where the hell was the tuna fish? He knew he had gotten it because it had taken him a good ten minutes to get the right brand and number of ounces.

He could have sworn, which is what he did, that he had gotten it and put it in his cart. And he was right, he had, but he also had put it in the collapsible "shelf" in the front, the one with the big gaps that things could easily fall through, including, apparently, the ultra-small can of tuna. The canned fish aisle was at the far end of the store, but as he started back, he caught a glimpse of a shopping cart whose user was looking for something a few feet away. There, in the center of her cart, was another can of the elusive fish. He felt like a pickpocket as he grabbed it and headed for checkout...never a dull moment when dealing with his mother – and himself!

CHAPTER SEVEN

The Plane To Perdition

Newark Airport

"American Airlines flight non-stop to Los Angeles now boarding for first class passengers at Gate 11."

The two sisters had been at the airport for hours, and the call for their plane seemed almost too good to believe.

"Let's go, Mare. That's us." They had checked their bags earlier, but they seemed to have a whole storefront of carry-ons. Somehow they managed to get everything in hand, including their purses, which were big enough to hold a body and contained just about everything else. They made their way through – literally – swarms of people on their way to and from the planes. Had they been a bit younger NFL scouts would have been keeping an eye on them.

"Oh, excuse me, sir," Elizabeth apologized as a well-dressed businessman and his coffee went flying.

"Why you say you're sorry? That man stepped right in front of you?" her sister admonished her.

"I was just trying to be polite."

"You're too nice, Liz. Come on, we're going to miss our plane."

They were actually just a few steps away from the gate for their plane, but by the length of the line, it wouldn't be leaving anytime soon. The sisters plopped their bags down, and it was then that they realized how many people were ahead of them.

"We're gonna be here all morning, Liz."

"We've already been here all morning," her sister replied, exasperated, aggravated, and exhausted. "I'm tired. You wanna just go home?"

"Go home? You know how hard my daughter works at her stinking job so she can send us on a vacation? We can rest on the plane. Look, the line is moving."

It was indeed moving, albeit rather slowly. Of course, the tickets had to be checked, as did the bags and passengers. It was a long, laborious process, and it seemed interminable to the two ladies. But, lo and behold, three couples had been checked through, and the sisters were within earshot of the entrance. And then all hell seemed to break loose, as the volume of an animated conversation between someone and an airline official reverberated throughout the terminal.

There were two women together and there seemed to be some problem with their tickets. One of them was short and dressed casually, and the other one was a bit younger and thinner, and very professional looking. She was dressed to the nines. They looked like they were in their mid to late sixties and from their appearance, they could have been sisters. In fact, they were sisters, and one of them was going at it with the harried airline official, who was doing her best to be courteous and still do her job.

The talkative lady turned to her sister, who was aghast with embarrassment.

"See, Marica, we wait all this time, and now we got to wait some more. It's cause they don't like what we look like. It's cause we're Greek! Just like when I was in sixth grade and they wanted me to clean up because I was an immigrant."

"They wanted you to clean up because it was a home economics class, and that's what you were supposed to do."

The "gatekeeper" had had enough.

"LADIES! You can settle your family squabbles on your own. I've got a ton of people to get on this plane, so I will have to ask you to leave and come back at the proper time. Is that clear?"

Meanwhile, the Sicilian sisters had been taking all of this in, and their disposition was turning sour in a hurry.

"Look at those two women, holding everything up. We've been in line forever, and now they are making it even longer. What is wrong with them?"

"I don't know, Mare. Some people have no consideration."

Just then the shorter of the two at the beginning of the line let loose with a a string of expletives in Greek, for which she was quickly berated by her sister.

"Mable, please. People are turning their heads."

"I don't care. We waited all this time. We're at the front of the line. We're next. It's our turn."

The airline employee took it all in stride, and in fact, broke out into a smile. Calmly, she addressed the two Greek sisters.

"Ladies, you can say whatever you want, in Greek or any other language. But the fact of the matter is, you're in the right place at the wrong time. Now, if you'll excuse me....Next."

Marica grabbed her sister by the elbow and the two of them headed back toward the seats, Mable cursing all the way.

The two Sicilians didn't miss a trick. Marie turned to her sister with an "I knew it" look on her face.

"Did you hear that, Liz? Greeks. Always causing trouble. I knew it, I knew it.

Just like that damn Greek that works with my daughter, that Pappas. Always breaking the rules, always after something!"

Liz nodded in acquiescence as they found themselves at the front of the line.

"Hello, ladies," said the relieved airline rep. "May I see your tickets?"

Marie and Elizabeth rummaged through their bags, and finally came out with their paperwork.

"Here, Liz, I'll give it to her," Marie offered. "Might as well try to make it easier for her cause she's had a rough time this morning with those damn Greeks."

Liz gave her paperwork to her sister, who couldn't resist a shot at the two previous sisters as she handed them to the woman behind the counter.

"I'll bet you are glad to be rid of those two. What a scene they made!"

The airline official couldn't resist a small smile as she looked at the tickets and handed them back.

"I'm sorry ladies. You're going to have to return in a bit. This line is for first class ticket holders only!"

CHAPTER EIGHT

Greeks and Sicilians

Marie and Liz managed to get back on the line when the call came over for the coach passengers, but the Greek duo was nowhere to be seen, and Marie was hoping they were on some other plane, or no other plane, or had gone home. She was not one to forgive and forget, but as she boarded the plane her thoughts did manage to turn back to the trip and their means of conveyance. She was not fond of flying, and neither was Elizabeth, a feeling attested to by the appearance of their rosary beads before they even entered the airplane. The flight attendant at the door nodded knowingly as the two ladies, their bags, and their beads paraded by.

"Aisle 14, seats A and B, ladies. Enjoy the flight," she said warmly.

The two sisters made their way toward their seats, reading the number of each row as they passed it. They finally reached their destination, and now the question became where to put their carry-ons and who was going to get which seat. There was a whole line of passengers behind them of, course, all waiting impatiently to get themselves settled. But they seemed to be oblivious to the plight of their fellow travelers as they debated who and what would go where.

"You wanna sit by a window, Mare? I know you like to see outside. Oh, this bag doesn't fit here What we gonna do?"

"Why don't you sit near the window, Liz. I just sit in the middle. It's OK."

"OK, thanks, Mare," Liz replied, relieved that the seats had been worked out. Of course, there were a couple of hitches to be resolved.

"But wait, Mare, what if someone sits next to you that you don't like?"

"Don't worry. I just turn and talk to you. It's OK."

Elizabeth still had a rather large bag on her lap in addition to her purse, but her sister sat down before that situation was settled, Of course, Marie had a bag and purse of her own. The ladies and their "luggage," all piled into two seats were quite a sight. It made stuffing a phone booth from the Twenties seem like a walk in the park.

Not to worry, though; Marie appeared to have an easy solution.

"Here, Liz, give me your stuff. I'll put it on the seat next to me. I got my stuff there. We'll just put them all on the seat. It looks like no one's sitting there, and the plane is almost full.."

Marie was correct with one of her conclusions. The plane was filling up, but the seat next to her was supposed to be occupied;but the passenger and her companion were late. Of course, the flight attendant wouldn't have allowed their belongings to stay on the seat, but she hadn't made her walk through yet, mostly because there seemed to be a bit of a rhubarb brewing near the door. Apparently, there were two late arriving passengers, and one of them was "fit to be tied," an expression she kept using over and over.

"If they had let us check in before, we would have already been on the plane," she said to her companion, who was also her sister.

"It was our fault. That line was for first-class passengers. If you hadn't insisted on calling your daughter, we would have been sitting already," her flustered companion countered.

"Well, if they had any pay phones in this damn airport, we wouldn't have had to go searching all over the place."

"Mable, I told you that we wouldn't find any. Everybody has cell phones now."

"Well, good thing I asked that woman at the car rental place. Now I don't have to worry about Jo Ann. Now that I hear her voice."

"You told the woman it was an emergency."

"Marica, it was an emergency. We gonna be three thousand miles away. I just want to be sure she will be OK."

"She does have a husband, you know."

"That good-for-nothing George? He can't even take care of himself."

Luckily, the two Sicilian sisters had closed their eyes; they were vigorously working on their worry beads as they focused on the imminent liftoff of the plane. They were able to get a brief respite from their one-sided feud with the Greek sisters since they didn't hear or see the altercation just a few feet away. But that was about to change! The flight attendant, who had been the same one taking the tickets just a short time before, had long since run out of patience.

"Ladies, could you take your family squabble to your seats, please? We will be taking off shortly, and there are several things the crew needs to do to prepare. Please come in and enjoy your flight...or fight. as the case may be."

"Ella, Melpo," the younger one pleaded. "Come on."

Mable did come on, though it took them a while to walk to their seats, since she stopped every step to berate the phone company, the airlines, and mostly her son-in-law. It took them a good five minutes to walk about forty feet, which was probably fortunate since the sound of the air fan and the engines warming up had put the two Sicilian sisters on the edge of the land of nod. They actually looked like a couple of kittens curled up in a basket, as Marie's head was resting on her sister's shoulder.

The Greeks finally arrived at their seats, only to find Marie's and Liz's luggage piled in a heap. Luckily one of the crew was just returning from the men's room, and before Mable could raise a big fuss, he threw them up into the overhead compartments along with the bags Mable and Marica had on them. As often happens, Marie's doze incorporated what was actually going on into her dream, and she poked her sister to wake her up.

"Liz, Liz, the Greeks stole our bags. The Greeks stole our bags!"

She turned toward the aisle only to see Mable sitting there, for once just minding her own business. Of course, Mable knew nothing about the Sicilians' animosity toward her and her sister, or the supposed theft of luggage. She looked at Marie and was about to introduce herself when the flight attendant came walking by to do the seatbelt check.

"Ladies, we are about to take off. Please fasten your seatbelts."

The tension was broken a bit, as Liz and Marie got them on easily, but Mable's was all twisted and gnarled, and she was starting to fume. Marie laughed good-naturedly as she offered to help. Her fellow passenger accepted her offer quite readily.

"Thank you so much. Bad enough my sister makes me wear the damn things in her car. She drives so slow that even if we hit something nothing would happen. My name is Mable."

Almost against her will, Marie began to warm up to this lady, nationality notwithstanding. She did seem friendly and down to earth, and it would be a long flight Might as well make friends. Besides, there was something about her that seemed to resonate with the Sicilian. It would turn out that there were quite a few things they had in common.

"You know, whoever is running this airline should be locked up – the way they treat their passengers," Mable began out of the blue. "You know my sister and I got all the way to the front of the line, and then they kicked us out. Just because we don't got first-class seats. We waited all that time. It would have killed them to let us come onto the damn plane?"

Marie broke into a big belly laugh.

"So that's what happened to the two of you? That's why you were yelling at them?"

"Yeah, and my sister, over there(she points across the aisle)...she gets all mad cause I raise my voice. They're lucky I didn't take off my shoe and smack that woman in the head."

"I know what you mean. The same thing happened to us. They waited till we were all the way in the front, and then they tell us. Terrible."

"I think maybe they don't like Mediterranean people," Liz added. "My name is Liz, by the way. Pleased to meet you."

"Endaxi," Mable replied in Greek. "I said that to my sister, and she got all upset. I know when people don't like me. I'll have you know we're from Cephalonia, the biggest island in the Ionian Sea. Where you from?"

"Well," Marie answered. "We're from an even bigger island – SICILY"

"Sicilians, Greeks....it's all good," Mable exulted.

A light went on in Marie's head. Where had she heard that before?

Just then another light went on, as the plane was ready for takeoff. A voice came over the speakers informing everyone to be sure their seats were in the upright position, their tables were secure, and their seat belts were on. The airliner began to taxi into position for takeoff. Mable glanced over at her sister, who was all set to go - of course. She smiled back at her to indicate that everything was OK on her side of the plane. An odd couple if there ever was one.

"My sister. She got mad at me cause I want to call Jo Ann to see if she is all right. Not my fault there's no more pay phones anywhere. I just want to be sure she is all right. We're gonna be gone a whole week to the other side of the country. What's so bad that I call her? I ask you?"

Marie was listening intently to Mable's narrative.

"Mable, who is Jo Ann?"

"Oh, she's my daughter. But . you know what Marica says – that's my sister's name - she says to me why I'm worried, she has a husband. Jo Ann, she means. Jo Ann has a husband. He will take care of her while we're gone. . Her husband, George. George the pushover and pain in the ass. He's gonna take care of her? George? Don't make me laugh. Only a mother knows. You have children, Marie? You love them but they break your heart. Why does she has to marry that idiot? His family's not even from Cephalonia. They're from near Sparta, somewhere. A mainland Greek. They're different. You have children?"

This woman could talk!! Marie could barely keep up with all the details and questions. But Mable wasn't finished by a long shot.

"All the damn Greeks in Washington Heights, she has to marry him! When she was going out with him he was always late. Always, you hear me? He doesn't have a damn watch to tell the time? I yell at him every time. You know what he does? He smiles. What kind of an idiot smiles at you when you yell at him? You'd think she would listen to her mother?"

By this time both Marie and Liz were captivated by Mable's rapid excoriation of her son-in-law.

"Did you tell her not to marry him?" Liz asked.

"Of course, what do you think? I tell her next time he comes for her I gonna lock the door. I wish I did. He ruined my hallway!"

"He did what?" Marie and Liz asked in unison.

"In those years, I lived in New York, in apartment. Fourth floor. There is a long hall leading to the other rooms, and I just had it painted. Not just painted, but stencil put on. You know how much that cost?"

Marica of course had heard this story many times and started to smile in anticipation.

"It's not funny!" Mable exclaimed as she shot a look at her sister. "I had a beautiful stencil put on the walls. See, the hall is not wide. And that damn George comes in carrying some packages with his elbow sticking out, and he erases the whole damn stencil all the way down the hall. I could have killed him. I told my daughter to break up with him right there. Does she listen? Of course not. And you want to know what he does? He starts laughing."

By this time Marie and Liz and Marica were all laughing, as were the people in the seats in front and back of the excited narrator. Almost on cue the engines suddenly picked up in intensity and the plane began to accelerate for takeoff. The Sicilians were laughing so hard they almost forgot about their worry beads, Marica had her hand over her eyes to cover the tears of laughter, and Mable just shook her head as she thought of George!

Everything went smoothly aeronautically, and soon they were at cruising speed and altitude. The pilot came on with the customary welcome and the flight attendants were seeing to the comfort of their charges. Mable broke the silence first. Shocker!

"So, you have children Marie?"

"Yeah. Three. My one daughter lives in California."

"Oh, so you going to go see her when we get out there and stay with her?"

"Ha! See her? Stay with her? She's not even gonna be around. I get a phone call just before we leave, and she tells me they are going away for a week or two. Did you hear me? A week or two! *Now* she has to go away? How often I get to California? Kids, they don't care about you at all. I mean, since my husband passed away, that's all I got. I give birth to them and they don't care if I live or die. I fly three thousand miles and they go away. It's awful to be old and be alone."

All the while Mable was nodding her head vigorously.

"I know, I know. We both widows, too, me and Marica. You kill yourself with worry and raise them and feed them and then they grow up and they don't care what you do. But I still worry. Then I try to call my daughter to see if everything is all right, and we almost miss the damn plane"

"I told my sister we should take the train. We could see something while we go out there – farms and cities and mountains. Now what do we see....clouds and sun and more clouds."

The other side of the plane chimed in.

"Mable, we went over all this. With the plane we're there in six hours, and we have more time to do things."

"My sister thinks she's so smart. Well, she is smart. But she's not always right." The "smart" sister just shook her head and went back to her magazine.

"I know what you mean," Marie exclaimed. "Just like my daughter. She's smart, too, but she's not as smart as she thinks she is. And she needs to treat me better."

Mable nodded her head. "I guess you're mad that she's not going to be there to see you."

"No, not that one. My other daughter, Maria. She teaches English in high school I think she read every book ever written, and she knows a lot of stuff. But she should still be considerate and treat me with respect. Don't you think?"

"Yeah, your daughter Maria sounds like my nephew. He's a pretty good guy, but sometimes he's too smart for his own good. I mean, he went to this fancy college, and he winds up being a teacher. He has a lot of kids and no money. Well, I gotta say this....he gave us this trip for a Christmas present. That was nice, I gotta admit."

"Hey, you know what's funny....that's why we're going to California. Maria gave this vacation to *us* as a Christmas present, too. And she paid for a cab to take us to the airport this morning. She got no money, either."

"I know, Marie. Those damn schools don't pay them shit," Mable exclaimed. Then the elder Greek started to chuckle and then segued into a rolling belly laugh.

"What's so funny, Mable?" Liz asked.

"I just thought of something! I think they gave us these trips just to get the hell rid of us!"

"You're right, you damn Greek!" Marie yelled out loud with a coast-to-coast smile. "You are so right!"

The three of them would have done the Three Stooges proud! Meanwhile, Marica, or Ricky, as most of her family called her, bore just a trace of a smile as she relaxed a bit with her eyes closed and her mind somewhere else as the plane streamed along with a quiet hum.

The two sisters could not have been any more different. They were both born in Cephalonia (which was, by the way, the largest Greek island in the Ionian Sea). They came to America as children with their mother and father. Marica was seven years younger, bright, and well educated. Her sister was not fond of school. People were her forte; she was outgoing and sociable and full of stories. When she would come out to visit from New York City out to Jersey, a forty-minute ride, she could relate the life history of just about everyone on the bus. She was also outspoken and not afraid to challenge anyone about anything. Just ask the flight attendant. It was little wonder that she and Marie hit it off.

"Hey, Marica," Mable called to her sister. "I want you to meet my friends. Wake up."

"I was just resting my eyes, I wasn't sleeping."

"Whatever," Mable observed. "Hey Marie, Liz, this is my sister, Marica. Very nice, very smart. I embarrass her all the time."

"Well, not *all* the time," came the quick response from the younger Greek. "Pleased to meet you, ladies."

There were smiles all around as the foursome got better acquainted.

"Your sister was telling us about her daughter and her son-in-law. He sounds like a character!"

"Yeah, I caught the destroy the wall story," Marica replied.

"Did that really happen?" Liz asked.

"What, you think I'm lying?" Mable scowled, with a big smile thrown in.

"No, no," Liz protested. "It just sounds like something from a movie or TV show."

"If they ever made a TV show about George they would call it *THE IDIOT..*"

Everyone laughed, and Marica felt obliged to come to the defense of both her sister and her beleaguered son-in-law. Still laughing, she assured their new Mediterranean acquaintances that the wall incident was indeed true.

"...and George, yes, he is somewhat of a character, but he has the sweetest disposition of anyone you'd ever want to meet. Can you imagine having my sister as your mother-in-law?"

But Mable wasn't quite finished with her son-in-law – actually, she would never be finished, but she was on a roll and she wasn't about to stop now.

"Listen, Marica, don't put it all on me. How about that time when he knocked all your figures off the speakers? I don't think you were so pleased with that, were you!"

Marica nodded her head back and forth and then broke into uncontrollable laughter, which was rare for her. She leaned across the aisle and directed her comments right at the

Sicilians so they could get the full effect of what she was about to say.

"So, ladies, it was Christmas Day, and George and Jo Ann came over for Christmas dinner. Now, try and picture this: when you come into my hall there is a large archway on the left into the living room. Book ending the entrance were two big, round speakers on the floor. My son had brought them home from when he was in the Army, and we had about six or seven porcelain Christmas decorations on each one."

Mable jumped in. "Also, you gotta know this: my sister's house is the cleanest spot on the face of the earth. Nothing is out of place. You could eat off the floor."

The younger sister gave Mable a quick dirty look.

"Well, it's true, Marica. Go ahead, finish."

"So George comes in with an armload of long Christmas presents, and as he turns to go into the living room, he knocks over all the knick-knacks on one of the speakers."

Everyone yelled "GEORGE!"

"And as he turns to see what he did, he knocks all the pieces off the other speaker." The Sicilians were crying they were laughing so hard, and Mable was doubled over in hysterics. Even Marica, who was shaking her head vigorously as she remembered George's "two-step," and couldn't keep the belly laughs away.

But the story wasn't quite over as Mable continued...

"And then, after everyone takes their coats off, my stupid son-in-law sits down on the couch and my sister brings him some hot egg nog. Now, in front of the couch is a marble table that must weigh two tons, and it's like new and my sister's pride and joy. There are at least six coasters right in front of that knucklehead George, and what does he do? He puts the HOT cup of egg nog right on the table. I thought Marica was gonna kill him!"

Liz was beside herself. "Listen, listen...my sister has a table just like that... marble with gold edging, right? Right?"

The Greek sisters nodded in unison.

Marie picked up the baton...."Yes, I do. And just last week, when my daughter Maria was over, she did the same thing, only with hot espresso coffee!"

"They have no regard for precious possessions," Marica stated matter of factly.! "And if you try to protect your things because they're valuable..."

"Or mean something to you," Marie threw in....

"Or BOTH!" Mable exploded.

"Then they say you're too fussy or too picky or just a pain in the ass!!" said Liz as she shook her head vigorously and rocked with a vengeance.

"Our kids have no idea how hard it is to keep beautiful things in good condition over many years. They're spoiled," added Mable.

"AMEN!!" echoed the "fearsome foursome" in unison!

Their unanimity was interrupted briefly by the flight attendant...

"Ladies and gentlemen, the movie for this flight will be starting in a little while. We have headsets for those of you who want to view it. I would recommend it, because it's funny and yet pretty true to life. It's a Steve Martin movie called *PARENTHOOD..*"

"Oh, I never see that one. How about you, Liz, you ever see that movie? You, Mable?"

The two ladies shook their heads to indicate that they had not.

"How about you, Marica, you ever see it?" Mable wondered.

"No, I haven't, but I like Steve Martin."

"*PARENTHOOD*. I bet it's about kids that don't listen to their parents, just like *MARTY*," Marie observed emphatically.

Marica was quick to agree: "*MARTY,* now there's a great movie."

CHAPTER NINE

To Sleep...For Sure to Dream

The four ladies were looking forward to watching the movie and were getting comfortable both in their seats and in their conversations.

"So, Marie, you see this movie before?" Liz asked.

"No, but Maria was telling me about it. Mable, you ever see it?"

"No, but like you said, Steve Martin is funny. He was good in *CHEAPER BY THE DOZEN,*" Mable answered.

"How about *SATURDAY NIGHT LIVE?*" Marica's voice bounced across from her solitary seat. "He was so funny in that!"

"Yeah, yeah," Marie echoed. "I loved that bit he did with Belushi about the Greeks owning the diner!"

"No Coke, Peksi. Czeeseburger, Czeeseburger," Liz chimed in.

Mable was doubled over laughing.

"They sure had the accent down good, especially not being Greek!"

As the credits started to roll, the eyes of the four women started to slowly fade, and soon they were all either asleep or in that twilight stage where you're half and half. Of course, Hamlet was right on the money when he said "to sleep perchance to dream...," because they did both as the film provided some sound sleeping background and the plane wound its way across the country....

Union, NJ – Ten Years Earlier....

"Hi, Aunt Mable, when did you get here? I didn't know you were coming out. Did you walk here all the way from the bus stop?"

"No, your father picked me up. I called him yesterday. I guess he didn't tell you? Well, whatever. I thought I'd stay a couple days and give your old man a break from cooking. Where's your brother?"

Mable was talking to her niece, a senior in high school. She had a brother who was a junior in college, and they, along with their widowed father, lived in a modest but comfortable home in a suburb about twenty-five miles from New York. Mable would come out to visit every so often, usually staying with Marica, who lived only a few blocks away. But this time she decided to stay with her brother-in-law and his two kids.

No matter where she was, Mable would assess the situation and take charge, especially where family was concerned.

"So, where's your brother?"

"He's got a rehearsal with his wedding band." Her brother, John, was a very talented singer and trumpet player. He was going to college but had a band as a sideline. They played for weddings and proms and parties. And they were good.

Just then Cathy sneezed, and she wiped her eyes, which were beginning to run a bit.

"You better take care of that cold!" Mable warned her. "It could develop into something worse, and you don't want to be sick your senior year."

Cathy assured her aunt that it wasn't anything to worry about and that it was mostly allergies anyway. They were about to go toe to toe on this when luckily the doorbell rang. It was Tony, a friend of her brother's. He and John had been good friends since grammar school, and he was almost like a member of the family. Mable had a bit of a scowl cross her face when she saw who it was because she didn't want her niece to get too "friendly" with him. He was a good guy and really very nice, but he wasn't in college and that was a no-no as far as Mable was concerned. He was on his way to work at the garage and just wanted to drop off a book he had borrowed, so it was a quick hello and goodbye. But Mable had to get a shot in any way.

"You know, your father told me that he doesn't work on the car engines, just the outside of the cars," she threw at her niece.

"Aunt Mable, I'm not gonna marry him; we're just friends," Cathy answered, as she put on a jacket.

"Where are you going?"

"To Nick's game."

Her cousin was a high school baseball coach, and they had a state tournament game just a few miles away.

"Are you crazy? With that cold you have? You see how cool it is out. You're gonna get pneumonia!"

"Aunt Mable, this jacket is warm. I'll be fine."

"And I'm telling you not to go. If you go I hope I get hit by a bus!"

As she tossed and turned in her sleep, Mable grabbed a hold of Marie by the arm and shouted loud enough for the stewardess to come check to see if everything was OK.

"I hope I get hit by a bus."

With a smile the attendant assured Mable and the now awake and startled Marie that there was no chance of that happening while they were in the air.

The quizzical look on Marie's face warranted an explanation and her new traveling companion told her all about the incident with her niece, who did NOT go to the game.

Marie nodded vigorously and patted Mable on her knee several times.

"I know just what you mean, Mable. I know just what you mean!"

"And she had a liking for that friend of her brother's – she wasn't fooling me. I mean, he's not a bad kid, but he's no genius either. He'll probably have to work for someone else his whole life. He doesn't have the brains to go to college or the spunk to be his own boss someday. You know?" She looked to her left and found Marie to be in a bit of a world of her own. "You OK?"

"Huh? Yeah, I'm fine. I just started thinking about my husband, God rest his soul. He had his own business, and he killed himself working. What a guy."

"What kind of business was it?" the Greek lady asked.

"He had a hardware store. HARRY'S HARDWARE."

"HARRY'S HARDWARE??" Mable inquired with astonishment. "You don't mean in New Jersey, do you?"

"Yeah, Jersey. Petersville, near the port. Do you know it?"

"Know it? We used to live around the block from it growing up. My father used to go in there all the time."

"My God, this is unbelievable. Liz, did you hear that?"

By this time Elizabeth had awakened and did indeed hear the conversation.

"You know, a lot of people we know – they started out 'down the port,' as people would say. They say it like it was something bad. But I liked it. It was cozy and friendly and everyone knew each other. Best part of Elizabeth, if you ask me."

Marie was a bit taken aback since her sister usually didn't go on and on like that.

But she nodded in agreement, as did Mable, who continued where Liz left off...

"Yeah, that's where we lived when we first came to America. Most of our neighbors were Greek, though there were quite a few Italians and Polish as well. Yeah, that was a nice neighborhood all right. But then we moved after a few years. I guess my father wanted to be closer to where he worked, or maybe it was the school? I don't know."

"Mable, what did your father do?"

"He had a restaurant, what else would a Greek do? It was a small one, but they served great food. POP'S PLACE was the name."

"On Orchard Avenue, right?" Marie interjected. "My husband used to eat lunch there every day, and he would bring home what was left over. Your father served some big portions."

"At home, too," Mable said laughing, as she patted her belly.

The jovial trip down memory lane was suddenly interrupted by the captain's voice – "Ladies and gentlemen, we are about two hours from Los Angeles, and we've just been alerted about some turbulence a few minutes ahead. It's nothing to be concerned about, but just as a precaution, we'd like everyone to fasten their seat belts, as the signs indicate."

The warning "bell" and the seat belt sign were in synch with the captain.

"Shit, I knew we should have taken a goddamn train," Mable shouted, as she did a quick right face with her head directed at Marica, who tried to reassure her sister by staying calm and keeping her voice very matter-of-fact.

"He said it was nothing to be concerned about."

"If there's nothing to be concerned about why is everyone on the plane acting VERY concerned, huh?"

"Yeah, damned right!" Marie added, as she quickly blessed

herself – followed closely by her sister. Mable was already on her second go 'round with her fingers flying across her chest the requisite three times.

In the midst of all the turmoil and fear, Elizabeth had a question for their Cephalonian aisle mate.

"Mable, I've often wondered why Greeks bless themselves three times, and from right to left, rather than left to right, and only once, like Catholics do it."

Mable's face turned from panic to deliberation, as she looked up and thought and thought. The two Sicilians were waiting on the edge of their seats, literally, for her reply.

"Well, ladies, first of all, we say 'Cross' instead of 'Bless,' and we've been going right to left three times for close to two thousand years. Why do we do it that way? IT BEATS THE HELL OUT OF ME!!"

The three of them burst into gales of laughter, and even the solemn sister across the aisle cracked a smile. They never did hit any turbulence, at least in the air...

CHAPTER TEN

Meanwhile Back in Jersey

Mondays were rarely really good school days, and this was no exception. It was cold and what the weather channel would call "partly sunny," although the sun made the "partly" sound more like "barely." It was pretty much a typical March day in Jersey, but another downside if you had cafeteria duty was that none of the kids would eat their lunch outside, and it also cut down on the students opting to walk into town to grab a sandwich or coffee. So the lunch room was pretty much standing room only. It was also mid-marking period, which meant that if you were a teacher, all your grades had to be up to date, and if you were a student, there were deadlines that meant business. Maria had just been notified that she was to be observed on Tuesday, and it would be during what she called her "all or nothing" class because it seemed like they were either great or awful. Just what she needed – not knowing what to expect. After thirty years of teaching she had learned to roll the dice, and with the punches, but having her supervisor observe a more consistent class would have been nice. Plus she was behind on a few of the things she had to grade – and now this. She stormed into the cafeteria to find Nick among the missing. Where the hell was he? Of all the goddamn days to be out.

Nick wasn't "out" in the literal sense, though he was not "in" in the literal sense either. He had taken a half a personal day to drop his mother and aunt at the airport, and he was just entering the parking lot when he heard the bell sound, signaling the start of lunch. Shit. He hadn't told Maria he would be out in the morning because he figured he'd be back in plenty of time. Dumb. Of course, if he had her cell phone number, he could call her, but he didn't. Dumber. Now he would have to face what he assumed would be her death stare scowl. Dumbest. He screeched into a parking spot and made a run for the door, praying that what he had heard was the warning bell, and not the late bell. All the close spots had been taken, so he had to sprint a good sixty yards while listening for the second bell that would be at least a reprieve. It never came....because it had already sounded. He was a good ten minutes late when he burst upon the scene, mumbling every apology he could think of.

Maria had actually calmed down a bit by the time Nick came panting over to their table, but she figured she'd play the situation for all it was worth as she dialed up a face that would have frozen Mount Vesuvius.

"Sorry, Maria. I thought I'd make it back in time. I hadn't counted on the detours or Monday morning traffic." She was looking right at him, face to face, nose to nose, about six inches between them, and not a crease or an eyelash moved even a centimeter. She was biting her tongue to keep from bursting out with a rolling laugh, but she was a master of subterfuge, and Nick was literally petrified as the sweat started to run down the back of his neck, which was as tight as a drum.

The silence was finally broken by a tight-lipped, terse question that got right to the point "Where the hell were you??"

"Newark Airport."

"Newark Airport?"

"Yeah."

"Why didn't you just get on a plane while you were there? It would have been nice if you had told me on Friday. The principal's already been here twice wondering why *you* weren't here. I don't get paid to cover for you, nor to run this damn lunch by myself! Shape up, man!"

Maria had him exactly where she wanted. Just pick a metaphor, and that's where he was: *behind the eight ball; up shit's creek; strike two; not a leg to stand on...and on...and on....!*

To make matters worse, the principal walked in. It was in reality his first trip that day, but Nick thought it was his third, and he began a string of abject apologies that would have been confusing even if he had had his facts straight.

"Sorry, you missed me before, Mr. Morgan. I had to go to my car to get some manipulatives for this afternoon's classes, and also the software for my "Back To The Past" computer project for my history class.

This was all too much for the Sicilian. She had never heard Nick use the words "software" or "manipulatives" in his life – and with good reason, because he *had* never used them. She was laughing up such a storm inside that her eyes were tearing so much that even Morgan noticed.

"Are you OK, Maria?"

"Allergies," she managed to stutter.

The headman got a quizzical look on his face. It was too early for allergies, but he decided to let it slide since he was still trying to figure out what Nick meant by his apparently sincere apology. So, like all leaders from Caesar to the Queen, his reply was a statement that had nothing to do with anything.

"OK, then, catch you both later. Have a good day."

Maria could finally let her laughter go, and did it ever go, that is. Of course, she wasn't quite finished with Nick, so she used the principal as the pretense for her frivolity.

"Man, he can be a real idiot at times...."

Nick nodded in agreement.

"Just like you, you damn Greek. Now, would you be so kind as to explain what you were doing at Newark Airport on a Monday morning, and why you didn't tell me about it??"

Well, at least she was speaking to him now, so Nick figured he was slightly better off than he had been. He was still not out of the woods as the saying goes. In fact, he was pretty sure he didn't know the way out of the woods, so he figured he might as well stick with the truth, spoken in his subservient, apologetic, "mea culpa" tone, which he had become pretty good at.

"I was dropping my mother and my aunt off to catch their flight to California, and I meant to tell you Friday, but I was preoccupied with trying to catch up with my grades and I forgot all about it. Then this morning I figured I'd be back with plenty of time.to spare. Don't be mad, OK? Please?"

Maria cocked her head slightly and broke out into what appeared to be a smile, tiny as it was.

"Was that today they were leaving?"

As traumatized as he was, Nick just couldn't let a straight line like that go to waste.

"I sure as hell hope so. Otherwise, they're going to have to hitch a ride back!"

His partner's reply was a swat on the head with a stack of papers she had been reading.

"Guess who else is flying to California this morning, you dunderhead..."

Nick opened his mouth and was about to speak when she headed him off....

"And don't say 'lots of people'...you Greek clown!" Her tone had changed, and he could now see the clearing at the edge of the woods.

"Wait! Don't tell me your mom and aunt were going out this morning as well?"

"Uh, yeah. I told you last week they were leaving Monday! For a smart guy, you certainly do some dumb things."

Nick was about to say to her that there were a lot of "Mondays," but he thought he'd better leave it at that. She had told him, and he had totally forgotten all about it.

"Sorry, Maria. Yeah, you did tell me. Did you drive them out?"

"Nope. Cab. I couldn't take the drawn-out goodbyes I knew would happen if I drove them.."

Nick was surprised, and said so: "You sprung for a cab?"

"Hey, it was well worth it!"

Nick suddenly had an epiphany....

"You don't suppose they're on the same flight, do you? And that they somehow meet?"

"Hmm....I guess there's a possibility that they're on the same plane. But there must be a half dozen flights going out to the coast over the course of the morning, so chances are they're on a different one. But even if they're on the same plane, there have to be two hundred people on board, right ? What are the chances they'd run into each other? Believe me, if our mothers and aunts, respectively, meet up with each other, I'm pretty sure I'll hear about it." She didn't know it then, but Maria was foreshadowing some imminent earth-shaking events that were huge even for California.

CHAPTER ELEVEN

The City of Angels...??

The four Mediterranean Mothers were in different stages of consciousness as the plane ate up the miles across the country, passing over the Rockies and fast approaching California. Marica was looking out the window in between several cat-naps, while her sister had taken out some crocheting and was counting and looping and humming an old Greek song. Liz was out cold, but Marie was awake enough to watch Mable with a great deal of interest and admiration.

"Wow, that's really good. What are you making, if I may ask?"

"Just a shawl for my sister over there. She likes what I do, and it's my way of saying thanks to her. Even though I'm the older one she has done a lot for me, you know!"

Marie nodded her head.

"Yeah, we're like that, too. We always have each other's backs," Marie added as she pointed toward Liz, who was totally in the land of dreams.

Their sisterly admiration society was interrupted by the voice of the pilot indicating that they were about an hour away from the airport, and if anyone had anything to attend to this might be a good time to do it.

Marie decided to go for a final restroom visit, which gave Mable and Elizabeth the opportunity to talk a bit. Marica was resting ('sleeping'), so it was just the two of them for a few minutes.

Elizabeth looked over at her companion and smiled.

"You know, Mable, you're not fooling me with all that huff and gruff stuff. Know what I mean?"

"Not really, Liz, no." And she didn't. Well, sort of didn't.

Liz smiled and shook her head. "As my niece Maria would say: 'Please....' In fact, you remind me of her a little. She's tough as nails on the outside, but not on the inside – although, she doesn't want anyone to know it. Like you."

Mable was touched by what she felt was a compliment, which was how it was intended.

"Well, thank you. It's hard being the older one. You have to be tough, especially with my sister. Like I said, she's smart, but she still needs someone to look after her!"

Then she added with a chuckle – "Know what I mean?"

"I know exactly what you mean, Mable. Exactly."

For probably the first time in their lives, the two new friends high-fived, just as Marie was making her way back to her seat.

"So, talking about me, ladies?"

Mable couldn't resist.   "It's not always about you, Marie," which was really Liz's line, but what the heck!

The landing at LA Ex was smooth and uneventful, and the four of them approached it in the way most befitting each one's personality. Elizabeth and Marie worked their worry beads to a shiny luster, their eyes closed, of course, with prayers emanating from their faces like water over rapids. Marica calmly looked out the window, although she might have done a quick, almost imperceptible cross as the wheels touched down. Mable? Clutching the arm rest as if her life depended on it, which to her seemed it did. Along the way she recited at record speed three "Our Fathers," two in Greek and one in English, and capped everything off, once the plane had come to a complete stop, with loud applause and a kiss for the aisle between the seats. The Sicilians pointed to her with respect, Marica shook her head, and the rest of the passengers gave her a standing ovation. Welcome to California!!

The ladies said their goodbyes to the crew of the plane, and whether it was because they provided somewhat of a diversion during the flight, or the personnel of the airline were glad to be rid of them – or a little bit of both – there were sincere smiles all around. The "Four Musketeers" had no problem finding the proper conveyor for their luggage, and they picked it up as easily as if they had been seasoned travelers. Of course, not to belittle native Californians, especially those who live in LA, their laid-back demeanor was no match for four tigers from New Jersey. They had their bags, a porter, and a taxi quicker than you could say Italians and Greeks. They were all a bit gassed from the trip, but they decided to meet the next day for dinner and talk about their first day and whatever else might come up. The taxi dropped the Mediterraneans at their respective hotels, but not before there had been hugs and kisses all around, even from the usually prim and proper Marica. So far, so good on this "Widows' Odyssey"!!

Their hotels were just a few miles from each other, and before they said their farewells, phone numbers, addresses, and seemingly enough information to complete a mortgage application changed hands several times. Everything got straightened out to everyone's satisfaction, and they were all looking forward to having a good time on Tuesday, their first full day in the City Of Angels. They promised to get in touch and make arrangements for dinner to rekindle their newly formed friendship and tell about their first day in California.

The four women were all pretty beat as they settled into

their hotel rooms. The Greeks were on the eighth floor and they had a great view of the city, which Mable absolutely loved as it reminded her both of her current apartment in New Jersey and her residence for forty years in Washington Heights, New York. Her sister took a peek out the window in between unpacking and putting her wardrobe in its proper place, which drew a comment from her older sister.

"A place for everything, and everything in its place, huh Marica?!"

"I just like to be organized. Aren't you going to unpack?"

"Maybe in a while. I want to call my daughter and tell her we got in all right. You want me to tell her to call Nick?"

"Might as well," Marica answered. "Nick's probably at work now, and he's never thrilled when I call him there. In fact, he's not thrilled when I call him anywhere." she said with a sigh. "Yeah, just ask Jo to call him later."

"Hey, he did give us this trip, right? That was nice," Mable responded as she fiddled with the phone in their room. A few misdials and several expletives later she was able to dial her daughter's number – only to get her voicemail. "Damn it all. Her stupid answering machine. Ugh! It was better in the old days with the old phone."

"Yeah, but at least now you can leave her a message," her sister reflected.

"I guess you're right"...."Hey, Jo, it's Ma. We got here OK. Give your cousin a call and let him know, and call me back when you get a chance. I left you all the Information on the hotel and everything. Love you. Ma."

She did love her daughter, and the feeling was mutual, although for a very long time the loads of guilt and mistrust had taken their toll. Jo Ann felt that her mother had been impossible to deal with and live with as she was growing up. Well, that's a story for another day, or at least another chapter, but suffice it to say that while most of the parents of Jo Ann's friends were somewhat controlling, Mable made a prison warden seem like a soft touch. She wouldn't let Jo Ann go to her prom, and Jo once told Nick that while she was growing up she hated her mother. Ah, but that was long ago, right...

The younger sister, serious as she usually was, did like to kid her older sibling when she got the chance, and this seemed like an easy one.

"You know, Melpo, you must be slipping as you're getting older. I'm just a bit disappointed in you!"

"What the hell you talking about??" To say this caught her off guard would be like a reverse hyperbole.

"Well, under normal circumstances, or perhaps when you were a bit younger, you would have gotten the skinny on just about everyone on that plane. Wha' happened?"

The usually stoic younger sister was loosening up. Actually, she would let her guard down once in a while, and maybe the trip to the coast was just what she needed.

"You know what happened as well as the next person. We ran into those two damn Sicilians and I couldn't shut that Marie up," Mable answered with a wide grin.

"She's probably saying the same thing about you right now."

Their analysis was interrupted by the phone.

"I got it," Mable volunteered. "Probably Jo Ann."

She grabbed the phone, assuming it was her daughter.

"Hey, just wanted to let you know we got here all right."

The answer was just a bit unexpected.

"I know you did, you damn Greek..We just dropped you off at your hotel. You getting senile on me, Melpomeni?"

"Marie?"

"Very good. I'm proud of you...."

"You think you're funny, huh?" Mable answered with a barrel-like laugh. "Well, you're not so funny!"

"We were just talking about you, you big-mouthed Greek."

"Yeah, same here, you frickin' Sicilian! What's up?"

"Well, Liz was just saying....why do we have to wait till tomorrow night to have dinner together? We got a lot of unfinished stories to tell."

"You're so right! I didn't even begin to tell you about all the heartaches my daughter dump on me!"

Marica had been listening in the background and, once more uncharacteristically, yelled out: "And I didn't even start!!"

Liz heard her across the rooms and across the miles.

"Was that the 'quiet one'?" she asked the older Greek. The two Sicilians thought that was a good moniker for Marica.

"Yup, it sure was," Mable answered. "I think being in California has done something to her – something good! Marica, the ladies want to know if we'd like to meet them for dinner tonight?"

"Hmm...that might be a good way to unwind, and then we can talk, and maybe I could get a word or two in. Yeah, let's go tonight!"

The question was what kind of food did everyone feel like, and how were they going to find a good restaurant?

CHAPTER TWELVE

Four for Dinner

Life can often be unpredictable, and it is hard to know what lies around the next bend, or in this case, in the next seat., Both sets of women had discussed the days happenings "intra-sister" and would later open up the conversation to include all four of the Mediterranean mothers. What were the odds that they would meet up with a somewhat mirror image of each other – albeit from across two seas – and also bond like gorilla glue. On the other hand, stepping back and examining the foursome, it seemed not only possible but inevitable that they would become the "Four" Musketeers, or perhaps the Fearsome Foursome, as Nick would later call them. They were, after all, widows, Mediterranean sisters, about the same ages, opinionated, and hell-bent on exacting many pounds of flesh from their progeny via years and years of intense and continuous histrionics and guilt trips, tears and smiles, scoldings and love. What a recipe for raising kids! Just standard fare for those of Italian or Greek descent.

So now that they decided *when* to eat, the question became *where* to eat! The two more talkative of the foursome were on the phone discussing that very thing as Marica and Liz offered their input to their sisters from across their respective hotel rooms.

"Hey, Marie, I don't care where we go as long as they have some Ouzo or Metaxa," Mable began with a smile that could probably be seen over the phone.

"So, you overbearing Greek," Marie replied kiddingly. "We meet you today and right away you want to take charge. I should have known. Actually, though, Greek food doesn't sound too bad. And something to wash it down besides coffee. Hmm. That might work."

Marica could sense the gist of the conversation, and interjected her opinion quickly and vociferously.

"That's OK with me, but it's got to be a *good* place, not some hole in the wall."

"Marie, my snooty sister wants to be sure it's a *good* place, not some hole in the wall and I quote her exactly."

Marie was transcribing her conversation for her sister, although Liz pretty much could tell what was happening, and the two Sicilians and Mable went into a belly laugh contortions. Even Marica cracked a smile.

"OK, smart ass," Mable said to her sister. "How do we find a good place?"

"Well, we could ask them at the front desk. They should know about restaurants and what they serve. And the reputations they have among the people. After all, the hotel workers live here."

"Did you hear that, Marie? My sister wants to ask the people at the front desk."

"Well, that might work, but..."

Her thoughts were interrupted by a quick question from Elizabeth.

"What might work?"

"Asking them at the desk."

Liz shook her head. "Don't like that idea. How do we know

we can trust the desk clerks? Maybe they have a relative who owns a place, or maybe they're getting paid off to send their guests somewhere. We need to talk to someone we can trust!"

Then the proverbial light bulb went off over Marie's head!

"Let's call Maria!"

CHAPTER THIRTEEN

When the Cat's Away…

It was about five o'clock on the west coast – around eight back in the East. It was also "College Night" where Maira and Nick teach, and they were both involved with various presentations. They lived within a few blocks of each other, so they decided to come in together, and since Maria's meetings were right across the hall from Nick's room, she dumped her purse and things on his desk.Maria's talk had already started when her phone went off, catching Nick not only off guard but also with very few options. He usually didn't answer other people's cells, but of course he knew her mom was out in California, and he was afraid it might be an emergency, either real or imagined. So he discreetly crossed himself and picked up the call.

"Hello, Maria? It's your mother. I'm calling from California."

The next four words would live on as a turning point in his sanity.

"Hi. This is Nick."

"*WHO* Is this?"

"Nick. Nick Pappas."

"Who the hell are you?"

"I teach with Maria. Maybe she told you about me."

"Why do you have her phone? Is she all right?"

"She's fine. She's right across the hall."

"Across the hall? Across the hall? Are you at her house?"

Nick started to chuckle, which was definitely the wrong thing to do.

"No, no. We're at school. We're at college night. See..."

Before he could finish Marie had a memory flashback and literally jumped through the phone as she exploded:

"Now I remember that name. Pappas. You're the damn Greek who has lunch duty with her, right?"

Once again Nick's choice of words left much to be desired: "guilty as charged."

"I'll bet!!!" Marie stated emphatically.

Meanwhile, Liz, Mable, and yes, even Marica, wondered what was happening, and to complicate things just a bit back in the East, Maria had left her speaker on and half the parents In Nick's session, who were waiting for things to start, wore puzzled looks as they tried to figure out the context of this surprising conversation. Of course, this was nothing new for Nick. He was used to taking a touchy situation and making it into an explosive one, and he lived up to this track record once more.

When the parents looked up at him for some sort of explanation about the "slightly emotional" female voice on the phone, there were a number of things he could have done to mitigate the damage and several things to make things worse. Of course, he chose something from the second group as he addressed the curious multitude.

"Hi, welcome to college night. My name is Nick Pappas, history, and I suppose you're all wondering about the person on the phone. Not a big deal, really, just a little mixup. She's just trying to talk with her daughter, who left her phone in here, and she sort of doesn't trust people...well men....who work with her. Men who work with her daughter, not her. Well, I mean she tends to be suspicious, and she is calling from three thousand miles away."

Nick was sweating profusely, and he was speaking faster and faster, a sure sign of panic. As he looked over those assembled, he almost felt he was in the middle of a class judging by the wide range of looks in people's eyes, which went from disbelief to laughter, and every stop in between.

Like a relief pitcher from the bullpen, Maria walked in to try to save the day. Luckily her group was on a break because there was no telling where things in Nick's room were headed. Maria had heard just enough to realize what was happening. She grabbed the phone, gave Nick a look and a wink, and apologized to the assembled parents and ducked into the hallway, turning off the speaker as she went.

"OK, Mom. What's going on?"

"What's going on? What's going on? Don't you think I should be asking *you* what's going on? I call to find out about a restaurant and I find myself in the middle of a modern *PEYTON PLACE....*"

Maria knew how her mother's mind worked, and though she was usually ready for just about anything, this caught her off guard just a bit.

"PEYTON PLACE?"

"Yeah, Maria, you know, the movie about the town where everyone is fooling around with everybody else!"

"I know the reference. What does that have to do with tonight?"

"Please, Maria. All I tried to do was get in touch with my daughter, and I get this damn Greek on the phone instead, and he's in some sort of 'meeting,' he says. I can just picture what's going on. Why does he have your phone, and where are you?"

Maria was in a precarious position because there were people constantly walking by, so she had to keep both her emotions and her voice low, but she couldn't stop herself from shaking her head and displaying the wry grin of all time as she rolled her eyes and almost shook her head out of its socket. This was like talking with Nick…

"First of all, how are things going on the coast? Are you and Liz OK?"

"Never mind changing the subject. Yeah, we're good *here*. How are things *there*? Or shouldn't I ask, 'Why does this Greek have your phone?' What's all that noise that I hear. Some kind of party? When the cat's away, Maria. When the cat's away."

"WHAT??"

"Very convenient. Your husband's on a business trip to Italy, and you send us packing to California. Quite a coincidence that we're all gone at the same time. Is there something you're not telling me?"

"Ma, listen….we had a meeting at school and we had to bring in a lot of stuff, so we just came in together. He lives about a half mile from me, that's all, so he picked me up."

"And then he's going to drop you off at your house? Listen, Maria, I didn't just get off the boat!"

The parents were changing rooms to go to different presentations, and the hall was filling up quickly, so Maria needed to end this as soon as possible.

"Ma, I'll talk to you about this tomorrow, OK? I really gotta go. Was there something you wanted?"

"You'd better believe we'll talk about it young lady or you're going to have to live with this guilt your whole life. How could you do this to your mother?"

Marie hung up and never did ask Maria about the restaurant. The next session was just about to start, and Nick quickly poked his head into the hall and caught Maria as she was stepping into her assigned room.

"Not good, huh Maria?"

She shook her head.

"Tell you about it on the way home, just don't get fresh you damn Greek," she said out of the corner of her mouth with just a hint of a smile.

"Huh" Nick exclaimed, for probably the five millionth time in his life.

"This is enough to make a girl start drinking....tonight." Maria thought to herself as she walked into her classroom. The parents were already there.

"Hi! I'm Maria Orlando. Let's see about getting your kids into college!"

CHAPTER FOURTEEN

Where Italians and Greeks Come to Eat

Marie told her sister about her conversation with her daughter complete with suspicions and threats – all directed at Nick. She vowed to get to the bottom of things once they got home at the very latest, but she was, after all not only Sicilian, but a widowed mother. What a combination! Had Nick known the tenuous position he was in there's not telling what he would have done. Although, the truth of the matter was that there was rarely a time that one could predict what Nick would do. Not even Nick!

While Marie was debating the fate that awaited the unsuspecting Greek in Jersey the hotel phone buzzed. It was Mable.

"Guess what, Marie! My daughter called!"

"Yeah, well, guess what, Mable. I called *MY* daughter! Wait till you hear what's going on with this guy she works with!"

"Can you tell us at dinner? Jo Ann said there's a really good place that serves Greek *and* Italian. It's called '*Where ITAL-IANS AND GREEKS – Come To Eat*' She said it's usually called just *ITALIANS AND GREEKS!* Supposed to have a good variety of food to pick from. Even my sister says it seems all right. How about you two? Sounds like a pretty good name!"

Marie and Liz held a quick caucus and it was unanimous.

"We're all good here, Mable. Do you want us to meet you at your hotel, or do you want to come here?"

Mable was hungry, and it didn't make any difference as long as they got going fairly soon.

"I'll have my sister call and make reservations for six thirty, and we'll grab a cab and pick you up in about an hour or so. How about that?"

"You got it, 'Melpomeni.'"

"Hey, Marie, that was really good. I'll make a Greek out of you yet," Mable answered with a laugh.

"Heaven forbid, Mable, heaven forbid," Marie grinned. "See you soon."

Before you could say "guilt trip" the four ladies were seated comfortably in a taxi headed for dinner. Marica was her usual prim self as she settled into her seat, Liz was commenting on all the sights of LA, Mable's stomach was growling, and Marie was so happy with the transportation that she temporarily put aside her recent run-in with Nick and Maria. She turned to her Greek compatriot.

"Mable, where did you find this cab? It's so comfortable and it has so much room to stretch out!"

"I can't take the credit. My sister did everything. She got it."

"Thank you, Marica!" Marie proclaimed. "Thank you. Hey, is it OK if I call you 'Rica'"? Marica, for her part, just nodded and smiled. It was the first time Marie had addressed Marica directly, but it wouldn't be the last!

"I love to stretch out while we're driving. There is so much room. You should see my nephew's car. You can barely turn your head," Mable proclaimed, exaggerating just a bit. Her observation drew a laugh from her sister and a comment from Marie.

"Yeah, just like Maria's car. Right, Liz? I think it was made for midgets." Her comment drew giggles all around, including the driver, but it also reminded Marie about her recent altercation with Nick and her daughter. She was about to "tell all" "to all," but the cab was just pulling up in front of their destination, so the story of intrigue and deception would have to wait – but only for a bit!

CHAPTER FIFTEEN

Friends Old and New

Before you could say "I'm starving," the cab pulled up to a very homey looking restaurant perched on the corner of two very picturesque streets. "ITALIANS & GREEKS" was highlighted in large, soft neon lights, with *Where....Come To Eat.* completing the name. The lights were a pleasing combination of light blue, purple, and crimson, and the restaurant had a traditional, inviting brick front which complimented the lighting and welcoming feeling it exuded.

A courteous doorman let them in and greeted them in Italian, Greek, and English, which pleased the guests more than one could imagine, and before you know it the ladies were seated at a very nice table with a beautiful view of the city. No fuss, no problems. Of course, they couldn't leave well enough alone; there had to be a comment, or rather a complaint, tied to their offspring.

Marie led off.

"Hey Liz, remember the last time we went out to eat? About a month ago. We were at my house and Maria took us out to the diner?"

For her part, Liz was already scanning the menu and had to ask her sister to repeat what she had said.

"That diner, Liz, where we went with Maria. Remember?"

"Oh yeah, the diner, couple weeks ago. Yeah. They had good food there."

"Well, they did. But do you remember how long it took us to find a table? I thought it was the damn Greek who ran the place, but now I'm thinking it was Maria This place is probably run by Greeks and it was smooth as anything getting seated.!" Marie emphasized her revelation with a snap of a breadstick.

"Hmmm, You might be right, Marie. I mean, Maria tries to help but I think sometimes it would be simpler without her," Liz answered.

Mable, meanwhile, had been nodding her head vigorously.

"I know just what you mean. When Jo Ann goes out with me she tries to take charge, like I was some kind of helpless old lady. Drives me crazy. And what's even worse is when her god damn idiot of a husband comes with us. I feel like killing him."

"Yeah, ladies, well, at least your kids *take* you out. My son hasn't done that since....lord, I can't even remember when the last time was When he was growing up we used to take him out to eat with us all the time, and then after his father died I would take him out every chance I had. You'd think he would remember that and return the favor. Nope. He acts as if I had some kind of disease, or that he's just embarrassed to be seen with me. I mean, it's the least he could do, don't you think ladies?"

"Damn right, Marica!" Marie exclaimed. "I know just how you feel."

Mable and Liz nodded vigorously.

"Don't expect nothing, Ricky, cause you're not gonna get nothing," Mable lectured her sister. "I tell you a hundred times."

Their complaints were interrupted by a smiling waitress, who brought a tray of bread, olives, and cheese for pre-dinner snacking, along with a "side order" of oregano, olive oil, pepper....the works. Mable, never shy, grabbed a piece of feta and a slice of Italian bread to get herself started. This drew a disdainful look from her sister, but the older Greek didn't care.

"You could have waited till she left, Mable."

"Hey, she brought it for us to eat, and I'm hungry. Anyway, I think better on a full stomach."

"Think? What do you have to think about?"

"I gotta think what I want for dinner. Ti kopsimo se troey?"

Mable's forceful rebuttable elicited laughter from the Sicilian sisters, even though they weren't quite sure about the meaning of the last four words.

The server, who was laughing herself, decided to help with the translation.

"It's an old Greek saying, and it means 'what's it to you?' But the literal translation would be 'what cramp is gnawing at you?'"

This brought more laughter all around, even from the usually prim and proper Marica, who thanked the lady for her help and complimented her on the explanation.

"I apologize, ladies, for not introducing myself. I got caught up in your conversation. My name is Christina, and it will be my pleasure to serve you tonight. This looks like a fun group. You guys must be good friends, huh?"

Marie jumped in with a big grin...

"Yeah, I guess we are good friends, huh, Mable?"

"You bet we are. Greeks (as she pointed to herself and her sister) and Sicilians (waving at Marie and Liz). The best of friends." Even Marica had to smile.

"Well, that's me, Greek and Sicilian. My father's Greek, my mom's Sicilian!"

This was too much...!!

All of the women were a bit taken aback by this revelation. Coincidence is coincidence, but this seemed like it might be something more.

Liz was the first to voice her surprise, and her comment was short and to the point: "Wow!"

"You got that right. You got that right!" Mable shot in. She rarely repeated anything so vociferously, and when she did it served as a double exclamation! "Something is going on here!"

Marie threw in a "Holy Cow," and even Marica chirped in with a "Hmmm," and nodded with an expression on her face that her sister always called "The Look."

Christina smiled but seemed just a bit puzzled at the reaction to her ethnic background. Marie decided to explain things and turned her head toward the slightly confused waitress.

"You were right when you said we appeared to be 'good friends,' cause I think we are, right ladies?" (There were nods all around). "But the truth of the matter is that we just met these Greek ladies on the plane coming out here today. They were sitting next to us, and we got to talking...." She passed the baton to Mable, who was more than happy to continue with the story of this apparent Odyssey   .

"...and it turns out we have so many things in common. We're all from New Jersey, two sets of widows..."

"....with ungrateful, disobedient kids," Marie added.

"And we're all from islands near Italy and Greece," Marica surprisingly contributed to the geography lesson.

"You know we're Sicilians," Liz reiterated.

"And we were born in Cephalonia," Mable stated proudly.

Christina's jaw dropped to her chest, and she broke out with a coast to coast smile. "Cephalonia?? That's where my father and his brothers were born. This is unbelievable!"

"You got that right, kid! You got that right." The four of them more or less shouted.

"My dad is off tonight, but my mother is here. She's back in the kitchen. I'm sure she'd like to meet you, but she's talking a new cook through the steps of a new dish, so she's a bit tied up right now. Wait till I tell her!!"

In all the excitement Christina turned and started to walk away without getting a single order. She was back in a flash with an embarrassed look on her face that was buried in her smile and apology.

"I'm so sorry ladies. I didn't take your orders."

"No apology needed," Marie sincerely replied.

Christina appeared relieved, but she was still smiling incredulously, as were the ladies.

"May I make a suggestion? My parents created a dish which is a combination of Greek and Sicilian cuisine. It's got a little bit of everything, and they named it 'Heaven On A Plate.' Would you like to try it?"

There were nods all around.

"Great!" Christina smiled. "I'll be right back with the salads to start you off!"

"See how easy it is without the kids here!" Marie proclaimed.

CHAPTER SIXTEEN

College Night Winding Down...

Despite all the extra-curricular problems courtesy of the West Coast, the night actually went pretty well, as parents came and went and Nick got his feet back under him. Of course, there had to be a wrinkle in the works, and it soon showed its face in the person of Brad Morgan, the principal. He was going from class to class and making his presence known, which was actually what he was supposed to be doing as the head guy. It put sort of an official stamp on the event, and it was good PR for the school as he said hello to different groups of parents at the various sites. And then he stuck his shiny bald head into Nick's room. One group of parents had just left and there was to be one more meeting in about ten minutes. The principal was not a welcome sight, although it did add a bit of levity to the night as the fluorescent lights danced and twinkled off of the top of Morgan's head. Nick scrunched his mouth into a knot to keep from chuckling out loud.

"Mr. Pappas, how's it going?" he asked with a phony smile.

"Not bad, not bad at all," was the reply from Nick. He figured that was about as non-committal as he could get. In fact, he said it a third time for extra emphasis but mostly to piss off the principal, who hated when things were repeated.

"Yes, Nick, I heard you the first thirty times," was Morgan's sarcastic response.

"Good hyperbole, Brad. Very nice," Pappas responded.

"It was actually an understatement...."

Nick decided to put an end to the tennis match of insults back and forth. He knew he could "one up" the principal indefinitely, but he wanted to get him out as soon as possible before the last group came in. Then he could get them out a bit quicker. Sort of a domino effect!

"I actually have one more presentation in a few minutes. Was there something else?" Nick tried to be as diplomatic as possible, which was normally a chore for him even talking with someone he liked, much less this dolt.

"Well, yes, there was. I understand you took a phone call during one of your sessions? You know that's a 'no-no,' right?"

Damn. One of the parents had ratted him out. Nick pinched the back of his thigh as hard as he could to keep himself from cursing out the unknown stoolie and to stop himself from pointing out that Brad had just repeated the 'no' sound three times. The "high road" was foreign to Nick, but he navigated it pretty well.

"Yes, I am aware of that protocol. But it was a family emergency. Thanks for understanding."

Morgan was ready for a confrontational statement, and like a batter getting a change up when he was expecting a fastball, this caught him totally by surprise.

"Well, this...uh, sure. Things happen," he stammered as he turned and walked out into the hall. "Have a good night."

Nick released the smile he had been holding in, and it was perfect timing as the final troop of mothers and fathers sauntered in.

CHAPTER SEVENTEEN

The Long Ride Home...

By the time the principal gave his "thanks for coming and have a good evening" speech over the intercom it was pushing ten o'clock. Why he had to say anything, and why any of the parents stayed to hear it was beyond comprehension, but, as people say, "it is what it is," and what it was, was, very late on a school night, with still more than half the week to go. Nick grabbed his car keys, Maria grabbed her purse, and they were off to the car, their path lined with the epithets cascading out of their mouths like mouthwash at a dentist's office.

"Why don't they start these damn nights earlier, or at least do them on a Thursday night, so we'd have only one day to go? Do you realize the week is just beginning?" It was Maria at her fire-eyed best.

All Nick could do was nod in agreement. Anything he said would be gilding the lily, as the saying goes. He was pretty good at complaining, but when it came to sheer vitriol, no one could top Maria. Or even come close.

As they were getting into the car he said something he knew he should not have, but after thousands of times doing just that, what difference would one more make?

"Maria, I know I probably shouldn't ask you this, but is everything OK with your Mom?"

She turned and gave him the death stare, and she didn't have to verbalize what she was thinking: "If you know you shouldn't be asking, then why the hell are you??"

He answered her unspoken query out loud...

"Yeah, yeah...I know...."

It was a scenic drive between the high school and the town in which they lived; the winding roads through the hills and past literally hundreds of trees made coming to work – and going home – a pleasant experience. Well, at least most of the time. By now it was well past ten and the scarcity of lights, which heightened the country feel in the daytime, made the night drive a bit hazardous. It wasn't made any easier by Maria's continual harangue at the phone for having poor reception and at Nick for "barely missing" several large trees. In reality, he hadn't come that close to them, but he knew that something unpleasant or embarrassing would come from the transcontinental communication between mother and daughter, so for once he kept quiet.

"I may as well wait till we get to my house. I need a minute or two to gather my thoughts." She glanced at the dashboard...."Hey Greek, you're going ten miles under the speed limit. Let's go, huh?"

There is a limit to anyone's resolve to go against their first instinct, and this constant nitpicking was more than Nick could tolerate even without an impending crisis at hand. Luckily, his comment was direct and non-provocative without any of his usual sarcastic inflection.

"Sorry, I thought you said you needed a moment or two."

His companion was about to give him what for when they turned the corner of her street. Nick was actually a bit astonished because it looked like Maria was somewhat apprehensive about the forthcoming call. He had rarely seen that expression on her face, so he decided to put away his "humorous" persona for the rest of the evening.

"You wanna just leave all the school stuff in my car?" he asked, as he pulled into her driveway.

"Yeah, either in your car or go back and dump it in the river!"

Ah, there was the woman he knew and loved.

"Hey, Nick, could you do me a favor?"

"Sure!"

"Stay here while I make the call. Just for moral support"

Nick had to use all his powers to clam up with a straight line like that. Given her mother's accusations from earlier in the evening, he was dying to make "moral" into "immoral," and then perhaps add a comment of his own. But, for the second time within the space of about an hour, Nick Pappas was a better man and took that little-travelled high road.

"Whatever you need me to do, you got it." Was knowing Maria actually making him a better human being? First with the principal, and now with this panicky Sicilian. He shook his head and dismissed that thought out of hand. No way. Or, as Maria might have said had she been privy to his mental battle with himself – "PLEASE..."

CHAPTER EIGHTEEN

We Don't Really Drink

While Maria and Nick were playing a guessing game as to the happenings in California, the four widows were off to a rip-roaring start to their evening. Christina not only brought the salads, which looked mouth-watering and turned out to be delicious, but also a double round of drinks – Disaronno and Metaxa for each of their guests.

"Oh, I don't think we ordered these," Marica began as the glasses were deftly placed in front of the ladies."

"And we don't really drink," Marie added.

"Speak for yourself, you damn Italian," Mable chided her while taking a big gulp of the Greek brandy. "Speak for yourself."

"Oh, everyone who dines with us gets something complimentary to sip on before dinner," Christina explained. "But when I told my mother about who you were and where you were from – she said to double the drinks and keep them coming!"

"That works for me," Liz added.

"Me, too," said the suddenly loquacious Marica, as she downed one and was halfway through the second.

"What the heck, I don't wanna break up the party," Marie concluded with a flourish of clinking glasses with her sister and friends and two big gulps of delicious booze!"

Their unbridled revelry was almost interrupted by a three-thousand-mile phone call, courtesy of Maria, who hit her mother's name on her phone, but after a few rings, it went right to voicemail. She tried again with the same result. Apparently not only drinking and driving don't mix, drinking and hearing a cell phone don't either. An apprehensive look spread across Maria's face as she turned toward Nick.

"Something's wrong, Nick. Something's wrong. My mother always has her phone with her, especially when she's somewhere other than her house. Why doesn't she answer?"

Nick was rarely any good in a crisis, but for once he appeared to have things under control, his mouth included.

"Hey, she probably is in the bathroom or maybe she stepped out onto her balcony. It's around eight out there, right? Maybe she's having a late supper. Just give it another shot."

These were unfamiliar waters for Nick. Usually, he went off half-cocked (no pun intended) and Maria was calm and cool. It actually gave him a good feeling – not to see her upset – but for once to play the rock instead of a flighty feather at the mercy of every slight gust of emotion.

"OK, I'll give it another shot. Thanks, Nick," Maria said sincerely as she squeezed his hand, took a deep breath, and pushed the button on her phone.

"Hello!" Maria's eyes lit up!

"Thank goodness, she got her," Nick surmised.

"Hi, Mom?"

"Yeah! Jo Ann? How did you get this number?," replied the voice from California.

"Jo Ann? This is Maria. Who is this?"

"This is Mable. Who is this?"

"Maria! Where is my mother? And who are you??"

"I'm Mable. Oh, wait. Wait a minute...." Came the response, as the lady on the west coast put down the phone.

Maria turned to Nick with her logic in disarray.

"Nick, someone has my mother's phone. Someone named Mable!"

Nick's eyes almost popped through the windshield.

"Mable? Mable??"

Meanwhile, the aforementioned Mable had given the phone to Marie, laughing all the while.

"Sorry, I picked up your phone by mistake. I thought it might be for me."

This was too much for Marica.

"Mable, how the heck could that be for you? Neither of us has a cell phone!"

Marica was not in the habit of cracking jokes, and this was about as far from a funny line as you could get. Yet it sent the four of them into howls of laughter. This was not lost on Maria, who was getting more bewildered by the second.

"Mom, is that you? It's Maria! Is everything all right?"

"Yup, it's your mother. Is this my daughter?"

"Ma, I just told you it's Maria...:"

"Well, there are thousands of Marias in this country. How do I know it's you and not some other Maria? Answer me that if you can!"

"Mother, have you been drinking?"

Marie pulled away from the phone and addressed the other three women:

"Someone named Maria wants to know if we've been drinking! What about it ladies....have we? Let's take a vote... Maria my daughter or just plain Maria, my sister Liz and our two Greek lady friends unanimously feel that you're damn right we've been drinking"

This sent them into an encore of their guffaws, only they

were louder and longer.

"Ma, look. I'll call you in the morning, OK?"

"OK by me. And remember, whoever you are, and whatever you've done, you can always go to confession!"

Maria shook her head in desperation and clicked the phone off to another chorus of laughs. She turned to Nick in disbelief.

"My mother never drinks, but she just vehemently stated that she and my aunt and two Greek women were all getting plowed. AND....she said I should go to confession! Nick, did you hear me? Confession!"

This was within a whisper of Nick's self-control, which was not that great to begin with. THREE TIMES in one night. Yes, three times, and somehow he had kept himself calm and even rational. And to top it off, the last two were with Maria. CONFESSION? Give me strength, he said over and over. Maybe it was divine intervention, or maybe he was just due for a stable response – but whatever it was, he managed to keep both his libido bottled up and his mouth shut, as he shifted gears.

"Yeah, I heard you. I heard you. But listen, the first woman you talked to...her name was Mable?"

"Yeah, so?"

"So, that's my aunt's name!"

"Holy crap, Nick. Holy crap."

"You can say that again, Maria!"

"Holy crap, Nick, you're in the wrong driveway."

CHAPTER NINETEEN

Stories and More Stories

Back on the "Left Coast," as Easterners often say, things were rolling right along, and the musketeers were traveling all over the map of their minds and their memories.

"What shall we drink to," Marica asked, as she downed another gulp of Disaronno. "You know, this drink is pretty good, and I never drink. Do I Mable?"

"You're full of shit you never drink my little sister. You never let anyone *see* you drink."

"Well, isn't that the same thing? Isn't it? Well, isn't it?" Marica paused to let the other ladies ponder her question, and to allow Christina to serve their specialty dish.

"Wow, this looks delicious," Marie proclaimed, as she took a big whiff of the steaming hot main course. "And, no, Marica, I don't think it's quite the same thing."

"Yeah, it's like the tree falling in the forest. I think it makes a sound whether or not someone is there to hear it!" Elizabeth piggybacked.

The only other sounds emanating from the mouths of the "babes" over the next few minutes were a few "Hmmms" but mostly "Ummms" as they tasted and then began to heartily devour the fare in front of them.

The food and the liquor and the company soon turned the evening into stories about who they were and why they had hit it off so famously and so quickly.

"You know," Marie said thoughtfully between forkfuls of spinach pie and bites of both feta and provolone, "I think you two ladies are really interesting. I mean, you could do a feminine Abbott and Costello skit very easily. You're very different, and yet you're a great team!"

"Maybe it's *because* we're so different!" Mable proclaimed.

"She's right there." Marica agreed wholeheartedly. "My sister is outgoing and talkative and very mischievous."

"Yeah, and *my* sister is prim and proper and smart as all get outs!"

"We figured that out pretty quickly," Liz added. "Pretty quickly!"

"You think you've seen the real Mable? You ain't seen nothing! Let me tell you a couple stories about my big sister. May I?"

"By all means," the Sicilians said almost in unison. "By all means."

"OK, girls, you asked for it," Marica warned. "Grab a drink and hold on while I take you back a few years."

"Thelo na pau mazi sou," said the little girl. She was about four and a half, and full of the devil.

"Oxi!" said her mother rather emphatically.

Her mother and father, Nick's grandparents, usually went out to work in the fields. Sometimes they would take Mable with them, sometimes they didn't. This day happened to be one that she would be left at home. That usually meant there was an extra amount to do and it would be easy to lose track of their little girl. She would be safer at the house, and her mom's cousin would probably stop by to check on her. Made sense, but not to Mable, who felt that she had asked very nicely, and that her mother's one-word answer – "No!" – was not acceptable. So she just put on a down-cast mask and whimpered softly.

"You play. We will be back before you know it," her mother said half consolingly.

However, "play" was not in Mable's plans for this day. The operative word was revenge. Her mother had about a dozen beautiful plants in pots displayed rather decoratively around the patio adjoining their modest house. There was a wide va-riety of blossoms, everything from roses to violets, and they were her pride and joy. Though it took the better part of the morning and a lot of sweat and exertion, the little girl man-aged to separate each of them from its respective receptacle and place it neatly on the ground. "That will show her," Mable thought to herself. "They're not going to leave me home again." And they didn't. Of course, she wasn't able to sit down for a few days, but it was worth it, as she thought of a partic-ular plant with each swat her father administered.

The Sicilians looked at her in awe.

"Weren't you afraid of what your parents would do to you?" It was Marie who asked what seemed to be the obvious question.

"Nah, not really. I just wanted to get even with them for leaving me home. And I did!"

Liz took a different tack: "Didn't you feel guilty about what you did to your mother's plants?"

"Why should I? They sure as heck didn't feel guilty about leaving me home all by myself! They started it by leaving me all alone!"

As the ladies were getting the scoop from the plant perpe-trator, Christina stopped back to see if everything was OK and whether the ladies needed anything else at the moment.

"Maybe another round?" Marica asked as she downed her remaining brandy.

"And, Christina," Liz joined in. "This dish you recommended is the best thing I've ever had!"

"Yes," Marie quickly added. "It is heavenly indeed!"

"Well, I'm delighted you like my dish," said a voice from a sultry-looking fiftyish lady coming up behind the waitress. "I'm Gina, Christina's mother" She made a hand gesture to her daughter to get another round, and one for her as well. "My husband, Ted and I run this establishment, and the 'piece of heaven' was sort of my idea."

"Bravo! Bravo!" Mable proclaimed   as she clapped her hands, a gesture in which she was soon joined by the other diners.

Marie did the introductions, including nationalities, as Gina exchanged handshakes and hugs with the fearsome four-some.

"I understand you just met, and yet you're good friends, right?" Gina tasted. They all nodded. "It's obvious how well you get along and fit together. Must be the Mediterranean in you. Would you mind if I joined you for a bit?"

"Would we mind?" Mable began....

"...we weren't gonna let you go!" Marie completed the thought.

"Please, sit down," Liz continued. "Rica was just telling us some stories from the time her sister was a little girl in Cephalonia."

"Ah, Cephalonia! My husband talks about it all the time. He was from a small village called Cardia. It means 'heart.'"

The Greeks suddenly became transfixed with their mouths open a country mile.

The three Sicilians' expressions all asked the same thing: "what's the matter?"

"That's the village we were born in," the Greeks said almost in unicorn.

As if it were choreographed, Christina had just returned with the brandy.

"A toast to Cephalonians, Sicilians, and my new friends," shouted Gina with a flourish. They all took a big sip and smiled. What an evening this was turning out to be.

"I believe someone said something about a story from the old country?"

"You're up again, Rica," Liz remarked.

"OK. I think you'll like this one even more...So you have to remember my sister was about five, and she was already on the road to being the biggest kidder and con artist you'd ever want to meet. Now, our village was up in the mountains, and while it was not very large, the houses were spread out a bit from each other, and the paths were very uneven and stony. One day Mable met a friend of hers walking toward the edge of the village. The little boy was carrying a rather large dish covered with a very elegant red dinner napkin, and he was walking very slowly and watching every step.

Besides being mischievous, Mable was always curious about everything, and this rather unusual situation piqued her interest.

"Hi, Ted, where are you going?"

"To my Yiayai's house."

"Why are you going there?"

"Well, she's not feeling well, so my mother made her some food and I'm taking it to her."

Mable shook her head, explaining to the lad that his grandmother lived such a long way off and that he didn't have to walk all the way over there. She could be very convincing.

"I don't?" questioned her patsy. "What do you mean?"

"That is a magic plate. All you have to do is let go of it, and it will get to your Yiayia's on its own."

"Wow! I didn't know that. Are you sure?"

"Swear to God," said the flim-flam artist extraordinaire.

So the boy let go of the plate and it smashed to pieces on the rocks beneath their feet. Ted went home crying, and Mable went home to another spanking. But she was laughing all the way.

Of course, all four of the musketeers were laughing, including Marica the storyteller and Mable the "star."

"Come on, Mable. Did this really happen?" Marie wondered.

"Oh, it happened all right. It happened!" It was Gina. "And I've heard that story many times....many times...."....she continued with a smile as wide as the Ionian Sea...."many times!"

"*You've heard it?*" Marica asked in amazement.

"You've heard it?" Marie echoed.

"From who, Gina?" Liz interjected

"Yeah, from who," asked Mable, the most puzzled of all.

The crowd at the restaurant was starting to thin out, so Christina had stayed for "story hour."

"I've heard it too, at just about every family gathering. Should I tell them Ma?"

Gina nodded vigorously.

"I heard it a thousand times, it seems like – and each time it gets funnier."

The guests were on the edge of their seats....

"I HEARD IT FROM MY FATHER! He's the one you got (pointing to Mable) to drop the plate. Wait till we tell him."

Gina, meantime, was on her phone.

"Hey Ted, you need to come down here right away. Yeah, I know it's your night off and a special on the Dodgers is coming on....And no, I can't tell you why. Just get your Greek ass down here."

She looked around the table and winked!

CHAPTER TWENTY

It's Been a Long Time

"Mable!" was the first thing Ted Micropolis said as he walked toward the table in his restaurant. "It's been a few years, huh? *Ti Kanis?*"

Gina was stunned, as was everyone else.

"Christina, did you tell your father what this was all about?"

"Not a word, Mom, honest," said the equally flabbergasted waitress, shaking her head. The other ladies were just as thunderstruck by what appeared yet another outlandish coincidence. The six of them looked at the owner, who smiled broadly and explained.

"It's very simple, really. The last time I saw a look like that on anyone's face was about fifty-some-odd years ago on a small path in Cardia. That sly, foxlike countenance becomes you, Melpo. Welcome to *ITALIANS AND GREEKS*!"

There were smiles and hugs all around, even before introductions, which were carried out with another round of drinks served by Ted himself.

"Before you ask, dear, these are all widows from New Jersey – two sets of sisters who apparently became good friends in less than a day," Gina explained.

Her daughter did the ethnic background – "Two Sicilians (pointing to Marie and Liz), and, as you must have deduced, two Cephalonians. They all met on the plane coming out this afternoon. Pretty cool, huh Dad?"

"Yes, pretty cool, but not surprising," Ted laughed. "You know the old saying, right? 'Olive oil is thicker than blood.'"

"He made that up, girls. You're terrible, Teddy."

"Well, what if I did? It was a long time ago, so it is *old*," Ted offered in his own defense.

"Leave the man alone, I like it," Marie added.

"You like *him*," Liz kidded.

"What if I do? He seems like a good guy....for a damn Greek," Marie countered with a smile as she downed another glass of Sicilian red.

By this time Ted was well into the frivolity everyone else was enjoying, and he was going with the flow with a vengeance. Waving his hand in a sweeping, circular motion to indicate he was speaking to all those assembled, he grabbed a glass, filled it with Metaxa, stood up, and made an impromptu but impassioned speech.

"Ladies, raise your glasses. I propose a toast to good people, good friends, and the islands off of Italy and Greece – with a special bravo to the six lovely women assembled here. OPA! How about some coffee and dessert – cannolis and baklava?"

Teddy got the coffee while his wife and daughter brought out some cannolis, baklava, and other assorted Italian and Greek treats. It had certainly been quite an evening between the new friends, the island connection, and a half-century reunion!., As long as the "plate dropper" had the floor and a drink, he decided to keep going, which was all right with the "gentler" sex, as all of them were busy with their coffee and selecting something sweet to finish off their meal.

"One thing I've learned is that you never know what each

day will bring. It's like a pitcher making a pitch – fastball, curve, ball or strike, swing or take. Just like baseball," Ted concluded – at least for the time being.

"If you couldn't tell, my husband is partial to baseball, especially the Dodgers," Gina threw in, giving Ted a hug.

"The Mets for my husband," Marie added proudly.

"Yankees for mine," Marica said with a wistful look.

"How long are you ladies staying? The season opens up in a couple of weeks. We could all go to a game," Ted said hopefully.

"Just a week for the Greek sisters," Mable answered.

"Same for the Sicilians," Marie added.

"Too bad. You really need more than a week to see California."

"Well, all we got is a week, My nephew gave us this as a Christmas present," Mable explained.

"Yeah, same here. My niece gave us a week as well," Liz added. And before the obvious question was asked, Marie finished up: "Yup, for Christmas."

"Wow, that was really nice of them," Teddy observed.

"Yeah, it was," Mable jumped in. "But I think they just wanted to get rid of us, right Marie?"

Marie laughed and nodded and laughed some more.

"You don't mean they pulled a fast one on you guys? Where would that personality trait come from, huh?" Teddy deadpanned, looking right at Mable. "But I think we might be missing the big picture, here..."

Christina and her mother looked at each other. Gina rolled her eyes as she half shrugged, smiled, and said: "Here we go. Here we go."

Apparently, Ted had to deal with this attitude before. Actually, thousands of times before, so he was used to his wife and daughter poo-pooing his ideas.

"Scoff if you will, but I think something bigger than all of us is at work here. Look at the facts: we've got four 'good friends' who just met because their "child" just happened to give them the same Christmas present and booked them on the same flight, and, of all the places to eat you could have chosen, you wind up in a place run by a Greek, a Cephalonian, and a Sicilian, and...."

"Oh my God," Mable interjected, "my daughter called us and recommended this restaurant."

Everyone stopped and looked around at each other as if they were expecting someone's head to go spinning around or to turn into a spirit and fly off. Perhaps they did, but, just for the record, no one's body, or body parts didbanything supernatural.

"And of course we have the 'Cephalonian Reunion,' Gina added. "Yeah, Ted, I think this time you might be onto something," as she gave him a quick kiss.

The four travelers were slightly overwhelmed by the events of the last twenty-four hours. They were also stuffed to the gills, and a bit more than *three* sheets to the proverbial wind.

Marie had yet to divulge the story behind her distrust of her daughter and Nick, which had been triggered by their phone conversations, but she was still convinced that the trip, while gracious and generous, was a way of getting her and Liz out of the way for a while. She gave the group a quick synopsis of what her suspicions were, and why she had them.

Oddly, it was not Mable but Marica, the "intellectual," who spoke first.

"You know, you might be right, Marie, when you said they were sending us here to get rid of us. I mean, my son is not bad, as kids go, but he rarely has been considerate or acceded to what I wanted. Then, out of the blue, he comes up with the Christmas present of all time. I think he might have just wanted to get me and my sister out of commission for a while, so he wouldn't feel guilty about all the things he did, and never did."

All the mothers at the table nodded and nodded and nodded.

"Well, my daughter's gonna get a piece of my mind tomorrow," Marie vociferously exclaimed. "And if I ever find out there was something going on with her and that damn Greek she works with, watch out!" And then, looking at the Greek sisters and Ted as well, she quickly added – "uh, no offense intended."

"None taken," Ted replied. "What a story you guys are living. You should write a book about it, People would love it...."

"And that's another thing, she and that damn teacher she works with are writing a book together. It's supposed to be about teaching, but I can just imagine what it's really about."

Suddenly a light went off in Marica's head, as she asked matter-of-factly.

"Marie, where does your daughter teach?"

"Uh," Marie stuttered as the brandy was impacting her sense of anything. "She teaches at....uh....Liz, where the hell does Maria teach?"

Her sister smiled. "Burns High School."

Marica jumped in with the follow-up. "Oh my goodness.! That's where my son teaches. Maybe they know each other. Did she ever mention a teacher named Nick, Nick Pappas?"

Marie almost choked on her coffee, as she gulped and coughed and spit it out all over the table...."Know each other? Know each other?, He's the one who's writing the damn book with her...and doing God knows what else." Then she caught the glare in Marica's eyes...."Well, at least thinking about doing God knows what else."

"Listen, I know my son. He treats me like garbage sometimes, but he is a family man and a perfect gentleman. And I resent any insinuations to the contrary."

Mable, of all people, was the calmest and became, as it were, the peacemaker and voice of reason. "You know what I think, I think that they got together and gave us these trips just to get us out of their hair, and to get us thinking and supposing just to drive us crazy. My nephew is not a bad guy, but he is sneaky. And Marica, don't get mad – I know he's married with a lot of kids, but he does like the opposite sex, and he always has. And he does like to tease people and flirt with beautiful women. That is part of who he is. A big part!" She looked over at her sister, who grudgingly nodded and sighed. Mable had a head of steam, and continued with her analysis, as everyone else listened intently. "And that book – about teaching? I don't think so. I think they're writing a book about us, about how horrible we are and how much we put them through their whole lives. They see a chance to get even, and they're taking it."

A hush of agreement fell over the crowd, as her "treatise" got an A+ from all concerned.

"We are in the presence of greatness, here," Ted finally said. "When the queen of practical jokes gives her analysis, that's it, brother. That's it."

The puzzle seemed to have been if not solved, at least parsed out into pieces, and the tension was broken. The good time became even better.

"How about it Ladies, one more quick round?" Ted buzzed, as he waved to a passing waiter/ Everyone soon had a fresh glass and a new outlook both on themselves and their friends, "Let's each propose a toast to mark this night of nights.... Christina, why don't you lead off...."

"To family."

"To my incorrigible husband," Gina put in.

"To new friends," Liz said with a smile.

"To Sicilians....and Greeks," from Marie.

"To stories yet untold," added Marica.

"To finding a new life ...and living it.... Ted said with simple sincerity.

"To old friends and new schemes," Mable concluded, as they all downed their drinks in one shot.

115

CHAPTER TWENTY-ONE

Problems by Any Other Name

...An Email Between Neighbors

To: Npappas@bhs.org

From: Morlando@bhs.org

Re: What the hell is going on

Nick had barely gotten home when he noticed the light on his computer indicating a new email. Probably the best thing to do would have been to ignore it. It was late and he was gassed, but Nick had a thing about messages, Whether it was a voicemail, a text, or an email, he had to check repeatedly to see who was trying to tell him what. So he flipped up the screen and read the rather frantic and cryptic message from Maria. The whole text was only slightly longer than the subject line.

"GREEK...WHAT THE HELL IS GOING ON?"

For once in his life Nick was succinct and also pretty much on the mark with his reply:

"Maria – I think they just want to have an adventure. Get some sleep. We'll talk at school OK? Don't worry....love ya, Greek."

"Thanks, man. I needed that. G'night."

Believe it or not, Nick was correct: the ladies were about to embark on an adventure that would include themselves, Maria and Nick, and actually quite a few others. But no one could imagine the roller coaster ride they were about to undertake!

The morning came much too quickly. It usually does under even normal circumstances, but after teaching a whole day, going through College Night, and then dealing with whatever was going on in Los Angeles, both Maria and Nick were pretty well beat to shit, to quote a popular and very fitting phrase. Nick's mind was on the events and implications of the previous evening and wasn't paying full attention to the road ahead, which was at that moment being crossed by three rather large deer. He looked up barely in time to swerve out of the way, and he forced himself to focus on his driving and not on what might or might not have been going on with their relatives. Of course, there were other items of concern. He was worried about Maria, who was normally a rock when it came to emotional matters, but who seemed both concerned and shaken up by what had transpired. He liked her a lot (no kidding) and he genuinely didn't want to see her hurt or upset, but being honest, he had a hard time interacting with his lunch partner even when she was in a good mood. When she became "pensive" (read "moody") – watch out.

He didn't remember driving the rest of the way to school, but apparently, he had done so because the next thing he saw was the big, gray building that housed his place of employment. "Holy crap, school," he said half out loud, as he turned the corner toward the parking lot. Nick tried to think of what he'd be doing with his various classes, but he drew a big fat blank. Hopefully, once he got to his desk, a glance at his lesson plans would kick his mind into gear. As he drove down the long sloping driveway to the parking spaces, he glanced into the rearview mirror and had to look twice more to be sure his sleepy eyes weren't playing tricks on him. It was Maria. She *always* beat him to school by at least a quarter-hour; her car was always there first. "Wow," he reasoned, she must be worried about her mom and aunt – and maybe herself.

Nick pulled into an empty spot and Maria parked right next to him. He walked over to the driver's side as she was pulling down the window.

"I don't know about you, Nick, but these College Nights really knock me out. It's like teaching two days in one."

"Yeah, you and me both. I'm gassed, and that's an understatement," Nick contributed, all the while shaking his head.

"Well, luckily they're having class meetings for the first hour, so we can just drop off our homerooms and then catch our breath a bit," she added.

"Class meetings! I forgot all about them." Nick breathed a sigh of relief. "Yeah. It will give me time to figure out what I'm going to do today. Is that why you got in later than usual? I was kind of worried about you after last night with your Mom."

"It's definitely been on my mind – most of the night. You wanna meet for coffee after we drop our classes off? My Mom was acting mighty strange, even for her. She said they were kicking up their heels with two Greek ladies? Who were they? Wait, I think I talked with one of them. Named Mable."

Suddenly Maria's face became a bit more solemn as she turned and looked directly at Nick. "Yes, Mable....!

"That's my aunt's name, Maria...Mable!! I thought you had said that last night, but everything was so jumbled I wasn't sure I heard you right."

"Nick, you don't suppose that our moms and aunts met up

with each other? Is that possible?"

Nick's countenance took on a serious, incredulous tone.

"But if it is my mother and aunt, it would mean they met on the plane and all of a sudden became dinner partners? How could that be? Maybe it's someone else, and the name is just a coincidence. There are probably thousands of Greeks in LA. It could very well be other Greeks. Or...maybe it is my relatives, and they all wound up at the same restaurant, and then were thrown together because it was so crowded. Isn't that a possibility?" He kept thinking out loud and clutching at straws as they walked up the stairs to the entrance to the school. "But I have a sinking feeling that they did meet on the plane and somehow hit it off. Could that have really happened? Lord, what have we done?"

"What do you mean 'we,' Nick?" Maria shot back. "I had booked this trip six months ago. When did you arrange yours? This is your fault, you frickin' Greek."

Things had gotten a bit out of hand, which could have been due to the lack of sleep for both the antagonists and the pressure of not knowing what was transpiring three thousand miles west and three hours later. But, truth be told, both Maria and Nick were hot-blooded to say the least, and every once in a while their vitriolic nature came bursting to the surface. They continued their "discussion" as they walked into the hallway, already populated by a few dozen students, several of whom turned toward the two animated teachers.

"Trouble in paradise, Mr. Pappas?" kidded one senior boy whom Nick had known for many years. His comment actually snapped Nick back to a semblance of reality. He stopped short and turned to face Maria.

"Sorry. Didn't mean to go off on you. Lots of stuff going on and my brain cells need a cup of coffee.

"Yeah, no big deal, Nick," she answered. "We can relax a bit and sort this out while the classes are meeting. OK?"

"Sounds good," Nick replied sincerely.

But things were about to get more complicated as another sound came cascading through the halls. It was the principal with an announcement.

"This is Mr. Morgan. Due to circumstances beyond our control, the class meetings have been postponed for today. We will follow the normal schedule for Tuesday. I repeat: class meetings canceled, normal Tuesday schedule. Have a good day."

"Shit!" Nick exclaimed, probably too loud.

"YUP!" Maria added. "Catch you at lunch, man...."

CHAPTER TWENTY-TWO

A Long Day

It was one of those days that should happen to someone else. Nick couldn't find the movie he was going to show to his first class, the principal stopped in "just to say Hi," and his mother and aunt were on his mind, especially the possibility that they had met Maria's relatives. God knows what they would be saying about him and her if that turned out to be the case. He thought about calling their hotel, but given the time difference it was too early to do that, and by the time lunch duty rolled around he was beside himself with worry, stress, and, yes, GUILT.

He and Maria got into the cafeteria at the same time, and she was literally fuming. He could almost see the smoke coming out of her head, and he *could see*, literally, the sparks flying out of her eyes. Today there were no prelims, no warming up – she started right in.

"So I call out there, and my mother doesn't answer her phone. Then I call the goddamn hotel, and they tell me she and my aunt are out. It's nine in the morning there – where the hell could they be going at nine in the morning? Something's not right. Something is up. Hi, Nick."

"Hey, Maria. Yeah, it's like they've disappeared off the face of the earth. I mean, we know they got there all right, and my aunt did call her daughter, but it's not like my mother not to let *me* know. I feel helpless. And guilty. Come to think of it, that's more or less how I felt during most of my life. Holy smokes...."

Just at that moment the principal and vice-principal walked in, but there must have been something else on their minds since they walked by the two teachers without so much as a perfunctory greeting, which was fortunate, because the mood Nick was in his reply would have probably been un-printable.

Maria had that look about her that told Nick she was about to add something important to their discussion, so perhaps the brief interruption by the two administrators was a blessing, as it were.

"Nick, I think that might be it."

"What might be it?"

"GUILT, you idiot. GUILT! They've been doing this to us our whole lives, and this situation is perfect for them....Guilt from a distance. Get it? They are still controlling us and mak-ing us feel guilty. Having said that, I am worried about them all, and, yes, I feel guilty, damn it. Damn it Greek."

Nick could only nod in agreement and shake his head in despair. She was right. Guilt was such a powerful weapon, es-pecially when practiced by Mediterranean mothers. But, to paraphrase an old axiom, they hadn't seen nothing yet! It was one thing to have done something, or not done something, and pay the consequences. It's like a little kid getting punished for a transgression he didn't commit, or for a misstep from so long ago, it was forgotten. Well, the seeds of Maria and Nick's guilt had been planted when they were both very young and nurtured to their current insidious level throughout their lives. But the genesis of their current confusion and worry had been devised and implemented in the previous twenty-four hours, as these clever ladies concocted a plan to throw their kids the ultimate curve ball!

CHAPTER TWENTY-THREE

Wednesday Morning
Calming Down

Tuesday went by without a word, or call, or text, or email –
nothing from the four wayward women. Maria texted Nick
first thing in the morning: "Still no word. How about you?
Worried."

"Ditto" was his succinct and pithy response.

The blank stares that each of the two teachers wore into
their encounter at lunchtime indicated that neither one of
them had heard or seen anything Trying to add a little levity
to what was becoming – despite the poo-pooing from both of
them – a worrisome situation, Nick, as was his wont, said
something he shouldn't have.

"Maybe your mother was right. Maybe you should go to
confession. Maybe we should both go," he offered with a
forced smile.

Maria was not in the mood.

"What the hell are you talking about? Greeks don't go to
confession."

"Just trying to lighten things up a bit...sorry, Maria."

"Don't worry about it," she replied. "I'm just edgy."

The lunch period rolled along, and the weather was surprisingly "springy," and unexpected for a day in mid-March. Many of the students took advantage of the sunshine and were eating outside at the picnic tables, which was fine with Maria and Nick since that meant fewer kids to watch. In actuality, they weren't paying much attention to any of the students, due to their preoccupation with their "missing" relatives.

"I just wish we'd hear something, anything," Nick blurted out after a long timeout from speaking, or doing much of anything at all. He probably wished he could have taken that statement back, as almost on cue he got an email, not from his mother or aunt, but from his mother's bank, where she and Nick had a joint account. It was to let him know that $10,000 had been transferred to a company account in California. He almost fell out of his seat, and it was all he could do to grab his partner's arm and point to the screen.

"MARIA! LOOK! Ten big ones. What the hell?"

Now, this was really his mother's account, and it was her money. Nick's name was on it for convenience and emergencies. But the question was, why would she transfer all that money?

"Nick, why would she transfer all that money?" Maria repeated, as if she had read his mind.

"That's what I was just asking myself??"

Just then Maria got a text. It was from her mother. Short and to the point: "CHK YR LPTP." She flipped up her screen and turned to email. There was one line of text – "THIS IS WHERE WE'RE STAYING," – and an attachment. Maria shot an elbow into Nick's side to get his attention. It would have done an NBA player proud.

"Nick, look at this...!!! Look at this....!!!"

The attachment contained a picture of the four smiling sisters standing in an elegant-looking yard with a pool, beautiful grounds, and a path leading down to the beach and the ocean. The Pacific Ocean!

"WHAT THE... Nick began to exclaim, but Maria shot a hand quickly over his mouth before he could finish. But her eyes were on fire with surprise and bewilderment, and they were both beside themselves, figuratively and literally. Holy Cow!!

CHAPTER TWENTY-FOUR

California Girls

The stories and laughter and eating and drinking continued long into the night, and the four Jersey girls were a bit worn out after their travels, both physically and metaphorically. Gina asked them if they had anything planned for the morrow. The day after a long trek is often more tiring than the first, and the four senoras had planned to sit and relax on a bus tour which had apparently been part of their vacation package. She looked over at her husband who was already shaking his head.

"Bus tour? I don't think so. We've been out here for thirty years, and we know "what's what" more than anyone else, tour or no tour. Why would you want to sit on a crowded bus when you can have two willing and eager servants at your beck and call? We can see the sights, eat the food, and take in the most beautiful part of this beautiful state. I'll bring our big and comfortable SUV, loaded with great songs, and with you – great people."

"Absolutely, Ladies. We won't take no for an answer," Gina added. "Like Ted said, we know the sights, and we also know the people. A lot of the 'celebrities' have been eating here for years and they've become our friends. Maybe you'd like to meet a few. I know they'd like to meet you!! And, oh yeah, wear something casual and comfortable!"

Mable and Marie jumped at the offer, notwithstanding Marie's comment to her sister about "Greeks bearing gifts." Liz said it sounded OK to her, too, but Marica, the studious thinker, was hesitant, saying that they didn't want to disrupt the couple's lives or put them out at all. But Ted, insisted, threatening to hold them hostage in the diner until they agreed to his offer. So it became a done deal! Gina and Ted drove them to their hotels, and indicated they would see them around nine in the morning.

"Get some rest, ladies, and get ready for a great day!"

Ted and Gina were as good as their word – they were at the ladies' hotels right at nine, just as they said they would be. Despite the seemingly exorbitant amount of alcohol they had consumed, none of them appeared to be hungover, which was astounding. In fact, they all felt great. Go figure....Anyway, it looked like it was going to be a glorious day weather wise, The sun was bright and beaming, and the temperature was supposed to hit the upper sixties. What could be better?

They stopped at *ITALIANS AND GREEKS* for breakfast, a "working breakfast" if you will to map out their day. After they were seated and coffee was served all around, Ted excused himself for a few moments.

"Something I said?" the younger Greek sister asked, as she fixed her coffee and took that all-important first sip.

Marie nudged Mable. "Your sister is starting to loosen up! That's good!"

"That's dangerous!" Mable kidded.

"My husband didn't mean to be rude. He thinks he makes the greatest pancakes in the world. He'll be back shortly!"

He was back quicker than anyone expected, carrying four orders of pancakes at once, with no hint of smashing any of the plates, and he couldn't resist taking a shot at his adversary from the old country.

"I was going to see if these were 'magic plates' and drop them, but I thought I'd better not risk it." he smiled. Mable stuck her tongue out and cocked her head.

He distributed the plates with the hotcakes steaming and giving off an aroma of home and good eating. Gina looked quizzically at her husband.

"Yes, dear, I'll be right back with ours!" he quipped as he headed back to the kitchen.

"These are absolutely delicious!" Liz began. "How in the world did he make them so quickly?"

"Don't tell my husband I told you this," Gina confessed, "but he always makes the batter the night before, and he had one of the cooks heat up the griddle before we came in."

"However he does it, these are out of this world," Marie added, in between bites and sips of coffee. "Out of this world!!"

Ted was back with plates for himself and his wife and a big smile, which seemed to .be a permanent fixture on his broadly handsome face. Marica made a complimentary re-mark about his disposition.

"Your hotcakes are a hit, Ted!" Gina informed him.

"Well, aren't they always?," he replied.

"And he's modest, too," Gina remarked.

Ted had barely sat down to take a sip of coffee when he stood right back up.

"Will you excuse me for a moment? I forgot to tell the cook about a luncheon party I had booked. Be right back." On his way, he tapped their waitress on the shoulder and pointed to the table.

"More coffee coming up, boss," she said pleasantly.

"Your daughter's not working this morning?," Mable asked.

"No, she's actually in college, at UCLA. I urged her to take a business course, but she wants to be a writer. There's so much competition, you know?"

Marica scrunched her face up and shook her head vigorously. "I know exactly what you mean; just like my son. He got a good teaching job and he says to me he really wants to be a writer. I told him to stick to what he was good at! There are thousands of people who want to be writers....with nothing to show for it but disappointment!"

"Just like my Maria," Marie added. "She's a great teacher, and even though her salary's not great, it pays the bills. But I know she's always wanted to do something else, too."

The mothers' symposium came to a halt when Ted returned carrying what looked like a bunch of travel brochures. He put them down next to his plate, had a swig of coffee, and took a big mouthful of hotcakes. He looked around at the Jersey girls with an expectant expression filling his face and the hotcakes filling his mouth.

Gina spoke up for everyone.

"Yes, dear, the reviews are in, and everyone loved the flapjacks."

Gina knew her husband. He couldn't have started his days without some praise for his breakfast, and he also couldn't stand the term flapjacks. She loved to see him smile and cringe at the same time (a reaction Nick often elicited from Maria, though in Nick's case it was unintentional).

"So, dear, where do we take this fearsome foursome on their first full day in paradise?"

Ted turned toward his wife, with a mouthful of coffee and was so anxious to get his thoughts out that he swallowed it while it was still a bit on the steamy side. Everyone chuckled as the slightly scalded host laughed at himself with a self-deprecating comment. "Well, I've always told my wife that I'm hot...."

It wasn't easy to calm himself down. Like most Italians and

Greeks, laughing uncontrollably was an intrinsic part of Ted's personality, and he felt that the best laughs are the ones at your own expense.

"Whew. Sorry ladies. I always said there's nothing like a good cup of coffee to get you going in the morning. OK, speaking of going....we, Gina and I, were talking last night, and there's no way you're going back to Jersey in one week. There's just not enough time to see all there is to see and meet all the people you'd love to meet."

Gina, sensing that their guests were somewhat "surprised" by her husband's comment, shook her head emphatically and "saved" him, which she had done countless times over the years of their marriage.

"What my talk first and think later husband meant, was, is that we'd love to have you stay out here longer, and we feel we've got a plan that you might like to consider."

"Thanks, Gina. What would I do without you?" Ted stated sincerely.

"The question is what am I to do *with* you?"

Ted smiled, gave his wife a quick hug, and began passing out the booklets he had brought to the table. A dealer in Vegas or Atlantic City couldn't have done it any smoother.

"I still have the good hands," he said, complimenting his own dexterity. "I think I could still play some shortstop if I wanted to..."

"...if you do say so yourself," his wife added, completing his thought with a chuckle. "Could you please just tell the girls what we discussed and save the self praise for later?"

The ladies had picked up their booklets and were immersed in the pictures and descriptions they contained.

"What a beautiful place this is," Liz began.

"This is all one city?" Marie asked with just a touch of awe.

"I think I've heard of this," Marica added. "Montecito, yeah, I've read about it."

"Is it as good as it looks?" Mable wondered.

"You'll soon see for yourselves, cause that's where we're headed. If that's OK with you that is," Gina asked semi-rhetorically

"It sounds wonderful! Marie exclaimed.

"If my son could see where we're about to go," Rica exclaimed loudly.

Ted thought he should fill in the blanks as they finished their coffee.

"Well, it's one of the most exquisite and exclusive places in the USA, actually, in the whole world. The list of celebrities who live there would knock you out – yet many of them are regulars here and we've become good friends. They hold their annual fundraiser at our restaurant, and the booklets you're looking at were an offshoot of one of the dinners. Melissa Topping came up with the idea. Perhaps you've heard of her?"

"Yes. She's on TV, right?" Mable asked.

"Yeah, Melpo, she's the hostess of that show uh, what's it called?" Marie threw in.

"IT'S NEVER TOO LATE," Liz said excitedly. "Right?"

"Would you like to meet her?"

"Sure, I've seen her, she's very smart," Rica said sincerely.

"And she's very nice as well, I listed her house," Gina stated matter of factly.

Everyone turned their heads in slight bewilderment.

"You did what?" Liz asked.

"Yeah, I'm a realtor part-time. I love it, and I got to get away from Ted sometimes, right dear?" she chided her husband, who smiled and shook his head. "It's not easy being married to a Cephalonian!"

"Don't we know it?" Marica and Mable said almost in unison. "Don't we know it!"

Everyone was in an expectant mood, eager to see the things Ted and Gina had been talking about, so they finished up their last sips of coffee and headed outside. All the ladies commented on how gorgeous the weather was. Ted smiled and shrugged: "Just another day in California."

The SUV was sparkling in and out. I looked like it had just been washed and polished, and it was roomy and comfortable. Marie and Mable took the back seats, Marica and Liz in the middle, with Gina riding shotgun. Ted slipped a CD into the slot, and they were all set.

"Hope you like the music. It's a variety of songs, all easy to listen to; I'll keep it low. Are we all set?" Ted looked back at his guests, who indicated everything was good.

"Talk is cheap, Ted. Let's go." his wife chided.

As they drove they were greeted by breathtaking views of the mountains, the beach, and the heavenly sun. Ted opened the sunroof and windows, and the gentle, cooling breeze was like a welcome mat beckoning the ladies to enjoy themselves. And were they ever enjoying themselves? Conversations were humming all over the car, covering everything: what they saw out the windows; how this whole adventure came about; what their kids would say if they could see them; the "feel" of being here and experiencing this place and these people. And there were questions for Gina and Ted about them, about their business, and especially about this fabulous part of the country. It was almost like a trip back to the 'old country: ("countries"), which all four of them desired but probably knew deep inside that they would never take. Their fanciful pipe dream was about to be reinforced by Ted the "tour guide"...

"You know, this part of the state was once a hideout for highwaymen, who robbed the people going from one town to another. But by the latter third of the 1800s the gangs were gone and a large number of immigrants from Italy began to settle here."

Marie poked Mable gently in the ribs.

"See, Italians know a good thing when they see it."

"They probably felt at home with the climate and coast, huh?" Liz added.

"Absolutely," Gina said. "This reminded them very much of Italy, and they grew produce as they used to do back home. And today this is one of the garden spots of not only California, but of the world, if you'll pardon the pun."

"Montecito! Can't beat it," Ted re-emphasized. "How about a look at the beach?"

They had been going for well over an hour, and a stretch of the legs, and the rest of the torso, seemed like a good idea to all parties. Ted pulled the car over and parked under a small grove of trees adjacent to one of the most beautiful stretches of sand one could imagine, with a stone wall just begging to be used for a natural seat and table. The word "idyllic" would have been a huge understatement, and the panoramic view left the ladies speechless, which was really saying something given their propensity for conversing with each other. The sound of the surf gently lapping onto the pristine sand evoked more emotions and memories than the sisters could count, and the aromatic scent of the ocean brought back other days and times, hidden hopes and secret wishes...

"I just love the ocean," Liz remarked. "I guess it's in my blood."

"Me, too, me, too." Mable agreed. " It is so relaxing." She seemed very subdued and pensive.

"It's who we are," Marie stated on behalf of all the sisters. "It's where we're from, The islands will always be a part of us!"

For her part, Marica just stared out at the Pacific, lost in thought.

Somehow a quaint picnic basket had manifested itself and was sitting invitingly on the sand....

"My husband *never* goes anywhere without 'provisions,'" Gina explained.

Ted just shrugged.

"Thought everyone could use something to snack on," he said, faking a defensive demeanor. "Just some iced espresso, oranges, almonds, and biscotti. How does that sound?"

"Damn good," Marica emphatically stated. "Damn good!"

Mable looked at Marie as her eyes widened almost to her ears.

Both Sicilians looked at Rica in disbelief. Who was this woman??

Gina took everything in stride and put things in perspective with her straightforward and sincere observation: "That's what Montecito can do to you, especially if you're Mediterranean."

"That's right," Ted added. "We came here for a vacation thirty years ago, and we never left..." He looked around at the four ladies. "Maybe the same thing will happen to you."

The sets of sisters became very pensive after his last comment, and the lull became almost eerie. Once again it was Gina to the rescue.

"Girls, if I can get your mind off what my husband said for just a moment, I have something else for you to wrap your heads around. But first, have a piece of fruit and a biscotti, and a few sips of coffee. Look At this marvelous setting, eat, drink, and relax!"

The ladies dutifully did as Gina directed, and before long they were their old selves again, no pun intended. Marie broke the ice with the question in everyone's thoughts.

"OK, Gina, from one Sicilian to another, what exactly was it you wanted us to 'wrap our heads around'?"

Gina cocked her head and grinned..

"What you think, Gina? We can't wrap our minds around what you're gonna say?" Mable threw in, half in jest.

"I agree with my Greek compatriot," Liz added in support.

"Yeah, Gina, spit it out, dammit," Rica interjected. "What

the hell is on your mind?" The "new" Marica seemed to have taken hold. Was this who she really was? Was it the bottled-up hostility coming out? It was like a bombshell! As Mable whispered to Marie: "My sister never was Pollyanna. She didn't hide her tough side, but I've never seen her like this! I wonder what my nephew would say?"

Mable was about to apologize for her sister, but Gina waved her off.

"Hey, that's a great lead into what I was going to say. Have some of the refreshments and think about what has transpired over the last day or so. It's about eleven-thirty, give or take, which means yesterday, twenty-four hours ago, it was about two thirty Jersey time. You were flying across the country. Now, less than twenty-four hours later, you're in a different place, with new friends – four of them I hope – (she pointed to herself and her husband), new feelings, new opportunities. But you're all still you." She noticed the puzzled looks on their faces and tried to address their confusion.

"I need two more sentences, OK?"

The ladies all nodded....

"I've heard you talk about a great number of things, including your ethnicity, your beliefs, your emotions – but mostly about the heartache of being mothers." She held up one finger for that sentence. "Why don't you put all your thoughts into a book and tell people what it's really like being who you are??" Two fingers from Gina.

"Yeah, why not?" Marie asked. "Our kids are writing one; let's beat them to the punch!"

"You mentioned that last night, but I thought you were just making conversation," Liz added.

"I was dead serious then, and even more serious now," Gina emphatically replied.

"A great idea," Mable contributed loudly. "A great idea. What do you think, Marica?"

"Best damn idea I ever heard!"

It was unanimous, Ted included.

"I can't wait to see this," he beamed.

"But how do we get started?" Marie wondered.

Gina's face lit up as she held up a small gray device about four inches square. It was an old-fashioned, portable cassette recorder. She explained what it was and that she and Ted always kept it in the car to record ideas for the restaurant and slogans to use when pitching a house. Sometimes, she indicated, she would just record her thoughts about...well....whatever she was thinking about.

"Pretty clever, Gina!" Liz remarked.

"Well, I have to tip my hat to Christina for this. She always carries a recorder with her to preserve ideas she gets for her writing." Gina paused as if she were hesitant to go one.

"And..." Rica prompted.

"Well, I have a small confession. I've had it on all morning, and I got just about everything you said. I thought that might make a good start. Am I forgiven?"

The grins all around were her answer.

"It's tough trying to keep up with this Sicilian of mine!" Ted smiled, as he gave his wife a big kiss. "But I agree with her totally on this. I think you guys could come up with a book that would put your feelings on the map. Christina already told us that she would help edit it if you would like. How could you miss?"

Everyone was all in, but Rica did have a caveat: "But when can we get this done?"

Marie agreed. "Yeah, we only have a week here, and we would like to see some more of California. Is it possible?"

"Maybe our lunch date will clear some of these things up and put your minds at ease. There are a couple more things I'd like you to see on the way. So just relax and take in the sights and feel of this beautiful day. They're expecting us in about a half hour or so, and I think my timing is pretty good. OK?"

"You gotta trust Ted on this one," Gina quipped as she turned the recorder back on. "All aboard, ladies!"

CHAPTER TWENTY-FIVE

Lunch with a Celebrity

The sisters were energized by the realization that they could do something to make their feelings known, but also that what they were about to embark upon would be a total blindside for their kids, and for everyone else they knew. The next half hour or so was very relaxing, as their "tour" showcased the beauty and grandeur of this garden of eden like place they had stumbled upon. They talked quite a bit, but the tone was low key and light as their vacation took yet one more unexpected turn. Both Mable and Marie felt that there was some other hand guiding their journey and easing them into what could only be described as heaven in every respect.

They wound around a number of quaint, picturesque streets with all different houses and landscapes. It was awesome and inspiring, and it provided a tranquility that perfectly blended with their mood. Ted pulled the car down a one lane street called Hillside Road, which was quite appropriate since it seemed to climb quickly up into the summit of the surrounding area.

"There's the house," Gina pointed out.

A narrow, winding walkway consisting of a variety of stones led up to the door. Beautiful ferns, trees, and other lush vegetation guarded either side of the walk. Mable got out of the car and was transfixed by the picture in front of her.

"What's the matter, Melpo?" Marie asked with just a bit of concern. "Are you all right?"

"Yeah, yeah, I'm fine. It's just that this reminds me of our village in Greece. It looks exactly the same. Marica was too young when we left, but I remember it like it was yesterday. It's like going back in time."

"This is what the towns in Sicily look like, too, from the pictures I've seen. Something or someone brought us to this place, Mable," Marie added with a bittersweet smile.

They hugged several times, and then realized there were other people viewing their nostalgic journey. But there were no worries. The ladies all were fighting back tears, and Ted made a comment about the sea air affecting his eyes. Gina clicked off the recorder, and motioned for everyone to come up to the front door.

"How about a picture, ladies, with the house in the background," Gina asked as she indicated a good place to stand. The sisters were all smiles, and they wound up posing for several shots: hugging, waving at the house, with arms spread to show the magnitude of their location. They took some with all six of them; separate ones of the two sets of sisters, Mable and Ted, Gina and Ted...it was glorious. No one noticed the front door being opened, or the comely, smiling woman standing there taking it all in. It was their host, Melissa Reynolds.

"I hope you know I charge a pretty penny for using my house as a backdrop!" she jokingly said, as she walked out to hug Gina and then Ted. "So, these must be the 'fabulous females,' you were telling me about at one this morning! Let's see if I can guess who's who!"

She batted a thousand as she pointed at each of the women

and called out their names: "Liz, Marie, Mable, Marica. Right?"

"Perfect Liss," Ted beamed.

"How'd you do that?" Marie wondered.

"Hey, you don't get our own show without learning a few tricks along the way," she admitted.

For her part, Gina swatted her husband hard on the back of his head.

"What's the matter with you? You called her at one in the morning?"

"Hey, I learned that from you. Strike while the iron is hot and all that other good philosophic advice you're always throwing at me. Well?"

"Yeah, yeah. Sorry, Liss..." Gina sincerely apologized.

"It's fine. The important thing is we're all here. Let's go inside!"

The inside of the house was spacious, yet cozy. There were rooms upon rooms, all decorated with the eye of someone who valued comfort and tradition. The furniture looked as if it might have been in a modest home in the Midwest rather than in a multi-million dollar residence in an exclusive California hillside. There was a room with a solid wall of books – much too lived in to be called a library, and the kitchen seemed to say "have a cup of coffee and stay a while."

"Some place, huh, ladies?" Gina asked rhetorically.

"You are the master of understatements, Gina," Marica offered.

"Some place? SOME PLACE!" Liz added.

"It's such a beautiful day that I had Maria set up lunch outside, If that is OK with everyone," Melissa offered as she opened two French doors.to reveal a vista usually reserved for a movie scene. There was a patio surrounded by lush plants and trees, and a winding path leading down to the beach about a hundred yards away.

"WOW" was written on everyone's face, as they made their

way out toward a rustic-looking picnic table right out of Norman Rockwell. The Pacific provided an elegant backdrop to the scene, and the soft sound of the waves was the perfect musical accompaniment to complete what surely had to be a dream. The table was set with paper plates and plastic utensils, more "picnic-like," their hostess explained.

The housekeeper seemed to know Gina and Ted, rather well, as she hugged the husband and wife and asked how their family was and how things were going at *ITALIANS AND GREEKS*. Ted answered the question on the ladies' minds before they asked.

"Oh yeah, Maria was like a part of our family..."

"You mean 'IS' part of our family," Gina corrected her husband.

"Yes, my wife is right. Maria 'IS' and always will be family. She helped us get our business started many years ago, and then Melissa stole her right out from under us," Ted said jokingly.

"Same name as your daughter, right?" Mable said quietly as she nudged Marie, who just put on a wry smile and nodded.

"Why don't we sit and have something to eat? Ted informed me that you had quite a dinner last night, so Maria prepared a light fare today, if that is OK," Melissa explained.

Apparently the meaning of "light" was different in California than it was in the East. There were platters of olives and cheese, warm chunks of Italian bread, containers of olive oil, tomatoes, and cucumbers, and a large variety of sandwiches cut into convenient triangular pieces, and San Pelligrino water with slices of lemon.

"My goodness, everything looks so delicious, Rica said.

"It sure does," Marie added.

"Please, dig in ladies. My husband really wanted to be here, but he had to go to LA to wrap up a book deal with one of the Dodgers. I told you about that, Ted, right?"

"Yeah, you did. I want an autographed copy, Liss!"

"Book deal?" Liz asked.

"Oh, yeah," Gina answered. "Peter Topping, president of *TOP SHELF BOOKS*."

"He publishes really interesting stuff with a personal touch," Melissa explained. "One of us has to like the premise before his company will consider it. His latest novel is a best-seller – *ACCIDENTAL LOVE*."

"Oh, I've heard of that," Rica said, as she took a big bite of bread.

The conversation began to take a back seat to their repast as the ladies began to dig in.

"You know what? We should get a picture of all of us with the ocean in the background."

"Good idea, Mable," Marie chimed in. "Maybe after we eat."

"Our mother used to say if you want to do something, you have to do it when you have the chance. Let's take a couple now, then we can finish, OK?"

"Yeah, let's do it, ladies," Liz agreed.

So, there was a brief intermission in the chewing, and a brief, fun filled picture session. They took every possible combination of people: each set of sisters; the fearsome foursome; Ted and Gina and Melissa; Melissa and the ladies; Maria with each of the combinations....and so on. The smiles were genuine, and when they settled back in to eat, everyone found that their appetites had been spurred by the photo ops!!

In between bites of chicken salad Marie had an epiphany.

"Hey, can I send one of these back to my daughter? It will knock her out!"

"Yes, yes," Mable jumped in. "Send one of the four of us, and tell her this is where we're staying. She'll probably show it to my nephew and they will go nuts!!"

"Well," Melissa began, "there could be more truth than not

in that statement."

"Huh?" Liz wondered

"Let's have coffee and dessert by the pool, and I'll explain the whole thing, if my accomplices (pointing to Ted and Gina) will help fill in the details..."

"We'll not only help with the details, we'll get the coffee and dessert," Ted offered genuinely. "Maria, take some food and take a break for yourself!"

Maria smiled and sat on a lounge chair, stretching and sighing. She smiled and saluted Mr. and Mrs. Micropolis. "You guys are the best."

"We know that!" Ted kidded.

After everyone was settled with coffee and crumb cake, all eyes were on Melissa.

"Ok, it's really pretty simple. We're opening our new season in two weeks, and I need to spend a lot of time in LA. So we're staying at our apartment in the city – it saves a lot of time on the commute, and it would ease things for both my husband and me work-wise and time-wise. Well, Gina was going to rent it out for me, but it's hard to do for that short a period of time, and I don't really like strangers in my house. Maria has a vacation coming up, and I really don't like to leave the house vacant. So...I thought, well, rather Ted suggested, that perhaps the four of you would like to stay here."

Fifty jigsaw puzzles could have been constructed from the looks of astonishment and confusion on the sisters' faces, which caused some chuckles on Ted's part and empathy from Melissa and Gina.

"Ladies, let Ted and me give you a refill and another pinch of cake, and we'll explain, cause I know you must have questions and concerns. Right?"

"First of all, let me say that I think that all this was somehow meant to happen. Yesterday at this time you were just landing at LA X, and I had no idea of what was going to happen. Right??"

They all looked at each other and nodded.

Gina took over. "We've known Melissa for many years. She helped us publicize *ITALIANS AND GREEKS*, and we knew some interesting guests that we got for her show." She waved her hand at Ted, who didn't miss a beat.

"So it all sort of fell into place when we met you all, and it seemed things had come full circle from when I was five. Melissa needed a house-sitter as it were, you guys want some adventure and you have a story to tell – it's a perfect match!"

"But what about the cost?" Marica asked.

"Yeah, we may have gotten loaded last night, but money wise we're not – loaded that is," added Marie.

Melissa couldn't contain her smile.

"Did Ted leave out that there will be no charge for your stay?"

"I thought he said that," Mable replied "Are you sure?"

"Absolutely. BUT – you will owe me something," Liss retorted with a big grin.

"I knew there'd be a catch," Rica said only half seriously. "What is it?"

"You agree to be my first guests for the new season of my show....two weeks from yesterday."

"That's it?" Liz asked.

"Well, we'd also like you to get your thoughts down into a book format....Christina will be on a break from school, and she'd LOVE to come out here and oversee the project," Gina explained.

"Well, everything sounds good, and you people are so nice....but what about our hotels?" Liz asked.

"The two managers are good customers and good friends. I called them while I was supposedly talking to my head chef this morning. If you decide to do this, they will move your reservations up two weeks, no charge, and my wife and I will see to it that you see whatever parts of this state that you'd like to see – at your service as a chauffeur and tour guide." Ted concluded with a huge bow, receiving an ovation from the seven ladies!

"Groceries will be delivered, the liquor cabinet is well stocked, and there will be a car here at your disposal if you'd like to go exploring! Do we have a deal?" Melissa earnestly stated as she bowed to the assembled sisters.

There were smiles and hugs all around, and too many "thank-you's" to record.

"Oh, Melissa, Mable had mentioned this before.. would you be able to send a picture to my daughter, with the caption: 'Look at where we're staying?'" Marie asked. "That will really throw them, right Mable, right Rica?" The Greek sisters high-fived the Sicilians, Gina included.

"Sure thing Marie. Maria is our resident computer expert – could you tell her where we can send it?" Melissa replied.

"Ou, ou," Marica shouted. "I have an idea that will really play with their brains. I have a joint account with my son, and the woman at the bank is a classmate from college. Gina, can you give me the name of your company? I'll call her and have her send an email to my son that I just withdrew ten thousand dollars and forwarded it to you. Combined with the picture, Nick and Maria will have to think it's for rent money, or maybe even a down payment! I'll have her send it during the day when he is at school, and he and Maria can chew on that for a while!!"

"I'm proud of you, Marica. You're starting to think like me!!" Mable said with gusto!

Another round of high fives was followed by some wine and brandy, and an exclamation from Ted: "You guys are something else! I would hate to have you mad at me!"

CHAPTER TWENTY-SIX

The Ladies Write a Book!

MEDITERRANEAN MOTHERS –

THE HEARTACHES & THE TEARS....

LIZ, MARIE, MABLE, MARICA

ACKNOWLEDGEMENTS

Based upon an idea by Gina Micropolis
Edited by Christina Micropolis

PREFACE

We decided to put this volume together because we felt that mothers in general, and Italian and Greek mothers in particular, get a bad rap from the population as a whole, and especially from their selfish, spiteful children.

Let us say right at the outset that while we will bring many of our own experiences into play, this will also be a global compilation of observations and events we have come to know over the cumulative years of our lives.

Who are we? Two sets of widowed sisters, Sicilians (Liz and Marie) and Greeks (Marica and Mable). As of this writing, we have been best friends for exactly seventy-two hours. That's right, just about three days. We met on a flight from New Jersey to LA, and if anyone thinks that things just happen randomly, think again, sister!

DEDICATION

*This book is dedicated to mothers everywhere
In the hope that it will help them deal with
Their ungrateful children*

INTRODUCTION

We were told by many "experts" that we can't have a PREFACE, a DEDICATION, and an INTRODUCTION. Who cares what they say? This is OUR book, and we'll do as we please.

So, what we'd like you to do is read this as if we were sitting right next to you, and this was more of a conversation between friends – mothers – rather than something to read. Make it personal. At the end of each chapter, we will pose an opinion question for you on what we said, and a second question relating to your own experiences.

How does that sound??

Go ahead, let's talk....

CHAPTER 1 – A MOTHER'S LOVE
IS THE ROOT OF ALL HEARTBREAK

Without love we wouldn't care, and if we didn't care, our lives would be a lot easier. I mean a LOT easier. Of course, this is true in other relationships: wives and husbands, siblings, friends. But there is nothing like the love a mother has for her child, and, on the flip side, there is nothing like the heartache, pain, and tears that your children can cause you to feel. There is NOTHING like the pain and emptiness a mother feels, and the reason is very simple: your children were once a part of you. For nine months you get fatter, you are saddled with morning sickness, throw up, can't eat what you want cause nothing tastes good. And then, to top it off, you have the distinct feeling that your lower regions were being ripped apart as the baby is born.

Husbands always say that they love the kids as much as mothers but how can they? They can't possibly have the depth of feelings and hurt that we experience. What exactly is it that they do? They get you pregnant, go about their lives for nine months, and then give out cigars. What a tough role!

And then....diapers, and rashes, and feedings, and baths, and crying, and not sleeping. Husbands make a big deal out of earning the money. Wow, what a sacrifice. That's what they've been doing their whole lives; nothing is different. It's like they go out the door with the attitude..."Well, I gotta go now. Let me know how things turn out." Please...

Q – What do YOU think causes you the most heartbreak?

Q – And, what has your husband done, or not done, that made (or still makes) you furious?

CHAPTER 2 – GETTING OLD STINKS –
AND BEING A WIDOW STINKS EVEN MORE

Let's face it, husbands are OK, but they can often be a pain. They never want to do what you want to do, they're on the lazy side at best, and they stick to their old habits as if they were afraid they would run away and leave them. Admittedly, they usually made a decent wage, but if you didn't watch them, they would waste what they earned on non-necessities, often involving some sort of alcoholic beverage or sporting event. Having said that, it was better to have them around from time to time. It was someone to talk to, complain to, threaten the kids with, and correct the behavior of. They were always suckers for the guilt trips we would lay on them, and they rarely if ever saw through our emotional outbreaks usually topped off with a layer of tears. Plus cutting the roast or turkey, taking out the garbage, cutting the lawn, and shoveling snow were all better left to the male of the species.

And where are they now? They all got up and left us, in a manner of speaking. They have died, passed away, whatever term you'd like to use. We feel bad, of course, and we miss them, but being left on your own is no picnic. People look at you and think you are feeble-minded at best and on the brink of kissing your life goodbye. You can tell by the way they look at you and talk to you. Like you're a doddering idiot. And please don't call us "seniors." Seniors are the last year of high school. We find the term very demeaning.

And your kids? You still worry about them, but it seems that they can't grasp what you are going through or what you need. They either suffocate you by making all your decisions or don't get in touch with you for weeks at a time.

> *There's no getting around it, getting old and being a widow is a double whammy we are all cursed with, and having kids is the razor's edge....heartaches and tears!!*
>
> *Q – What is worse, being old, or being a widow?*
> *Q – What would you change about society's view of mothers, young or old?*

The ladies and Christina had been working hard on the manuscript, and they got quite a bit done in one afternoon. They had spent the morning, with Ted and Gina's help, getting all their things together from the hotel and moving into Melissa's house. The whole thing still seemed a bit unbelievable.

"I think you're on the right track, ladies. Keeping it simple and to the point will attract a lot more potential readers and help you get your message across. Rather than being an all-encompassing warehouse of guilt, your book will highlight where you want the reader to go with her thoughts and let them flesh out each chapter with their own experiences and perspectives. Really seems to be working well so far. I think we're on the right track, and I also think we could use a quick coffee break, huh?

"Good idea, Christina. Thanks so much for helping us with this. Your mom's recordings of our conversations gave us a good starting point, and your guidance has been indispensable," Rica began.

"Absolutely," Marie piggy backed. "My daughter is always saying how hard it is to write. It's not really that hard at all, is it?"

"It's not hard when you have the right combination of people doing it. And we have the perfect combination!" Liz added emphatically.

"Damn right," Mable agreed. "Why don't we sit out back. I'll make the coffee"

"I got the snacks, Melpo," Marie volunteered.

Liz and Marica made themselves comfortable in the yard, while Marie and Mable attended to the refreshments. There was a cooling breeze wafting in from the Pacific, and the sun was in its late afternoon glow. Just like a postcard!

"So, what do you think about your new friends, Mable? Do you like us?" Marie said half-jokingly.

"Like you? We love you!!" Mable responded, giving Marie a big hug. "You know, my best friend when I came here from Greece was named Maria, and you're Marie, and your daughter is named Maria, right? Funny how things turn out, huh?"

Christina was in the front yard recording some observations on her recorder. She was truly enjoying doing this project, and she figured she may as well save her thoughts and ideas while they were still fresh. Who knows, she figured, maybe they would provide her with the groundwork for a book of her own someday. She was enjoying working with the women. They were nice people, they had fascinating stories and takes on things, and it was like going on a tour of her Mediterranean island(s) heritage. One thing she had learned from her parents, who worked harder than anyone she knew, was that you had to push, but you also had to learn to get your rest when you could. To say the ladies had been going on a breakneck pace the last few days was understating all the amazing things that had happened.

Christina decided to suggest that they knock off for the day, and have a quiet evening watching the sun go down over the ocean. She walked out into the back to find Liz and Rica almost asleep in the lounge chairs, and Mable and Marie talking quietly. Marie held up a finger to her lips to indicate they should all be quiet. Christina nodded.

"I'll hustle up something light for dinner and bring it out here. We can eat under the stars. How does that sound?" The smiles on their faces indicated their grateful approval. They would get back to work tomorrow!

CHAPTER 3 – BEWARE OF KIDS GIVING GIFTS...

Ironically, our children (Marie's and Marica's) unknowingly set up this friendship and this book by giving us a week in California as a Christmas present. Now, even though they work together, we don't think this was a coordinated endeavor. In other words, they just happened to give us, the two sets of sisters, the same days in California and to book us on the same flight. Why do we say that this was accidental (but not coincidental – more about that in a moment)? Because if they knew we were on the same flight they could have been smoother about it – when Marie called and talked to them they were clueless, and when Maria called back, they were even more in the dark. PLUS – would they want us to meet like this – and unite?? DOUBTFUL!

However, we feel that the motivation on each of their parts was to get rid of us for a while. Perhaps they didn't coordinate things, but we're pretty sure they tossed this option back and forth while they were on their "lunch duty," whatever the hell it is they do there. At the very least they wanted us out of their hair, if you will, and at the most they had things they wanted to do without us around. In either case, or if it were something in between, they wanted us out of the picture. That's why we say: BEWARE OF KIDS BEARING GIFTS. There's always a catch, always, and the sooner you realize it the better off you will be!

Now, we said before that our meeting was not coincidental, and what we meant was that there were too many things that "just happened" to bring us all together to have occurred by chance. I mean, what are the odds of bringing two Sicilians and Cephalonians together to become such good friends with so much in common and so much to look forward to? Nope, there was some sort of fate working here. They say God works in strange ways; why not through those two bratty kids?? Something to think about!

Q 1 Why do you think our kids gave us this trip?
Q 2 What gift have your kids given you that appeared to have strings attached?

CHAPTER 4 – OLIVE OIL IS THICKER THAN BLOOD...

It's really fascinating, and almost eerie, how this book came about. We all met each other on a flight out to LA from Newark, and everything just clicked into place like a slick Hollywood script – except that this all really happened. But you have to wonder if we would have been so compatible had we not all been from Mediterranean Islands: Sicily and Cephalonia. There's something about that part of the world that's unique and distinct. All the rest of the countries half nastily remark that we all have olive oil in our veins. Well, we don't see anything wrong with that. It's what makes us tick – or flow would perhaps be a better word. But it's also about being from an island, where the sea washes your homeland on all sides, and you never lose the feel, the mysticism of the water, and the aura it created over countless decades and centuries of kissing the shore of your homeland. That is what the four of us have, and motherhood solidifies and cements that part of our persona.

Now, we are not saying that Mediterranean mothers are any better than moms from other ethnic groups, but we do take issue, albeit in a minor way, with those groups who think they have a monopoly on pain and hurt because of their children. And, it is often these same groups who think they have cornered the market by doling out guilt to their offspring. Give us just a small break. First of all, you can't spell GUILT without a "G" (GREEKS) and an "I" (ITAL-IANS), but that is merely setting the stage. When it comes to rolling up your sleeves, 24/7 (justifiably) making your children feel bad for something they may have done, or which you imply they may have done, no one does more bloodletting than us: Italians and Greeks. Of course, that is a metaphor, but not by much.

Let's face it, our mothers did it to us, and we survived. It made us tougher and better able to deal with the world, even, to some degree, to put up with and "guiltify" the bratty children we raised. I know we've said this before, but children, whether they're four or forty, think that the relationship between them and their parents is a one-way street. Think about it, we feed them, change them, get them dressed, take them places, Stay up with them when they're sick, buy them things, worry about the people they hang around with, double worry when they get serious with someone – and all we ask in return is a little respect and concern. Is it too much for them to show us that they give a damn if we are alive or dead? Call the damn house, come over.

We used to get whacked when we didn't do what was right. Maybe we should have done that to our own kids when they were little – or now, when they are big. I know some of you cringe at the thought, but a swat or two never hurt anyone, least of all an Italian or a Greek. That's what kept those civilizations – the Greeks and the Romans – as the preeminent cultures of the ancient world. And that's why we say, today, some two thousand years later, that although you can take the "olive oil" statement as a metaphor, and apply it to any ethnic group, there's still, in our humble opinion, nothing so lethal as a Mediterranean Mother who is out for revenge....nothing!

Q – What caught your attention the most in the above passage? Why?

Q – What can you emphasize using your own ethnicity to get your kids to give a damn about you?

CHAPTER 5 – MARIA & NICK, –
FOUR LADIES TALKING...

We thought we should give you some specifics in our dealings with our children, and rather than going through a long list of happenings and situations, we decided to use these examples and show just some of the pain and heartache they've caused their mothers. This chapter will be essentially a conversation among the four of us, with Marie and Marica in the lead with regard to Maria and Nick, since essentially they are responsible for getting us tougher here in California, and thus this book. In fact, in a number of ways they seem to be joined at the hip – NO PUN INTENDED. We're sure some of these observations will hit home with you as we unroll our thoughts, and that you will revisit your own experiences as you read along.

MARIA –"Well, Maria is a pretty good daughter," Marie began, "and niece, for the most part," Liz added in. "BUT," Marie continued, "for a smart woman who teaches other people's kids, she really misses quite a bit. She can't understand why I stay in our house, the place where I had my kids and lived for more years than I can count. She keeps telling me the house is too big. Too big? It wasn't too big while she was growing up, did it suddenly grow in size? I feel comfortable there, and so what if the neighborhood has changed? Things never stay the same. She's a hot shot teacher...wouldn't you think she would know that? Of course, she was gone for quite a few of those years when she moved to California to teach and live her life."

"Kind of ironic, huh, Marie? She left for California, and now here we are IN California," Rica added.

"I gotta say, Marie, she's a good niece, and she tries to do the right thing," Liz chimed in.

"Yes, she does, she just doesn't do it often enough. How many times have I wished she would at least call to see if I was still breathing? And she always thinks her opinion is the right one. She has no patience with me at all. Let me tell

you, she was not an angel growing up – or now, for that matter. I had to have plenty of patience with her. You'd think she would at least let me know that she cares. And now apparently, she's teamed up with that Greek she works with, and they are working on a book?? God knows what they are saying about us."

"Hey, not to worry, we're gonna have the last laugh on both of them," Mable triumphantly added. "Keep the faith, ladies!"

NICK – "Let me tell you some things which most people don't know or don't care to know because number one they are not mothers, and number two they are not HIS mother. Everyone keeps telling me what a great son I have, and he's done this and done that and he went to such a good school. BULLSHIT. He is where he is, wherever that 'is,' because of me."

"I was the one who read to him, who took him places, who made him aware of things, who taught him Greek, who took him to piano lessons, and who got him interested in the college he went to....and, I was the one who paid for his damn college. ME, I did it. You'd think he would show some appreciation. I had to care for my father, my husband, and my son. Do I get any thank you's, or phone calls, or has he ever taken me anywhere? No, no, and NO."

"Wait, Rica, I don't mean to interrupt, but when you said 'piano lessons' it rang a bell. Did he take lessons on Werner Street, in Hilltown?"

"Yes, how in heaven's name did you know?"

"Maria told me! That's where my house is. Holy smokes."

This is Liz...."As the reader can see, or read, as it were, this chapter is basically four women talking about the heartache involved with kids....we didn't know which way it was going to go, but we tried to get everything down that we were saying just as we said it...another amazing 'coincidence'...time out....

---quick break....get something to drink, your choice---

"OK, we're back. Whew. Go ahead, Marica. You were say-ing..."

"Thanks, Marie. I was about to tell you more about Nick, but you seem to know more about him than I do," Rica said with a big smile. "I'm just kidding with you, but over the years there have been other people telling me things about my kid that I never would have known."

"You know how many times that has happened to me with Maria?"

"And to me?" Mable threw in

"Ditto...!" Liz concluded, finishing up the round robin. "You were saying, Rica?"

"Well, everyone thinks he's the perfect kid. First of all, there is no such thing. Secondly, they sure as hell didn't con-sult me on that description. Would a perfect kid go play baseball on Mother's Day? Or buy theater tickets as a pre-sent for his mother and then go on a date with his girlfriend so I had to go with someone else? Or write a song and not show it to me first?? It's like he's ashamed to be seen with me. Or how about a phone call once a day to see how I am? How long would that take? Two minutes? Tears and heart-ache, heartaches and tears, and lack of consideration to the nth degree. That trip he gave us was out of guilt, so he could feel better and, so he wouldn't have to call me. Well, all I have to say is that it doesn't make up for all the things over and over again through all those years of neglect. Heart-aches and tears."

Q – What did one of your kids do that was similar to what Maria or Nick inflicted on their mothers?
Q – How do you propose we get even with them?

CHAPTER 6 – GETTING EVEN....
AND THEN SOME...

This may sound harsh, but sometimes, wherever you can actually, you as mothers need to reassert who you are and make your kids take notice, at the very least. They need to be "spanked"(figuratively), so they can see what it's like to hurt and feel pain. This is nothing new, by the way. It goes back to the beginnings of history – actually, to before the beginning of history Just imagine it's ten thousand years ago, and a woman is cooking over an open fire and taking care of her children. Her husband, so to speak, is out supposedly hunting for dinner, although the men probably stopped for a drink or two at a nearby watering hole – a real watering hole, as opposed to the bars and gin mills of today. (Although, we suspect that they had hollow gourds filled with some sort of intoxicating beverages hidden somewhere out in the brush). Meanwhile, the women are taking care of the elders, the cooking, and the overactive children, who find out at an early age that their mothers are the source of food, and cleansing, learning how to speak, and how to acquire the skills needed to grow up. Then, of course, the men come home (sometimes, but not always, with the kill of the day) and it's playtime regardless of the success or failure of the hunt. There are stories to tell the children and demonstrations of daddy's prowess with the spears....but NEVER any help from the damn men....that's where the children get their "we are owed this, Mom" attitude.

Now, we're not advocating physical punishment, which I'm pretty sure was number one on the prehistoric hit parade – no pun intended. Although, truth be told, a forceful swat on the butt now and then certainly gets the point across. But we're talking words here, which, when coupled with emotions and some sobbing, take a grip on the soul which is hard to shake. We are pretty sure that Maria and Nick are not writing about their teaching experience as they claim, but about us, as their mothers and aunts and all the guilt we have doled out over the years. Too bad. If they feel guilty, it's because they deserve to feel guilty. If they had given us our due, we wouldn't be in the wretched places we often find ourselves as mothers, as aunts, as Mediterranean widows, as people, for goodness sakes.

So, while this is not really a "how to" book, here are some tips when dealing with your children. Use whenever the situation is appropriate, or, for good measure, whenever the mood strikes you. The best long-term technique is to start when they are very young. Two reasons for this – First, this will become part of their upbringing, and while they may never consider it "normal," they will figure it's a necessary evil that comes with growing up. Secondly, they will get so tired of hearing it time and time again over the years they will often do whatever you want them to just so they don't have to listen to it another time. (We believe Maria would call it "negative reinforcement") Whatever it is, it works when applied often with feeling.

Here are a couple of examples so you can see how this works. Remember, you have to adapt your tactics to who you are and what your kids are like, but a general rule of thumb, which we are using right now, by the way, is that repetition is always good. If you keep repeating the same thing It may not only get the desired result, but then later you can truthfully say things like, "I've told you this a hundred times" and "Don't you ever listen when I tell you things?" Your emotional tone can vary from situation to situation. Often a loud shriek is effective, and at other times a soft, barely audible tone will have them wondering what you are up to.

You might remind them about all the things you have done for them their whole lives, and are still doing for that matter. "Love" is a keyword. You tell them how much your actions have shown how much you love them, and that all you're asking in return is for them to have some consideration to ease your pain. "Is that too much to ask?" is always a good question to throw in.

Q – How would you settle at least one score with your kids right now?

Q – Is there something you wish you could have done differently or reacted to differently?

CHAPTER 7 – AN EMPATHETIC MESSAGE FOR THE KIDS...

We sort of assumed that our readers would be mothers looking for some solace and a shoulder to lean on through all the ups and downs of motherhood. And that's probably true. But maybe, just maybe, our book was sitting on the coffee table or on the counter in the kitchen, and one of the "children" happened to pick it up. So, to be fair, this chapter is going to be written with you in mind. I mean, after all, we do owe you something, cause without you we wouldn't be mothers, and this book would never have been written.

Most children from five to fifty have the preconceived notion that mothers are out to get them at all costs, and that guilt is the primary weapon in this lifelong battle. The truth is, "GUILT" is all we have left to us. It's not that we don't love our children – we do. And we know that for the most part, they love us. The problem is that we need to be shown that love by actions, not words. We realize that you have your own lives, with husbands, and wives, and children, and careers, and concerns. We feel that we could probably help with these things, and instead of welcoming our assistance, we are turned away, and you often use the other aspects of your lives as an excuse for not showing more consideration and sharing more of what you do – good and bad – with us.

How about it....will you at least take what we just said into consideration? The joys you have brought us are the reason for our heartaches and tears. Love leads to heartaches – it's as simple as that.

Q – If you're a "kid," regardless of age, is there something you could do to make things better? If so, what would it be, and do you think you will do it?
Q – If you're a mother, do you think your children, your child, or any of them will follow through on the above question? Hmmm....

CHAPTER 8 – WHAT LINDER DID

Linder killed her mother. Well, she didn't take a gun and shoot her, but she might as well have.. Linder and her mother used to live on the corner, just down the street from us. They were just an ordinary family with a single parent and one child, and they had the normal ups and downs that any family has. Things seemed more or less OK. But then, for no good reason, Linder moved out, and that's when the heartaches and tears went out of control for her mother. Why did she leave? Was it just to be out on her own, or was it to punish her mother? They had a whole big house to themselves, with plenty of room for each one of them to go about her business without bothering the other one. The yard was gorgeous! There was a lush green lawn, rose bushes, and a trellis that Linder's father had built that was covered with grape vines. There were fresh grapes all through the summer and into the fall, and the back porch was a shady place to rest, or read, or just enjoy the day.

I remember running into the mother at the grocery store just a few days after Linder left. She waved to me from across two aisles, like someone who had fallen overboard and needed to be rescued.

"Marie, I'm so glad I ran into you. I don't know what to do."

I asked her what the matter was, and she told me the whole story, how they had a big fight and Linder accused her mother of trying to control her by making all the decisions for her and ruining her life.

"I've had enough. I can't stand it anymore," was what Linder said to her, and the next day she left.

I told her not to worry, that her daughter would keep in touch with her, and once she found out how hard it was to live on your own, that she would be back. The words seemed comforting, but it never happened that way. Linder rarely called, and she never came back, not even for a visit. Her mother lost all her drive to lead her life, and the last thing I heard she was in a nursing home. That's the last I heard of her. That Linder –she killed her mother. And they used to live right down the street from us; right on the corner.

Q – Do you know someone like Linder?
Q – Why do you think children treat their mothers this way?

CHAPTER 9 – AND SO...

We could go on and on and on, as our children might say, but this was not meant to be an all-inclusive look at the challenges of being a mother and the many factors that play into the picture. Rather, we wanted to highlight three major things:

1) How tough it is just being a mother, and how it becomes harder exponentially if you are a widow, and yes, as you get older

2) A mother's love cannot be duplicated by anyone, nor can the heartaches and tears she feels because of her love.

3) GUILT is often the only way mothers have of getting their children's attention, and no one does it better than mothers with olive oil in their blood.

We would like to say thank you once again to:
Gina Micropolis for suggesting this project ...

Christina Micropolis for her invaluable aid putting this all together...

Melissa Topping for turning our feelings into a real book.

One final word: call your mother, or suffer the consequences!!

EPILOGUE

If you'd like to get in touch with us with a comment, a question, an anecdote, or just to talk, PLEASE call us or drop us an email:

1-800-MOTHERS
{MediterraneanMothers@Tears&Love.com}

With love...
  THE Mediterranean Mothers:
  Marie, Liz, Marica, Mable

CHAPTER TWENTY-SEVEN

It's Never Too Late

(A daily TV show on at 10 AM Pacific Time, 1 PM in the East.
It is broadcast nationwide.
The host is a local newswoman, Melissa Topping.
The program is broadcast live. There are about 300 people or
so in the audience).

> THEME MUSIC PLAYS IN THE BACKGROUND
> With CHORUS SINGING........
> SONG: IT'S NEVER TOO LATE.
>> *Got something you want to do well*
>> *It's never too late*
>> *As long as you start right now*

SONG CONTINUES AS THE CURTAIN OPENS...

SET: What looks like a living room...there is a large
couch and a smaller piece of upholstered furniture, all
covered in clear, thin plastic. There is also an impos-
ing, large marble table One of the features of this program is that the decor is matched, as much as possible,
to the guests of each particular day.

(As the TV and studio audience see the people on the set, the theme song of the show fades out and is replaced by mandolin music playing traditional Italian and Greek songs, and, there are four women, yup, "the" four women, sitting comfortably and sipping dark coffee. The spotlight falls on the host, an attractive woman about fifty or so, sitting on a bench that resembles something you might see at a game. She is sporting a large, genuine smile and bows her head in appreciation for the applause she receives.)

"Hello everyone, I'm Melissa Topping, and I'd like to welcome you to *IT'S NEVER TOO LATE*, where we highlight people who have made a sharp turn in their lives, who have gotten off the bench, and into the game. Tonight we have a special treat: four "Mediterranean Mothers," actually two sets of sisters, who, believe it or not, met their counterparts less than two weeks ago. In that short span of time, they have become best friends, rented a house here in California, charmed the heck out of everyone they met, and written what I'm sure is going to be a best-selling book! Less than two weeks!!"

She held up a book for the camera, which focused in on the cover, which had, of course, the title: *MEDITERRANEAN MOTHERS – THE HEARTACHES AND THE TEARS* a very becoming picture of the ladies, and only their first names as the authors.

"What I'm holding up is what they call a galley edition, sort of a 'scrap copy' or 'rough draft,' if you will, of what the final product will look like. These four women tell some amazing stories in the book, but their own story of how all this came to pass is even more amazing. Let me introduce our guests, from left to right as you're seeing them: Liz, Marica, Mable, and Marie. Ladies, welcome to *IT'S NEVER TOO LATE,* where we highlight people who have made a dramatic turn in their lives, and the four of you have certainly done that. Before we get to the journey that brought you together and led you to our show, let me ask you about the accommodations here in the studio. Does the seating arrangement meet with your approval? How's the coffee? And the koulouria and cannolis?"

"Excellent." "Coffee is great." "Love the couch and the table!" "Coffee and something sweet is the best combination."

"I'm glad you like what my producer rounded up. And he and everyone else seem to like everything as well," the host exulted, as she swung her hand to indicate that the camera should sweep around and take a shot of her backstage crew, who were stuffing their faces with the pastries and savoring the dark coffee. For that matter, so were many in the audience, which was a bit of a surprise to the host. She looked back at her producer, who just shrugged and explained:

"Everything looked so good I couldn't resist letting the folks out there have some, too."

Kiddingly Melissa wondered if he had sent some home to the TV viewers.

"But, seriously, Greg, where are my coffee and pastries?"

Her producer, Greg Harris, was sincerely apologetic as he brought a tray out himself.

"I beg your forgiveness, oh queen of the morning. Sorry, Liss," he said with a quick salute!

"Yeah, yeah, Harris. Talk is cheap," she shot back with a huge smile. It was obvious that the two of them were not only co-workers but also good friends, and that the host was not only quick on her feet but had a genuine fondness for people.

"My producer is really a good guy, but he also likes to draw his salary, so I'd better get on with what I am paid to do so he has a show to produce." Her demeanor was infectious, and soon everyone on and offstage was laughing, which was just as it should be!

"You still here, ladies? Good. Ladies and gentlemen, my guests this morning are Italian sisters – Liz and Marie – raise your hands so they know...and Greek sisters – Marica and Mable. More precisely, they are from islands, Sicily and Cephalonia, respectively. I was introduced to them by the proprietors of a famous local eatery, *Where ITALIANS AND GREEKS Come To Eat,* where I dine at least twice a week. If you've never been there, go! How is the food there, Ladies?"

"Best I've ever had," Mable jumped in.

Marie gave Mable a high five, while Liz and Marica nodded and gave the OK sign with their fingers and their smiles.

"I'll set the stage, and then I'll let the ladies take over. *ITALIANS AND GREEKS* is owned and operated by a married couple, Gina and Ted Micropolis. She is Sicilian, and he was born in, you guessed it, Cephalonia. I believe they are here today...Ted and Gina, could you stand up please?"

Gina and Ted stand up and wave. The studio audience gives them a hearty welcome. Melissa continues with the background on her guests... "Now, this is only one of the many apparent 'coincidences' in this story. Ladies, you're up!"

Liz thought she'd better start, because once her sister and Mable got going, it would be like trying to swim up a waterfall.

"Well, my sister and I were on a vacation that my niece gave us as a Christmas gift, and on the flight from New Jersey we met these two Greek ladies and we started talking, and we became not only friendly, but good friends, and then one thing led to another and here we are."

Marica jumped in. "Yes, coincidentally, my son had given my sister Mable and me the same thing for Christmas, at the same time, on the same flight."

"Coincidence my foot. It turns out that my daughter and Rica's son work together every day, they're teachers at Burns High School – is that right, I always forget the name of their school," Marie went on. She looked over at Marica, who nodded slightly.

"OK, Burns, yeah. Anyway, I think they gave us this trip to

get rid of us for a while, and they planned it so the dates would be the same so they could be free to do whatever...."

A murmur went through the audience.

"'Whatever' covers a lot of ground!" the host observed.

"Exactly!" Marie emphatically stated. "Exactly!

The murmur turned into smiles and giggles.

"What they didn't plan on was that we'd meet. I don't think they would have wanted that. Now we have everything out in the open, and there is strength in numbers, right girls?" Mable interjected.

The four protagonists high-fived each other, the host smiled and chuckled, and the people watching in the studio, including the staff, went into cascades of laughter.

But Maria and Nick weren't laughing. They were watching on their computers while ostensibly on lunch duty. Luckily there were no emergencies, because from the time the show started to the first commercial break, they could have been on Mars. Students were signing in and out for the restrooms, no administrators came in, and the lunch period was winding down while their eyes were glued to their computers. They were so wrapped up in their thoughts that they seemed to have missed Marie's reference to their place of employment! They also missed the bell signaling the end of lunch, and didn't notice the two hundred some odd students walking by them on their way out of the cafeteria.

One of the last kids out was a senior who just had Nick the period before. He stopped at the table where the teachers were seated and asked a very pertinent question:

"Hey, Mr. P, don't you have a class or something coming up?"

Startled out of their daze, the two of them suddenly realized what was happening.

"Oh, yeah, Will, thanks," Nick replied. "We just got involved with a video for our next meeting; lost track of the time."

The student chuckled. "Yeah, they got some good stuff on that show; what is it called – *IT'S NEVER TOO LATE?* Ironic, huh? Since you guys are gonna be late! See ya, Pappas!"

Will was right, as the late bell had just sounded. But, for once in this whole catastrophe, luck was on their side since they each had a prep (what used to be called "free") period coming up.

"Let's watch this down in your room. If we hurry, we can get there before this commercial is over. I don't want to miss anything!" Maria barked with a sense of extreme urgency in her voice. "Let's go, man!"

Nick grabbed both computers and threw them in his bag along with everything else that was on the table, including two packs of Tic-Tacs, a paper towel, and the seeds from an orange he had been eating. It was about 40 yards to Nick's room, and they were there in what had to be record time.

"I think we just qualified for the Olympics," Nick joked, as he threw open his door (which he never kept locked) and dropped his case on his (luckily padded) desk chair.

Despite the perceived urgency of the situation, Maria couldn't helpbut observe, tongue in cheek: "I've never seen you move so fast, Greek!"

"I'll give you a rain check on that comment, Maria," he shot back They both indulged in a quick, much-needed laugh.

"And we're back," the host began with a broad smile. "For those of you just joining us, our guests are four Mediterranean mothers – widows –from New Jersey: two sets of sisters who have seemingly at warp speed turned their lives in a different and exciting direction, apparently helped along by the hand of fate! Does that sort of summarize what's been happening, ladies?"

"You'd make a good TV host," Mable quipped.

There were smiles all around, except from her sister, who chided her just a bit.

"Can't you be serious, just for once?"

Marie jumped in to defend her new best friend.

"Go easy, 'Rica. After all, it *was* your sister's connection that changed our lives, and got us here, right?" She didn't say it in a nasty way, and when Rica looked a bit askance at her, Marie countered with a smile and a quick rebuttal: "As my daughter often says, I was just stating an irrefutable truth."

"An irrefutable truth, and an incorrigible sister, and, I admit, an iconic prank." Marica conceded graciously.

"YES! That would be a great place to start." The quick-witted host shouted. "A great place." She looked directly out to where the restaurant owners were seated. "Hey, Gina and Ted, you want to do the honors? Come up and join us. How about it, folks, do you want to hear a great story from the horse's mouth, as it were?" The loud applause indicated that they did, and Gina and Ted were up in a flash.

"It was like a trip back to my childhood," Ted began...

Maria and Nick were aghast, which is not a strong enough word to describe their state of mind. In fact, only one word would not have been even close to being enough to cover the emotions they were feeling and the questions they had. Bewildered, puzzled, perplexed, worried, embarrassed, guilty, confused, angry, guilty, dumbfounded....well, you get the idea. They had heard from their relatives only a few times, and after that initial night with Maria's mom, all the rest were perfunctory quickies left on voicemails, both Maria's and Nick's. All the calls came when they were teaching, at times their relatives knew they couldn't answer their phones. Oh, and of course, there was the email from the bank to Nick regarding the ten grand, the picture of the four ladies at what were apparently their new digs, and the email to both Nick and Maria telling them to watch the TV show – that there would be some people they knew as guests. Too many moving parts as one of the phys ed teachers was fond of saying. Way too many!

Meanwhile, Ted was relating the "magic plate" story, which had the audience literally slapping their knees as they bubbled over with laughter loud enough to cause a sonic boom.

Melissa was nothing else if not considerate of her friends, and she always went out of her way to credit them with whatever was needed to be said. "Just so the audience knows, Gina and Ted and I have been friends for a long time, and when they told me about the ladies, of course, I was very interested. I am always on the lookout for a great story, especially if it's something we can use on the show. But, to be honest, nothing could have prepared me this fearsome foursome, or the 'sisters,' as they are sometimes called. They are dynamic, personable, well-spoken, imaginative, tough – but at the same time lovable. Their book contains many of their experiences and feelings, and, it looks like everyone here and probably at home has a feel for who they are and what they want from life. So I thought we would open things up for questions from our audience and from those at home. Those of you in the studio who would like to ask something of our guests please raise your hand and one of our staff will get a mike to you. Those of you watching at home, call 1-555-TOO-LATE."

A plethora of hands shot up in the audience, many of them waving vigorously.

"Why don't we start in the second row? Please tell us your name and where you're from, and to which of the ladies your question is directed. Thanks."

"HI. Caroline from Cincinnati. First of all, I want to say thank you, Melissa, for all your shows but especially this one," as Melissa nodded a thank you of her own in appreciation. "My question is to any of the ladies, or maybe even each one could answer? It would just take one word."

Melissa nodded approvingly.

"How would you describe what has happened to you since

you boarded that flight back in New Jersey with just one word?"

"Whoa, that's a great question to kick things off....ladies, what do you say? Marie, you want to lead off?"

"Unbelievable," Marie answered emphatically. "Simply unbelievable."

"Fascinating," Rica added, followed by a different tone in Liz's: answer – "Comfortable..."

"How about you, Mable?" the host asked imploringly.

"FATE. Had to be fate!"

A murmur went through both those on the stage and the audience.

"How about that gentleman toward the back being next up," Melissa indicated. "What's your name, sir, and where are you from?"

"Frank, from Helena, Montana," came the answer from a comely looking gentleman who looked to be about thirty-five. "I just want to say how much these ladies remind me of my mother."

"Which one of us?" Marie asked.

"All of you," came the answer. "It seems as if there's a piece of my mother in each of you. I travel a lot on business and this was the next best thing to going home. Thanks, ladies, thanks very much." His sincerity was evident, as were the happy smiles on just about everyone there.

"I think we'll take one more from the audience, and then right after the commercial break, we'll hit the phones for a few," the host explained. "I don't want to cut anyone short – your comments have been riveting. How about the lady in the third row....yes, the one in the red dress. You're up..."

The person addressed was a very pretty woman who looked to be in her late thirties. She seemed a bit tearful, though she tried to cover her emotional state by stating that she had a cold.

"I'm Sophia from Toledo, Ohio. I was touched by the title of your book: *TEARS AND HEARTACHES,* and I started thinking about all the memories, good and not-so-good ones, with my own mother. She lives in Torrance, not too far from here, and right after the show I'm gonna give her a call. I owe you one, ladies, and you, too, Melissa."

Three thousand miles away Maria and Nick were fixated on their computer, watching every move and hanging on every syllable. Maria reached for her phone.

"What the hell are you doing?" Nick shouted. It was one of the few times he had actually come right out with a statement with both force and clarity. There was no mistaking his meaning or intent.

"What do you think I'm doing?" she shot back. "I'm going to call my mother and get to the bottom of this. This is all unraveling like a bad dream. We send them three thousand miles away and they are still doing it – they are still controlling us with guilt. Personal guilt is bad enough – I can almost handle the one-on-one stuff. But now they're on television, and they've written a book? Who do you think are the bad guys in the book? You and me, bud, you and me."

One thing about Maria, when she gets mad, she gets mad, and it's like a volcano and a tidal wave all in one. She was right, of course, and Nick was vexed and perplexed himself, but he didn't relish getting into an argument on the air, nor did he want to see Maria and her mom go toe-to-toe on national television. He wished he could calm his colleague down just a bit, but, as usual, his intentions were good but his tactics were lacking. He couldn't risk getting into an argument with her in school, or anywhere, for that matter, and she was essentially going to bat for him as well, so he calmed himself down and eased up, which was fortunate for both his mental and physical well-being.

"Sorry, Siggi, I didn't mean to yell. I'm just as worried and hung up as you are, and we're better off with you talking this out with them than with any approach I could take."

Her eyes softened just a bit, and she nodded and put her hand on his shoulder, her usual way of saying that she got it and not to worry. She picked up her phone and hit her mother's key, but of course, her mother didn't have her cell phone with her on the air. The commercial was just finishing up as Melissa welcomed everyone back and reminded the audience at home that they were taking calls at 1-800-TOO LATE. It took Maria three tries to get it right, and then she was put on hold, although when she told them who she was they said they would put her through. She relayed this information to Nick, who was just finishing a silent prayer capped off with some nonstop crossing for good measure.

"Well, ladies, before we get to the phones, I was wondering if I might ask you a couple of things which perhaps some of our viewers had thought about as well."

The four women nodded and said "sure" and "of course" and "anything you want," or words to that effect.

"I was wondering if this adventure, this Mediterranean Odyssey, has changed you in any way, and also, what your plans are for the future."

Mable jumped the gun, as usual.

"Well, I don't know if it's changed me at all, but my sister has loosened up and actually appears to be enjoying herself. How about it Marica? Life can be fun, right?" Mable looked at her sister and laughed, and for her part, Rica just shook her head while trying to hide her smile.

Marie was already smiling and from her countenance looked as if she were dying to get something out, so when Melissa waved her way she seemed to be at full speed already.

"Well I gotta say that I love these two women, and I'm beginning to think that Greeks aren't so bad after all, huh Mable." She gave her new friend a light jab in the ribs, but

Mable was laughing so hard she hardly felt it. "Of course, I'm keeping an eye on that Greek my daughter is hanging around with..."

"That's a good plan, Marie. Greek men are unpredictable, and sneaky, to say the least!." Mable admonished her friend

"How about you, Liz? What's your take on this," Melissa asked quietly. Her thoughtful answer turned the discussion into a more philosophical direction, to say the least.

"I think all of us have learned that you have to embrace life as it comes to you, and that we're not just mothers and widows, but people..."

"With a lot to offer," Marica added.

"And a lot to enjoy," Mable threw in.

"And as for our next move," Marie began, taking the forum back to the original two questions, "who knows. We'll just have to wait and see, right girls? I think we all love what's happening out here. We'll see...."

Her three cohorts were in unanimous agreement, shown by their suddenly quiet countenance and pensive posture. Melissa got things going again with a pertinent yet rhetorical question: "Do you ladies think you're ready for a few phone calls before we wrap things up? I've got Maria on the line."

When she heard the name Marie's head spun around like a top, and the other three ladies suddenly sat straight up.

"Maria, you're on *IT'S NEVER TOO LATE,* but for some reason I don't have where you're calling from. Where are you?"

"Oh, I was so excited I forgot to say. I'm in Pennsylvania. Altoona, Pennsylvania."

A big "whew" came out almost simultaneously from the ladies...

"Pretty town," Melissa added "OK, Maira, what's your question?"

"Well, it's not really a question, I just want to say what a fabulous group this is. They make me laugh, they make me smile, they make me glad to be alive."

Meanwhile, *the* Maria was on hold and her fuming rate was only accelerated by this caller. She smacked Nick on the head with the back of her hand to be sure he was paying attention.

"Are you listening to this fawning, sophomoric drivel this idiot is saying on national TV? Our relatives make her glad to be alive? Where the hell does she live, in Hades? And on top of everything else, her name is Maria. Are you kidding me? Nick, Nick! Did you hear me? Are you listening?"

Truth be told, Nick was half listening, but he was still fixated on the comment Maria's mom made about him, or, as he was better known, "That Greek my daughter is hanging around with."

"Hey, Maria, whatever it is your mom has against me, does she have to tell the world about it? It's bad enough I embarrass myself all the time; she doesn't have to help me. Well, luckily, I don't think anyone has any idea who or where we are. Yeah, at least that's something."

"I would love to have any one of them as my mother," Maria from Altoona went on....

"Is she nuts? Have my mother as her mother? Yeah, OK...maybe I can arrange it...." Maria stopped in mid-sentence as something suddenly dawned on her...."Greek, we're screwed. They do know who we are. SHIT."

Nick was confused. Shocker.

"They? They who?"

"The whole damn country, which includes everybody here. I'm pretty sure that earlier in the show my mother mentioned where we worked."

"Damn, you might be right. Yeah, I think she did. Listen, you'd better hang up. HANG UP."

Maria shook her head.

"The horse is out of the barn now, Nick. We might as well get our money's worth."

Getting their money's worth would have to wait just a bit, since Maria from Pennsylvania went on and on gushing about the ladies while the host was trying to get her off the air without hurting her feelings. As he often did, her producer came to her rescue by walking quickly onto the set and whispering vigorously in Melissa's ear.

"I understand," she said quickly and loudly! "Maria, we are about to receive an important public service announcement, so we have to say goodbye. Thanks so much for your call."

Melissa looked over to Greg, who slid his hand across his throat. She nodded slightly and mouthed a "thank you" to him, and then explained to the audience....

"Well, it turns out the announcement has been postponed for an hour, so let's go to New Jersey, and... another Maria!."

At the sound of the name and the state the ladies just shook their heads with an expectant smirk.

"Hi, Maria. Melissa Topping. What do you have for our guests?"

"I have plenty for one of them I want to talk to my mother!"

Melissa looked over at her producer, who hit his palm against his head three times, the signal that a hard break was coming up – a legitimate break.

"Maria, we have a quick thirty-second break that I am required to take. Can you hang on?"

"You're damn straight I'll hang on...!"

Thirty seconds was just enough time for the host to have a quick consultation with the ladies, and for Maria and Nick to both go at each other and to curse the ironic, sadistic nature of fate.

Melissa had been doing live TV for a long time, and though something like this might have thrown a lesser host, she knew it was part of the dynamics, and often an agitated caller was good for an ensuing discussion and for ratings as well.

"That's my daughter," Marie began. "I guess she's watching the show....

"Probably with my son," Marica added.

"Yeah, Christina emailed them both, so they knew about it," Liz interjected.

"They're jealous that we're on our own, and doing so well, And we're famous....when were they ever on television?!" Mable added.

"So, you're good to take this call?"

A resounding "YES" from all four of them reverberated across America.

And, across America, the two teachers were so vexed and perplexed that a rarity occurred: Nick calmly made a pretty good suggestion to his co-conspirator, as they sometimes referred to each other.

"Siggi, you'd better take a breath. They have the numbers."

Maria looked at him with the mother of all death stares.

"Nick, don't you realize what they are doing? They are playing the sweet, innocent, heartbroken widows so they can get the sympathy of that damn host and all the idiots watching across the country. AND – they're pointing the finger at you and me so that we come off as the guilty parties in front of apparently everyone in California, Jersey, and everywhere in between. It's the ultimate guilt trip. I'm not going to let them get away with it without a fight."

Nick crossed himself again and again and again...

"And we're back," the host announced. "Maria from Jersey, are you still there?"

"You bet your ass I am," Maria answered.

Of course, thanks to the seven-second delay, which is common with with most live talk shows, the "double S" word was deleted. The "children" heard it in person but it didn't make it to the airwaves. Notwithstanding, this didn't deter Maria in the least; if anything, it got her even more aggravated and revved up as the words were flying out of her mouth almost as fast as the sparks were shooting from her eyes.

"Am I on the air? May I speak with my mother – right now? Or are my First Amendment rights meaningless on your show?"

Her mother, emboldened both by her surroundings and the favorable reception the ladies appeared to be receiving from all concerned (minus their kids), decided to play Maria just a bit.

"Is this Maria?"

"Mother, you know it's Maria. Knock it off."

"Well, we just had a Maria on the phone, and she was from someplace in Pennsylvania. This happened to me once before, about a week or so ago when we were at dinner. Do you re-member? Or wasn't that you then, or you now? There are so many Marias, you know what I mean? And it seems that we have two in a row. – that is, if Maria is really your name. How do I know you are who you say you are, Maria?"

There was a tidal wave of laughter once again through the studio, and most probably throughout the country. Except in room B66 in Burns High School, where Nick turned to his col-league with a pale look on his face:

"Your mother's really playing hardball, Maria."

"Yeah, well this next one is going right under her chin," was Maria's quick response...

"Listen, mom, I'm trying to be nice. *We're* trying to be nice, me and Nick, but your 'gang' is off on some wild spree in Cal-ifornia and we don't hear from you in days and we don't know what you're doing or anything."

Marie was very proper and calm as she answered her daughter softly yet firmly. "And how does that feel, Maria?

How does that feel?"

Maria looked at Nick, who shrugged. All she had was a "huh" in response.

"How does it feel not to be called, not to be included, to be left out? How many times was I expecting a call, praying for a call, and you were probably 'too busy.' How many times didn't you know whether I was still alive? Did you even care? How many times? And this isn't just for me, I'm speaking for all mothers, especially widows!"

There was an immediate standing ovation, including the crew and the host, who later said she couldn't help but support this courageous woman.

Maria seemed ready to explode, which caused Nick to ask one of his stupidest questions ever, and that is saying a lot...

"Do you want me to take over?"

"Over my dead body," she screamed. Luckily, only part of her statement came over the air.

"What was that, dear? I couldn't quite hear you," her mother stated sarcastically.

"I was talking to Nick," Maria shot back.

"Oh, is your Greek friend there with you? Correct me if I am wrong, but wasn't he with you the last time we spoke? Wasn't he, Maria?"

"Mom, that was during 'college night.'"

"Oh, is that what you call it?" Marie replied with a twinkle in her eye.

Laughter and pandemonium roared through everyone within earshot of the show, led by the host, Melissa Topping, who was trying to control the tears streaming down her face from her uncontrollable convulsions of laughter while at the same time slapping her knees.

She whimsically wished out loud: "Boy, if I only had a video of this it would by itself turn anyone's bad day around, not to mention what a marketing tool it would be for the show!

Oh, wait, what am I saying? We do have a video!!"

Melissa glanced over at Greg, who was holding up two fingers, the infamous two-minute warning till the end of the show. She knew that this mother and daughter slugfest would probably be good for another half-hour at least, but there was nothing she could do about the time constraint. On the other hand, this might be a blessing in disguise, since she could tell the combatants that they had to get in their last remarks, and a hard-hitting summary often made for great TV.

"Ladies, we've got two minutes left in the show. Can you tell each other, and the rest of us, what you feel is the most important thing to remember from your – shall we say – discussion?"

Maria jumped in before her mother could blink.

"I'm worried about you, Ma. What are you and Liz going to do when your vacation is done?" All the while Nick was waving frantically at Maria, who got his message and nodded to him. No words were needed.

"And Nick is worried, too, about his mother and aunt. What are you all going to do?"

Marica jumped into the fray with two words: "WE'LL SEE!"

"Perfect, Rica. Yes, Maria – WE'LL SEE!" her mother shouted out, and then repeated for emphasis. "WE'LL SEE!" Liz and Mable gave a vigorous thumbs up in support of their answer.

Maria and Nick looked at each other in stunned silence.

Maria had a sudden change of both tone and volume, as she softly and sincerely asked her mother: "You mean, you all might decide to stay there, and not come back to Jersey? What about your houses and your cars and everything?"

Liz jumped in: "Details, small details in the grand scheme of things, Maria."

"You gotta take life as it comes," Mable concluded.

Maria was momentarily speechless, as was Nick, which was probably a good thing. Quickly, however, she got a grip on herself, and asked her mother whether she hadn't always been "there" for her. The answer was on point, for an elder widow or for anyone.

"The thing was, Maria, what I wanted was for you to be *here* for me. See the difference?"

"Yes, Ma," Maria answered. She knew when she was beaten, so she figured she might as well throw in the towel. "What do you want me to do?"

"Read our book, and then we can talk."

"But what are *you* going to do next?"

"We'll see, we'll see. Oh, and if you are feeling guilty right now, maybe it's because you have something to feel guilty about! But no matter what it is, or how you feel, you should DEFINITELY go to confession" Marie glanced over at Marica, who was nodding and raising her eyebrows almost to her hairline – "And take that damn Greek with you."

The audience roared with smiles and laughs, as the hostess waved to highlight her guests, who are all smiling, shaking hands, and sharing hugs with their new fans. Melissa is holding the book up and references it once more: "The book is called *MEDITERRANEAN MOTHERS – THE HEARTACHES AND THE TEARS*, and the ladies are Elizabeth, Marie, Mable, and Marica. You can love them, fear them, or be riddled with guilt – but you'd better treat them with respect because you can never beat them!!"

....

EPILOGUE

As of this writing, the whereabouts of the four Mediterranean Mothers is still unknown. If you're ever in the town of Montecito or are dining at *ITALIANS AND GREEKS* in LA, and happen to hear unbounded laughter coming from four classy-looking ladies, please get in touch with Maria or Nick. They would be most grateful!

ABOUT ATMOSPHERE PRESS

Atmosphere Press is an independent, full-service publisher for excellent books in all genres and for all audiences. Learn more about what we do at atmospherepress.com.

We encourage you to check out some of Atmosphere's latest releases, which are available at Amazon.com and via order from your local bookstore:

Finding Us, by Kristin Rehkamp
The Ideological and Political System of Banselism, by Royard
    Halmonet Vantion (Ancheng Wang)
Unconditional: Loving and Losing an Addict, by Lizzy and Adam
Telling Tales and Sharing Secrets, by Jackie Collins, Diana Kinared,
    and Sally Showalter
*Nursing Homes: A Missionary's Journey Through Heaven's Waiting
    Room*, by Tim Eatman Ph.D.
Timeline of Stars, by Joe Adcock
A Boy Who Loved Me, by Wilson Semitti
The Injustice in Justice, by Charmaine Loverin
Living in the Gray, by Katie Weber
Living with Veracity, Dying with Dignity, by Alison Clay-Duboff
Noah's Rejects, by Rob Kagan
A lot of Questions (with no answers)?, by Jordan Neben
*Cowboy from Prague: An Immigrant's Pursuit of the American
    Dream*, by Charles Ota Heller
Sleeping Under the Bridge, by Melissa Baker
The Only Prayer I Ever Have to Say Is Thank You, by M. Kaya Hill
Amygdala Blue, by Paul Lomax
A Caregiver's Love Story, by Nancie Wiseman Attwater
*Taming Infection: The American Response to Illness from Smallpox
    to Covid*, by Gregg Coodley and David Sarasohn
The Second Long March, by Patti Isaacs
Me & Mrs. Jones, by Justine Gladden
Echoes from Wuhan, by Gretchen Dykstra
Through Her Eyes, by Maheen Mazhar

ABOUT THE AUTHORS

Maria Orlando, native Jersey gal, well schooled in Italian guilt. Teacher of English for 30+ years.

Nick Pappas - in Jersey his whole life. First generation Greek/American, grandfather, Vietnam Vet, history teacher 30+ years.

*Other Collaborations
by Maria and Nick:*

LUNCH WITH MARIA - A SICILIAN ODYSSEY
(published 8/5/22)

IT'S WHAT WE DO –
SNAPSHOTS FROM 65 YEARS IN HIGH SCHOOL